The Writings of Frithjof Schuon
Series

T0169139

About this Book

"With this new book, James Cutsinger shows he is an authority and teacher of the first rank on the work of Schuon. Professor Cutsinger has a kind of genius for organization, for discovering an ordering principle in the author's work and using that principle to guide his own decisions. His editorial hand in the choice of texts and the notes is sure and unobtrusive, letting the master speak for himself while opening pathways of understanding for readers of all levels."

> —**Vincent Rossi**, Director of Education for the Jerusalem Patriarchate of the Orthodox Church

"In this remarkable book Schuon, attentive doctor of the soul, exposes the soul's sophisms and denounces its weaknesses while honoring all the modalities of the inner life, from the simplest to the most vibrant, from personal prayer to the most elevated form of quintessential orison."

> —**Patricia Reynaud**, Miami University

"In the words of Marco Pallis, any religion is doomed to more or less rapid disintegration [without] ... the dimension of spiritual, intellectual, and physical integration [that is so well articulated in] *Prayer Fashions Man*."

> —**Brian Keeble**, author of *Art: For Whom and For What?*

"This new collection makes Schuon's work more accessible than ever, which is a great boon to those prepared to contemplate religion in universal terms. Here Schuon the metaphysician speaks as a spiritual master, placing the focus on the essential method of the spiritual life—prayer. His exposition of the dimensions and depths of prayer is traditional in the strictest sense, yet by no means confined to archaic forms. New readers will discover what experienced ones already have: that to read Schuon is not only to understand prayer anew, but to be drawn into it."

> —**Carl N. Still**, St. Thomas More College

"This extraordinary book is *sui generis*. Lean, lucid and graceful in style, *Prayer Fashions Man* offers profound and pivotal views the likes of which have not appeared in the western world since the times of Meister Eckhart and Dante Alighieri.

"*Prayer Fashions Man* is proof that Heaven has not left itself without witness even in these terminal 'dregs of time'".

—**Alvin Moore, Jr.** co-editor of *The Selected Letters of Ananda Coomaraswamy*

World Wisdom
The Library of Perennial Philosophy

The Library of Perennial Philosophy is dedicated to the exposition of the timeless Truth underlying the diverse religions. This Truth, often referred to as the *Sophia Perennis*—or Perennial Wisdom—finds its expression in the revealed Scriptures as well as in the writings of the great sages and the artistic creations of the traditional worlds.

The Perennial Philosophy provides the intellectual principles capable of explaining both the formal contradictions and the transcendent unity of the great religions.

Ranging from the writings of the great sages of the past to the perennialist authors of our time, each series of our Library has a different focus. As a whole, they express the inner unanimity, transforming radiance, and irreplaceable values of the great spiritual traditions.

Prayer Fashions Man: Frithjof Schuon on the Spiritual Life appears as one of our selections in the Writings of Frithjof Schuon series.

The Writings of Frithjof Schuon

The Writings of Frithjof Schuon form the foundation of our library because he is the pre-eminent exponent of the Perennial Philosophy. His work illuminates this perspective in both an essential and comprehensive manner like none other.

Books by Frithjof Schuon

The Transcendent Unity of Religions
Spiritual Perspectives and Human Facts
Gnosis: Divine Wisdom
Language of the Self
Stations of Wisdom
Understanding Islam
Light on the Ancient Worlds
In the Tracks of Buddhism
Treasures of Buddhism
Logic and Transcendence
Esoterism as Principle and as Way
Castes and Races
Sufism: Veil and Quintessence
From the Divine to the Human
Christianity/Islam: Essays on Esoteric Ecumenicism
Survey of Metaphysics and Esoterism
In the Face of the Absolute
The Feathered Sun: Plains Indians in Art and Philosophy
To Have a Center
Roots of the Human Condition
Images of Primordial and Mystic Beauty: Paintings by Frithjof Schuon
Echoes of Perennial Wisdom
The Play of Masks
Road to the Heart: Poems
The Transfiguration of Man
The Eye of the Heart
Songs for a Spiritual Traveler: Selected Poems
Form and Substance in the Religions
Adastra and Stella Maris: Poems by Frithjof Schuon

Edited Writings of Frithjof Schuon

The Essential Writings of Frithjof Schuon, ed. Seyyed Hossein Nasr
The Fullness of God: Frithjof Schuon on Christianity,
ed. James S. Cutsinger

Prayer Fashions Man
Frithjof Schuon on the Spiritual Life

Selected and edited by
James S. Cutsinger

Foreword by
Philip Zaleski

World Wisdom

Prayer Fashions Man: Frithjof Schuon on the Spiritual Life
© 2005 World Wisdom, Inc.

All rights reserved.
No part of this book may be used or reproduced
in any manner without written permission,
except in critical articles and reviews.

Translated from the French by Mark Perry in collaboration
with Jean-Pierre Lafouge, Deborah Casey,
and James S. Cutsinger.

For the French editions upon which the present translation is based,
see the listing of Sources, pages 237-40.

Library of Congress Cataloging-in-Publication Data

Schuon, Frithjof, 1907-1998
   [Selections. English. 2005]
   Prayer fashions man : Frithjof Schuon on the spiritual life / selected
and edited by James S. Cutsinger ; foreword by Philip Zaleski ;
[translated from the French by Mark Perry in collaboration with
Jean-Pierre Lafouge et al.].
      p. cm. – (The writings of Frithjof Schuon) (The library of
perennial philosophy)
   Includes bibliographical references (p. 237) and index.
   ISBN 0-941532-65-8 (pbk. : alk. paper)
   1. Prayer. 2. Spiritual life. I. Cutsinger, James S., 1953- II.
Title. III. Series.
   BL560.S38 2005
   204'.3–dc22

                                                    2004025692

Printed on acid-free paper in Canada

Cover Art: Painting by Frithjof Schuon

For information address World Wisdom, Inc.
P.O. Box 2682, Bloomington, Indiana 47402-2682

www.worldwisdom.com

Control thy soul, restrain thy breathing, distinguish the transitory from the true, repeat the holy Name of God, and thus calm the agitated mind. To this universal rule apply thyself with all thy heart and all thy soul.

Shri Shankaracharya

The true saint goes in and out amongst the people and eats and sleeps with them and buys and sells in the market and marries and takes part in social intercourse, and never forgets God for a single moment.

Abu Said ibn Abi al-Khayr

Abba Lot went to see Abba Joseph and said to him, "Abba, as far as I can I say my little office, I fast a little, I pray and meditate, I live in peace, and as far as I can I purify my thoughts. What else can I do?" The old man stood up and stretched his hands toward Heaven. His fingers became like ten lamps of fire, and he said to him, "If you will, you can become all flame."

Sayings of the Desert Fathers

CONTENTS

Foreword by *Philip Zaleski*   xi
Introduction by *James S. Cutsinger*   xv

1. Dimensions of Prayer   1
   Spiritual Perspectives I   5

2. Fundamental Keys   13
   Spiritual Perspectives II   19

3. Prayer and the Integration of the Psychic Elements   29
   Spiritual Perspectives III   37

4. Modes of Prayer   57
   Spiritual Perspectives IV   77

5. Trials and Happiness   89
   Spiritual Perspectives V   95

6. What Sincerity Is and Is Not   107
   Spiritual Perspectives VI   113

7. Dimensions of the Human Vocation   119
   Spiritual Perspectives VII   125

8. Microcosm and Symbol   139
   Spiritual Perspectives VIII   151

9. Meditation   153
   Spiritual Perspectives IX   163

10. The Servant and Union   169
    Spiritual Perspectives X   177

Appendix: A Sampling of Letters and
Other Previously Unpublished Materials   183

Editor's Notes   209
Sources   237
Glossary of Foreign Terms and Phrases   241
Index   253
Biographical Notes   267

Frithjof Schuon in 1952

FOREWORD

Frithjof Schuon (1907-1998), the most important twentieth-century exponent of the *philosophia perennis*, came to wide public attention in the English-speaking world with the publication in 1953 of his first major work, *The Transcendent Unity of Religions*. What drew many to this book was the endorsement of T. S. Eliot, who had received the Nobel Prize for Literature in 1948, the same year that Schuon's book had appeared in its original French edition. "I have met with no more impressive work in the comparative study of Oriental and Occidental religion," wrote the great poet, who had himself read deeply in the religious literature of East and West. Those who not only purchased but actually read Schuon's book discovered it to be all that Eliot promised: a masterful examination of the metaphysical and historical roots and flowerings of the world's revealed religions in the light of exoteric and esoteric teaching and practice.

Crucial to Schuon's exposition in *The Transcendent Unity of Religions* is the central importance that he accords to prayer. He concludes his study by speaking of prayer's role in "perfecting the natural participation of the human microcosm in the divine Metacosm"—that is, deification, or perfect union with God. In context, this remark refers specifically to the quasi-miraculous action of the Jesus Prayer, "a divine act in us and thus the best of all possible acts". But Schuon's observation may be taken to apply, in one way or another, to all prayer, for all prayer brings us to God, which is in the final analysis the only thing that matters in life (and in death). "Prayer fashions man" runs the title of the volume you hold in your hands; one could go even further and say that prayer *is* man, at least insofar as man is man—that is, insofar as he accepts his nature as image and likeness of God, answers the divine call, and thus fulfills his obligation to worship, praise, and, under grace, participate in divine life. The man who does not pray is half a man, the possessor of a truncated mind and a wounded heart, and this great truth Schuon has put in the forefront of his teaching.

Hence the importance of this landmark compendium of writings on prayer, skillfully assembled by James S. Cutsinger from the vast range of Schuon's published and unpublished work. Some of the material collected here, it should be noted at once, makes strong demands upon the reader. Schuon's thought can be complex, multi-leveled, elusive—in keeping with the material that he presents. A close reading of Professor Cutsinger's excellent introduction, in which he explains the author's tripartite division of prayer into personal, canonical, and invocatory modes, will help bring out the main themes, which focus upon man's tasks both as knower and lover in relation to God. Even if we occasionally find it difficult to thread our way through Schuon's tightly woven thought, we gain much from his brilliant aphorisms and apercus, which illuminate many difficult matters. Consider his definition of faith as a cognitive act that involves the entire person: "Faith is nothing other than the adherence of our whole being to Truth, whether we have a direct intuition of that Truth or an indirect idea"; or his dismissal of the cult of suffering: "Clearly what matters is not that man should suffer, but that he should think of God." This sort of penetrating, practical insight reaches its apotheosis in the lengthy appendix, drawn from Schuon's letters, memoirs, and other private writings. In these previously unpublished extracts, we hear Schuon speaking in a new key, more personal and tender, although hardly less authoritative. Who cannot benefit from his counsel when beginning a new way of prayer: "One must dedicate oneself to a discipline that is not above our strength—that may even appear to be beneath it—but one must dedicate oneself to it totally. And one will then see, over time, that it is above our strength, but that everything is possible with God's help; nothing is possible without it"; or from his advice on how to overcome sorrow: "To fight sadness, we have no other means than to fix the gaze of the intelligence and the soul on the Infinite, which contains everything that is perfect and lovable." I earnestly hope that more of Schuon's unreleased writings will appear in public in the near future; we will all benefit thereby.

This is not to say that Schuon's teachings will not present problems for some readers. I myself, as a Roman Catholic, find it difficult to reconcile orthodox Christian theology with Schuon's belief that the personal God is the "relative Absolute", beyond which lies the "pure Absolute". Adherents of other religions may encounter similar difficulties, as is so often the case when encountering a profound attempt to describe an overarching *sophia perennis et universalis*. This caveat notwithstanding, *Prayer Fashions Man* offers a bounty of penetrating insights into the nature and purpose of prayer and deserves to be welcomed into the library of everyone who wishes to understand how a man or woman, faced with the degradations and distractions of modern life, may yet remain faithful to God and become what he or she was created to be, chosen "before the foundation of the world, that we should be holy and blameless before Him" (Ephesians 1:4).

Philip Zaleski

INTRODUCTION

The title of this book deserves careful thought, for the full measure of its implications may not at first be evident.

Some readers will be surprised by the words we have chosen,[1] thinking that the truth of the matter is just the opposite. Is it not man who fashions prayer? Prayer is an act, and human beings are the agents of that act; whether what they say is prescribed by a religious tradition or uttered spontaneously in a moment of sorrow or gladness, men and women themselves do the praying, and their prayers, be they only imprecations, reflect in some way the kind of persons they are, giving form to their aspirations and fears and affording insight into the quality of their inner life. How we pray—whether only reluctantly and in moments of crisis or according to a regular discipline, and whether our prayers are of a purely devotional and discursive kind or include as well a contemplative and methodic aspect—can be a revealing testimony as to who or what we really are.

Others may respond less with surprise than a ready acceptance. Of course prayer fashions man, they will say. More than a monologue, as unbelievers suppose, our expressions of petition and praise constitute a genuine communication with God, and the answers we receive can bring about real change in our life. As a sculptor fashions clay or a poet words—as the wind or a stream gives shape to a dune or a valley—so do a man's prayers, faithfully and persistently repeated over the course of his life, come in time to transform the substance of his soul, eliminating the faults in his character, providing him with an increasing strength and stability, and bringing him step by step with God's help toward the fulfillment of his vocation to perfection. Anyone who doubts this truth, refusing out of pride or despair to call upon Heaven, has only to consult that most dazzling of proofs which is the existence of saints.

Each of these perspectives contains an element of truth; prayer both fashions and is fashioned by man, and the writings here assembled will serve in part to corroborate and amplify these important

[1] They are in fact Schuon's own formulation; see "Spiritual Perspectives X", p. 182.

insights. But if we are to grasp the full scope of what follows, there is a further-reaching and more elusive fact to be noticed. Fashioning can refer to a process of shaping or forming, the existence of the thing fashioned being presupposed in this case; but the word also has a constitutive and not merely formative sense and can be used more profoundly, as it was often used in times past, to signify an act of creation, the bringing into being of something where there was nothing before—as God fashions man in His image and likeness.

As we shall discover, this deeper significance is central to this book. "The very fact of our existence is a prayer and compels us to pray," its author has written; "I am: therefore I pray; *sum ergo oro*."[2] If we could see ourselves as we truly are, we would realize that human nature, made to serve as *pontifex* for the rest of creation, is itself a mode of prayer, and this being so it is impossible for us not to pray, whether well or ill; even more remarkably, it is only because, or insofar as, we do pray that we can truly be said to exist, human existence being derived, with or without our awareness, from the prior reality of prayer. Man's innermost being, and not just his personality or character, is in some mysterious way interwoven into the actual fabric of prayer, and without the generative force of his orisons, he would be "without form and void". In short, prayer fashions man in making him real. What this could mean, and how we might best make sense in our own experience of so striking a claim, are questions lying at the heart of the following meditations.

The author is uniquely qualified to aid us in our search for answers. Widely acknowledged as one of the twentieth century's foremost authorities on the world's religions, and the leading exponent of the traditionalist or perennialist school of comparative religious philosophy,[3] Frithjof Schuon was the author of over twenty books, as well as numerous articles, letters, texts of spiritual instruction, and other unpublished materials; the depth of his insights and the masterful quality of his early writing had brought him interna-

---

[2] *Understanding Islam* (Bloomington, Indiana: World Wisdom Books, 1998), p. 155. The Latin phrase *sum ergo oro*, "I am: therefore I pray", is deliberately used as a corrective to the famous expression of René Descartes: *cogito ergo sum*, "I think: therefore I am".

[3] René Guénon, Ananda Coomaraswamy, and Titus Burckhardt were also important figures in this school.

tional recognition while he was still in his twenties, and by the time of his death in 1998 at the age of ninety, his reputation among many scholars of mysticism, esoterism, and contemplative traditions was unsurpassed.

Schuon was more than a scholar and author, however. An accomplished artist and poet,[4] he was above all a man of prayer, whose fundamental message, whatever its particular thrust in any given article or chapter, was always linked to the importance of faith and spiritual practice. "Even if our writings had on average no other result than the restitution for some of the saving barque that is prayer," he once explained, "we would owe it to God to consider ourselves profoundly satisfied."[5] Whether his focus was metaphysics and epistemology, traditional cosmology, sacred art and symbolism, mysticism and esoterism, the modern world and its errors, human nature, or the spiritual path—Schuon wrote extensively on all of these subjects—his fundamental concerns were always of an operative or maieutic order, as he sought to lead readers, not simply to a deeper understanding of the religious traditions, but to a more lucid discernment of the presence of God in their lives. Never satisfied with a purely cerebral or academic approach, Schuon was well aware that "knowledge saves only on condition that it engages all that we are: only when it constitutes a path which works and transforms, and which wounds our nature as the plough wounds the soil".[6]

In the years since his death, a number of his close associates have begun to publish biographical memoirs, and it is now widely known that Schuon's own practice was undertaken within the con-

---

[4] The painting on the cover of the present volume is by Schuon. A number of his other works have been collected in *The Feathered Sun: Plains Indians in Art and Philosophy* (Bloomington, Indiana: World Wisdom Books, 1990). Schuon's English poems, several of which are featured in this anthology, can be found in his book *Road to the Heart* (Bloomington, Indiana: World Wisdom Books, 1995). During the last three years of his life, he composed nearly thirty-five hundred lyric poems in German; four volumes of these poems have been published to date: *Glück, Leben, Sinn,* and *Liebe* (Freiburg-im-Breisgau, Basel, Vienna: Herder, 1997). Bilingual editions of the poetry—German with an English translation—include *Songs for a Spiritual Traveler: Selected Poems* (Bloomington, Indiana: World Wisdom Books, 2002) and *Adastra and Stella Maris: Poems by Frithjof Schuon* (Bloomington, Indiana: World Wisdom, 2003).

[5] *The Play of Masks* (Bloomington, Indiana: World Wisdom Books, 1992), p. vii.

[6] See "Spiritual Perspectives II", p. 24.

text of Sufism and that he served for over sixty years as a master of the traditional Shadhiliyyah-Darqawiyyah lineage.[7] He himself did not speak of this role in his published writings, however, for he wished to distinguish very carefully between his function as a spiritual master, on the one hand, and his teaching as a metaphysician and philosopher, on the other—a teaching that is universalist in its scope and intention and worlds apart from any proselytizing, sectarian, or authoritarian aim. Born in Switzerland in 1907, where he was brought up as a Protestant before becoming a Roman Catholic, he knew that those who were aware of his background might falsely conclude that he had renounced Christianity and had "converted" to Islam. In fact, his Sufi affiliation was simply a matter of vocation, the result of his quest as a young man for a form of spirituality he had been unable to find in the Western Church, and it did not conflict with his remaining an adamant defender of traditional Christological doctrine and other essential Christian truths, nor with his having a special affinity for the Christian East and the Hesychast method of prayer. "Being *a priori* a metaphysician," he wrote, "I have had since my youth a particular interest in *Advaita Vedânta*, but also in the method of realization of which *Advaita Vedânta* approves. Since I could not find this method—in its strict and esoteric form—in Europe, and since it was impossible for me to turn to a Hindu guru because of the laws of the castes, I had to look elsewhere; and since Islam *de facto* contains this method, in Sufism, I finally decided to look for a Sufi master; the outer form did not matter to me."[8]

Although Schuon made a home for himself within this spiritual framework, he was in no sense an apologist for the Islamic tradition, but maintained close ties throughout his long life with authorities and wayfarers in a wide variety of orthodox religions, each of which, he insisted, is a saving expression of a single Truth, which he variously referred to as the *sophia perennis* or *philosophia perennis*, that is, the "perennial wisdom" or "perennial philosophy". Until his later years he traveled widely, from India to North Africa to America,

---

[7] This is an unbroken succession of Sufi *shaykh*s which traces its beginnings to the thirteenth-century master Abu al-Hasan al-Shadhili (1196-1258) and which includes among its subsequent branches an order founded in the early nineteenth century by Mawlay al-Arabi al-Darqawi (1760-1823).

[8] From a letter of January 1996.

and his personal friendships ranged from Hindu swamis to Native American chiefs and shamans, while hundreds of correspondents and visitors from nearly every religious background looked to him for advice. A traditional master in the midst of modern life, Schuon drew upon the insights and vocabularies of Christian, Muslim, Hindu, Buddhist, Plains Indian, and other spiritual patrimonies, and his books, by bringing the ancient teachings to life in a way that speaks directly, and deeply, to the problems and possibilities of contemporary men and women, continue to serve as a bridge between the great saints and sages of the past and our own experience in these opening years of the twenty-first century.

Our aim in this anthology is to give the reader some sense of the range and variety of Schuon's writings on prayer and the spiritual life, though the full scope of his doctrine on these momentous subjects can by no means be covered in a single volume. In a sense everything Schuon wrote was on the subject of prayer. Asked in a series of interviews during the last years of his life what his advice would be for people in general, he consistently replied by stressing the importance of prayer. "If you understand what is essential and what is absolute," he said, "you want to assimilate it; otherwise one is a hypocrite. . . . We may think that God is God: *Brahma satyam.* But it is not enough to think it; we must assimilate it—we must 'eat' it, just as the Christians eat the body of Christ and drink his blood. . . . And in order to assimilate the truth of the Absolute, you must pray. . . . I say to people, 'You must pray, always pray.' . . . To be a human being means to be connected with God; life has no meaning without this."[9]

There is no need to discuss Schuon's perspective in any detail in this context; the following pages will provide a clear and ample picture of his views, and it makes better sense to allow him to speak for himself. On the other hand, it will perhaps be useful, by way of anticipating one of his most fundamental ideas, if we provide at

---

[9] See "The Basis of Religion and Metaphysics: An Interview with Frithjof Schuon", *The Quest: Philosophy, Science, Religion, the Arts*, Vol. 9, No. 2 (Summer, 1996), p. 78; also "Frithjof Schuon: Messenger of the Perennial Philosophy", a biographical video based on interviews with Schuon in 1991 and 1992 (forthcoming). The Sanskrit phrase *Brahma satyam* means "the Supreme Reality is the truth", or simply "God is real"; it is part of a formula, traditionally ascribed to the advaitic sage Shankara (788-820), which Schuon often cited in summary of his own metaphysical outlook: "God is real; the world is appearance; the soul is not other than God."

least a glimpse of what he says concerning the principal dimensions or levels of prayer. Some readers, hearing that the author was a spiritual master and supposing without examination that they know what this means, may mistakenly conclude that his writings are not for them—that his advice will be too exotic or "technical" to speak to their condition—while others, motivated by a taste for the exotic precisely and looking only for the most advanced of pranayamic or samadhic techniques, may be surprised to learn that Schuon always began from the premise that every man, whatever his spiritual temperament or degree of intelligence, must become "as a little child", placing himself under the sacramental aegis of an orthodox religion and building his spiritual life on a firm foundation of trust in God.[10]

It is true that the Schuonian message is intended above all for esoterists—for seekers, whatever their tradition, who are motivated by a desire for *gnosis* or knowledge, who have an innate affinity for the essential Truth in all traditions and a sensitivity to the sacred in virgin nature, and who find themselves naturally drawn to a life of inwardness and contemplative prayer—and such readers will be offered much by this book. But at the same time Schuon never forgets that the esoterist is still a human being, and that there are certain fundamental temptations, struggles, and confusions that must be dealt with first before anyone can hope to make real progress in the spiritual life. While his writings are certainly demanding and often difficult, they nonetheless include a practical, down-to-earth quality, featuring acute observations on men's foibles and fantasies, and refreshingly pragmatic advice on how to deal with the world and with life; it is our hope that this collection can therefore be a source of nourishment and encouragement for many.

The multidimensionality of Schuon's spiritual writing is well illustrated by his teaching that there are three basic levels or modes of prayer: personal prayer, canonical prayer, and invocatory prayer. In personal prayer, which is essentially free and spontaneous, the praying subject is the individual person, or "such and such a man";

---

[10] In a list of key features of his teaching, Schuon included the qualification of "childlikeness"; it is essential to "retain alongside metaphysical science a childlike faith", "not to be exclusively adult", and to cultivate "a childlike heart capable of delighting in little things" (from an unpublished document titled "Our Perspective in a Few Words").

in this case one stands before God as a particular human being with needs and concerns, and reasons for thanksgiving, all one's own. Schuon often pointed to the Psalms as models for the personal dimension of prayer, and he frequently stressed its fundamental importance in the spiritual life, strongly criticizing those pretentious enough to suppose that they need only some advanced method of meditation or concentration and can therefore bypass this most fundamental form of communication with Heaven. Having created us with the gift of speech, God speaks to us, and He expects us to respond, externalizing our thoughts and feelings and maintaining a continual conversation with Him. Schuon writes in his autobiographical memoirs of having prayed in this way as a matter of course when he was a little boy growing up in Basel, and once he was older he was surprised to learn that everyone had not cultivated the same sort of trusting relationship with God.

A second level of orison is canonical or liturgical prayer, which is distinguished from personal prayer by the fact that the praying subject is humanity in general, or "man as such"; whether prescribed in the scriptures of a given religion or by some other traditional authority, the words of a canonical prayer are meant to express the intentions and needs of other people as well as our own, and in this way they remind us that a man is to love his neighbor as himself because in fact, metaphysically, there is only one Self. This universal dimension can be discerned in the use of the first-person plural, as in the Jewish *Shema*: "Hear, O Israel: The Lord *our* God is one Lord" (Deut. 6:4); in the Christian Lord's Prayer: "*Our* Father who art in heaven . . . give *us* this day our daily bread, and forgive *us* our debts as *we* forgive *our* debtors" (Matt. 6:9, 11-13; *cf.* Luke 11:2, 3-4); and in the Muslim *Fâtihah*: "Thee (alone) do *we* worship; Thee (alone) do *we* ask for help; show *us* the straight path" (*Sûrah* "The Opening" [1]:4-5). Schuon noted that the Lord's Prayer is introduced in the Gospel with an imperative, "When ye pray, say" (Luke 11:2), implying that the canonical prayers of one's religion, far from being mere suggestions or options, are incumbent on all the faithful and should be treated as an obligatory part of everyone's spiritual efforts.

Finally, there is a third and highest mode of prayer, variously referred to by Schuon as quintessential prayer, Prayer of the Heart, ejaculatory prayer, and invocatory prayer; this is the capstone of the spiritual method he taught and the form of prayer he accentuated in all his published and unpublished writings. Like the first two modes, invocatory prayer presupposes man's distinctive gift of speech, but its essential value lies not in the discursive meaning of what is said—not in the propositional significance of the formulations as such—but in the fact that the words enshrine a revealed Name of God, the Name in turn serving as a vehicle or embodiment of the Divinity. Even as the bread and wine of the Eucharist are the "Real Presence" of Christ, so also is the Name of God understood to be God Himself.[11] Thus, in contrast to the first two kinds of prayer, the subject or agency of invocation is not primarily human—it is neither the individual human person nor men in general who initiate the act—but rather divine, and it is for this reason that Schuon regarded invocatory orison as the most perfect and complete kind of prayer. Noteworthy examples of the practice include the Jesus Prayer in Christianity, the method of *dhikr* in Islam, the *nembutsu* in Pure Land Buddhism, and the various forms of *japa-yoga* in Hinduism, where the Names of Krishna and Rama can be found among a variety of invocatory *mantra*s. Building as it were on the two "lower dimensions" of prayer, invocation gives "solidity" to the spiritual life, providing seekers of every aptitude with that greatest of boons, which is to have arrived at the goal even while one is still in the midst of the journey. In Schuon's words:

> All great spiritual experiences agree in this: there is no common measure between the means put into operation and the result. "With men this is impossible; but with God all things are possible," says the Gospel. In fact, what separates man from divine Reality is but a thin partition: God is infinitely close to man, but man is infinitely far from God. This partition, for man, is a mountain; man stands in front of a mountain that he must remove with his own

---

[11] Schuon liked to quote the words of the Hindu saint Ramakrishna (1834-86), "God and His Name are identical" (see Chapter 4, "Modes of Prayer", p. 60), but the same essential idea can be found throughout the world's religions, including traditions as diverse as Judaism, in which respect for God's holiness required that the sacred *Tetragrammaton*—the four Hebrew consonants (transliterated as YHWH) of the Name that God gave to Moses on Sinai (Ex. 3:14)—never be pronounced aloud except by the high priest on the day of Yom Kippur, and the Buddhist sect of *Jôdo-Shinshû*, where the efficacy of invocation is based on the vow of the Buddha Amida that all who repeat his Name will experience the blessings of his Pure Land. "Why speak at length?" asks Saint Gregory of Sinai, referring to the grace of the Name. "Prayer is God, who accomplishes everything in everyone" ("On Commandments and Doctrines", *The Philokalia*, ed. G. E. H. Palmer, Philip Sherrard, and Kallistos Ware [London: Faber and Faber, 1995], Vol. IV, p. 238).

hands. He digs away the earth, but in vain; the mountain remains. Man however goes on digging, in the Name of God. And the mountain vanishes. It was never there.[12]

The following chapters have been chosen from Schuon's published corpus of twenty-three books. Written originally in French,[13] the selections are here presented in a fully revised English translation; bibliographical details, including information about previous English editions, may be found in the list of Sources at the end of this volume. As it happens, most of Schuon's books are themselves anthologies, which he periodically assembled from articles that had been initially published, beginning in 1933 and continuing through 1997, in a variety of European, Persian, and American journals, including *Le Voile d'Isis, Études Traditionnelles, Studies in Comparative Religion, Sophia Perennis, Connaissance des Religions,* and *Sophia: The Journal of Traditional Studies.*

Many of these articles were occasional in nature, having been composed in response to a broad range of questions and problems, often posed by those who sought the author's spiritual counsel. As a result, Schuon's writings are often more meditative than discursive in character, with any given essay ranging across a number of fascinating subjects and including illustrations drawn from an astonishing variety of sources. The selections presented here are filled with insights, not only on the subject of prayer itself, but on the presuppositions and goals of the spiritual life in general. Specific topics include the importance of self-domination as a prelude to self-transcendence, the differences between intrinsic morality and social benevolence, beauty and the aesthetic function of intelligence, the reason for trials and suffering, ontological levels in man and the cosmos, the relationship between method and grace, the interpenetration of knowledge and love, symbols and themes of meditation, the necessity of the virtues—above all, humility, charity, and veracity—for assimilating metaphysical truth, the spiritual significance of

---

[12] *Stations of Wisdom* (Bloomington, Indiana: World Wisdom Books, 1995), p. 157. The scriptural quotation comes from Matthew 19:26 (*cf.* Mark 10:27).

[13] With the exception of his first book, which was written in German and has not been translated into English, *Leitgedanken zur Urbesinnung* (Zurich and Leipzig: Orell Fussli Verlag, 1935), all of Schuon's published writings were composed in French; some of the letters and other previously unpublished selections included in the Appendix to the present volume were also originally written in German.

the regions of the human body, initiation and initiatic or esoteric techniques of concentration, and the "two planes of relationship" between the servant and the Lord and the Intellect and the Self.

Because of the wide-ranging nature of Schuon's work and its poetic—one might say musical—quality, a firm categorization of his writings is impossible; he himself spoke of the "discontinuous and sporadic manner" of his expositions, acknowledging that while "there is no great doctrine that is not a system", there is equally none that "expresses itself in an exclusively systematic fashion".[14] As the chapters of this book unfold, the reader will be asked to traverse a spectrum of ideas extending from the prerequisites of the spiritual life as a whole to the ultimate aim of that life, namely, self-realization in God. But the movement is by no means strictly linear; we have chosen in fact to highlight the "discontinuous" style of the author by punctuating the text with several of his English poems as well as with two chapters of shorter, aphoristic reflections or *leitgedanken* that are of an especially "musical" character, the sections of these chapters being interspersed throughout the book in a numbered series of "spiritual perspectives".[15] As in our previous anthology of Schuon's writings,[16] the book concludes with an Appendix of previously unpublished materials, including spiritual texts written for his disciples; selections from his autobiographical memoirs, "Memories and Meditations"; and samples of his extensive correspondence with seekers from many different traditions.

The breadth of the author's erudition can be somewhat daunting, especially for those not accustomed to reading philosophical and religious works; his pages frequently contain allusions to ideas, historical figures or events, and sacred texts that illumine or amplify his meaning, but a citation or other reference is not usually provided. With this fact in mind and as an aid to the interested reader, we have included a series of Editor's Notes in this volume; in order

[14] *Survey of Metaphysics and Esoterism*, trans. Gustavo Polit (Bloomington, Indiana: World Wisdom Books, 1986), p. 1.

[15] The chapters in question, "Knowledge and Love" and "The Spiritual Virtues", come from Schuon's book *Spiritual Perspectives and Human Facts* (for bibliographical information, see p. 238-39); their style is reminiscent of the genre of "centuries" found among the Orthodox fathers of *The Philokalia*, whom Schuon frequently quotes in these chapters, and in such writers as Thomas Traherne (*c.* 1636-74).

[16] *The Fullness of God: Frithjof Schuon on Christianity* (Bloomington, Indiana: World Wisdom, 2004).

to be as unobtrusive as possible, we have chosen not to interrupt Schuon's prose with asterisks or other symbols, leaving it to the reader to consult the notes when in need. It should be understood that this editorial apparatus does not presume to offer an interpretation of Schuon's teaching; as remarked above, we prefer to allow his writings to speak for themselves. Organized by chapter and tagged to the relevant page numbers, the notes are designed simply to provide helpful supports for those who may be unacquainted with the names of various philosophical writers and spiritual authorities or with certain religious and other traditional teachings. Chapter and verse citations are given for quotations from the Bible and other sacred texts; dates and biographical summaries are provided for historical figures; brief explanations are offered concerning the fine points of theological controversies and the principal doctrines of various schools of thought.

One final point should be mentioned. It is customary for Schuon to use a number of technical terms in his writings, drawn from a multitude of traditions and involving several classical languages, including Sanskrit, Arabic, Latin, and Greek, and a Glossary has therefore been provided as well; here one will find, in transliteration, foreign words and phrases appearing both in Schuon's text and in our editorial notes, together with translations and definitions.

James S. Cutsinger

1

Dimensions of Prayer

Man must meet God with all that he is, for God is the Being of all; this is the meaning of the Biblical injunction to love God "with all our strength".

Now one of the dimensions characterizing man *de facto* is that he lives toward the exterior and furthermore tends toward pleasures; this is his outwardness and his concupiscence. He must renounce them before God, for in the first place God is present in us, and in the second place man must be able to find pleasure within himself and independently of sensorial phenomena.

But everything that brings one closer to God partakes of His beatitude for that very reason; to rise, by praying, above the images and noise of the soul is a liberation through the divine Void and Infinitude; it is the station of serenity.

It is true that outward phenomena, by their nobleness and their symbolism—their participation in the celestial Archetypes—can have an interiorizing virtue, and each thing can be good in its season. Nevertheless detachment must be realized; otherwise man would have no right to a legitimate outwardness, and otherwise he would fall into a seductive outwardness and concupiscence that are mortal for the soul. Just as the Creator by His transcendence is independent of creation, so man must be independent of the world in view of God. Free will is the endowment of man; only man is capable of resisting his instincts and desires. *Vacare Deo.*

* * *

Another of man's endowments is reasonable thought and speech; this dimension must therefore be actualized during that encounter with God which is prayer. Man is saved not only by abstaining from evil, but also, and *a fortiori,* by accomplishing the Good; now the best of works is that which has God as its object and our heart as its agent, and this is the "remembrance of God".

The essence of prayer is faith, hence certitude; man manifests it precisely by speech, or appeal, addressed to the Sovereign Good. Prayer, or invocation, equals certitude of God and of our spiritual vocation.

Action is valid according to its intention; it is obvious that in prayer there must be no intention tainted with ambition of any kind; it must be pure of all worldly vanity, on pain of provoking the Wrath of Heaven.

Wholehearted prayer not only benefits him who accomplishes it; it also radiates around him and in this respect is an act of charity.

* * *

Every man is in search of happiness; this is another dimension of human nature. Now there is no perfect happiness outside God; any earthly happiness has need of Heaven's blessing. Prayer places us in the presence of God, who is pure Beatitude; if we are aware of this, we will find Peace in it. Happy is the man who has the sense of the Sacred and who thus opens his heart to this mystery.

* * *

Another dimension of prayer stems from the fact that on the one hand man is mortal and on the other he has an immortal soul; he must pass through death, and above all he must be concerned with Eternity, which is in God's hands.

In this context, prayer will be at once an appeal to Mercy and an act of faith and trust.

* * *

Man's fundamental endowment is an intelligence capable of metaphysical knowledge; as a consequence, this capacity necessarily determines a dimension of prayer, which then coincides with meditation; its subject is first the absolute reality of the Supreme Principle, and then the non-reality—or the relative reality—of the world, which manifests that Principle.

However, man must not make use of intentions that surpass his nature; if he is not a metaphysician, he must not believe himself obliged to be one. God loves children just as He loves sages; and He loves the sincerity of the child who knows how to remain a child.

This means that in prayer there are dimensions that are imperative for every man, and others that he may greet from afar as it were; for what matters in this confrontation is not that man be great or small, but that he stand sincerely before God. On the one hand, man is always small before his Creator; on the other hand, there is always greatness in man when he addresses God; and in the final analysis, every quality and every merit belong to the Sovereign Good.

*   *   *

We have said that there is a dimension of meditative prayer whose content is the absolute reality of the Principle and then, correlatively, the non-reality—or the lesser reality—of the world, which manifests that Principle.

But it is not enough to know that "*Brahma* is Reality; the world is appearance"; it is also necessary to know that "the soul is not other than *Brahma*". This second truth reminds us that we are able, if our nature allows it, to tend toward the Supreme Principle not only in an intellectual mode, but also in an existential mode; this results from the fact that we possess not only an intelligence capable of objective knowledge, but also a consciousness of the "I", which in principle is capable of subjective union. On the one hand, the ego is separated from the immanent Divinity because it is manifestation, not Principle; on the other hand, it is not other than the Principle inasmuch as the Principle manifests itself, just as the reflection of the sun in a mirror is not the sun, but is nevertheless "not other than it" inasmuch as the reflection is solar light and nothing else.

Aware of this, man does not cease to stand before God, who is at once transcendent and immanent; and it is He, not we, who decides the scope of our contemplative awareness and the mystery of our spiritual destiny. We are aware that to know God unitively means that God knows Himself in us; but we cannot know to what extent He intends to realize in us this divine Self-Consciousness; and it is of no importance whether we know it or not. We are what we are, and everything is in the hands of Providence.

3

Synthesis

Truth, Way, and Virtue: threefold is the Path
From Earth to Heaven. First, discriminate
Between Reality and Dream; then pray:
Invoke the Name and reach the Godhead's Gate.

Then Virtue: for we must conform our selves
To That which we believe, adapt our soul
To That which saves. Our very breath should be
One with our Faith and with our highest Goal.

Spiritual Perspectives

I

Whence does certainty come to saints and prophets regarding their supernatural inspirations? Why did Joan of Arc believe in her voices? It is because there is ontological evidence in the inspirations themselves: believing in them is as obvious as believing in one's own existence.

The same is true of ordinary inspirations, which are "natural" in their mode, that is, related to intellectual intuition and not revelation: metaphysical truths are accepted not merely because they are logically evident, but because they are ontologically evident; being logically evident is only a mental trace.

Ontological evidence is part of our very existence, part of the universe, part of God.

* * *

The theological distinction between faith as belief, and therefore as a relative darkness, and the certainty of the blessed in Paradise is analogous to the distinction between theoretical knowledge and a knowledge that is effective, "concrete", "realized".

* * *

Christ's words to the Apostle Thomas could not mean that those who do see are not blessed; otherwise the elect of Heaven, who see God, would be deprived of beatitude. The blessedness of those who do not see and yet believe lies in the future, like the blessedness of those who mourn and will be comforted; but the blessedness of those who see and thus have no more need to believe is in the present, and that is why it is not mentioned in the Sermon on the Mount.

A man may have metaphysical certitude without possessing "faith", that is, without this certitude residing in his soul as an ever-

5

active presence. But if metaphysical certitude suffices on doctrinal grounds, it is far from being sufficient on the spiritual plane, where it must be completed and brought to life by faith. Faith is nothing other than the adherence of our whole being to Truth, whether we have a direct intuition of that Truth or an indirect idea.[1] It is an abuse of language to reduce "faith" to "belief"; it is the opposite that is true: belief—or theoretical knowledge—must be changed into the faith "that moves mountains".[2] For the Apostles there was no difference in practice between an idea and its spiritual exploitation; they did not separate theory from realization: hence the word "love" as a way of indicating all conformity to divine Truth.

He who has faith acts as if he were in the presence of what he believes—or knows—to be true. One can neither cast doubt on the fact that simple belief is already an adherence to Truth, nor affirm that metaphysical certitude by itself implies an adherence of our whole being; for every man, whether he "knows" or "believes", perfection is "to adore God as if you saw Him, and if you do not see Him, He nonetheless sees you".[3]

* * *

[1] Evagrius Ponticus teaches that faith, fortified by the other virtues (fear, temperance, patience, and hope), engenders "apathy", that is, spiritual indifference or impassibility, which in its turn engenders charity, the gateway of contemplation; he also says that "apathy" precedes charity, and charity precedes knowledge. It may be added that, according to the Hesychasts Barsanuphius and John, "continual prayer measures itself against 'apathy'."

[2] This is the *credo ut intelligam* of Saint Anselm.

[3] This saying of the Prophet is considered the very definition of Sufism. For Saint Simeon the New Theologian, faith must live in works of holiness and thus in all that conduces to contemplation, and this leads him to conclude that the saints alone are effectively baptized. Far from wanting to replace baptism by an initiation that would go beyond it, Saint Simeon wants on the contrary to make baptismal grace come alive again through spiritual tears and through diverse disciplines and benedictions, and he founds his teaching on these words of Christ: "He that believeth on me, out of his belly shall flow rivers of living water." Now it is clear that this formula does not institute any rite. "According to Saint John Climacus, 'Repentance is a renewal of baptism, but the well of tears after baptism is a greater thing than baptism.' This judgment may seem paradoxical if one forgets that repentance is the fruit of baptismal grace; this same grace, if only it is acquired and appropriated by the person, becomes in itself the 'gift of tears', a sure sign that the heart has been melted by divine love" (Vladimir Lossky, *Essai sur la théologie mystique de l'Église d'Orient*).

There is a long-standing illusion that consists in wanting to approach the Absolute with the aid of the mind, as if there were not a measureless discontinuity between the most refined concept and Reality. The extreme point of a concept, of a doctrinal symbol, far from touching Reality, is like a needle poised against limitless space. A theoretical conception may acquire an infinite complexity as a result of intellectual intuitions; it is nothing by comparison with the Real. And yet this speculative meditation is all-important to the man who, with the help of a revealed idea and by assimilating its most profound aspect, puts himself into the required state of readiness in order that the miracle of intellection might be accomplished; now this state of readiness essentially implies faith and therefore also the virtues that express and nourish it.

Faith, even if it is only belief, always contains some measure of certainty, and in metaphysical certitude there is always a measure of faith: faith is a luminous obscurity, and certitude is an obscure light.

* * *

What God requires above all from man is faith: an attachment with the very depths of our being to the Truth that transcends us; now this Truth is invisible to human nature as such.

If faith is the adherence of our whole being to Truth, then the trials of life will have the divine and spiritual function of proving the quality of our faith and also of increasing our faith by purifying it; suffering, "trial", thus becomes the criterion of our real attachment to immutable, divine Truth, that is, of the integral and fundamental nature of our adherence. In relationship to this function, the trial is essentially "sent by God"; in other words it is looked upon from the point of view of its divine cause in connection with our spiritual weakness.[4]

---

[4] The Bible—especially the Book of Job—the Koran, and other revealed Scriptures clearly show this link between "trial" and "faith"; the Koran says: "Do men imagine that they will be left in quiet if they say, 'We believe' and that they will not be put to the test?" (*Sûrah* "The Spider" [29]:2). "And We (God) will test you by fright, by hunger, by loss of goods, of lives and harvests" (*Sûrah* "The Cow" [2]:155). "We shall alternate such days (of misfortune) among men that God may know which are those that believe . . . in order that God may test those that believe" (*Sûrah* "The Family of Imran" [3]:140-41).

It is fire that "tests" the true quality of metals; fire, by its incorruptible purity, plays the part here of divine criterion.

*   *   *

The great requirement of Islam is to believe in God, who is One. The question Sufism puts is this: "What does it mean to believe in God?" To believe is to prove one believes: to prove it to God, in whom one believes, and to prove it to oneself, that is, to him who believes.[5] And it is proved by the participation of our whole being in the conviction of the mind—"as if you saw Him, and if you do not see Him, He nonetheless sees you".

Trials, which are sent by God, have an analogous function, though it is in a sense the inverse, since the initiative, if one may put it this way, is on the part of God; He tests the faith of man, which man must prove.

Sincere, integral faith always implies renunciation, poverty, privation, since the world—or the ego—is not God.

God tests by removing; man proves by renouncing. The renunciation may be inward and independent of facts; in that case it is detachment. He is detached who never forgets the ephemeral nature of what he possesses and who looks on these things as being lent to him, not as possessions.

Faith, trial, patience, sincerity: the virtue of patience (the *sabr* of the Sufis) remains meaningless without faith and without trial; it is the criterion of sincerity (*sidq*).

*   *   *

The annoyances or adversities that come to man always have three causes: man himself, the world, God. According to the point of view adopted, we may take into consideration one or another of these causes, but we cannot deny any of them.

Man is the author of his misfortune insofar as it is experienced as suffering; the world is its author insofar as the misfortune seeks

---

[5] "Faith (*îmân*) is a confessing with the tongue, a verifying with the heart, and an act with the members" (*hadîth*). "He has the greatest perfection in faith who has the most beauty of character" (*hadîth*), or according to another saying, "who most fears God".

to keep man in cosmic illusion; and God is the Author inasmuch as the misfortune comes to man as a sanction, though also as a purification and thus as a trial.

The same thing is true *mutatis mutandis* of happy events: we can never say they do not come from God, or that they do not come from the cosmic surroundings, or that they do not result from our own nature. These events are also trials in their character of temptation;[6] the corresponding virtue will be renunciation or detachment (*zuhd*). The spiritual "traveler" (*sâlik*) should be not only "patient" (*sabûr*) but also "detached" (*zâhid*).

* * *

It is clear that suffering does not necessarily have the character of a trial; the impious man may suffer, but in his case there is nothing spiritual to be tested.

According to Meister Eckhart—who was nevertheless far from attributing to ascetic practices any role other than that of a quite contingent, preparatory means—there is nothing nobler than suffering; this is the doctrine of ascetics and martyrs because it is the doctrine of Christ: "And he that taketh not his cross, and followeth after me, is not worthy of me."[7]

It is this spiritual aspect of suffering that made it possible for Buddhism as well to be founded on the experience of distress.[8] Other perspectives are founded on the experience of beauty and sometimes even on the experience of earthly love;[9] everything that has an aspect of nobility or limitlessness can by definition be a vehicle for spiritual development.

* * *

[6] "And We shall test you by ill and by good in order to try you, and you will return to Us" (*Sûrah* "The Prophets" [21]:35).

[7] "For as the sufferings of Christ abound in us, so our consolation also aboundeth by Christ" (2 Cor. 1:5).

[8] Buddhism is a kind of "Hindu Christianity", and this doubtless explains the interest it has for Westerners; but it goes without saying that in other respects—precisely because it is Hindu and not Western in origin—it is much further from Christianity than are Judaism and Islam.

[9] This is the story of Majnun and Layla, of a love that pierced through appearances to the infinite Essence of all beauty. An analogous example is that of the role of Beatrice in the life of Dante.

The negation of pleasure, of the world, of manifestation is equivalent to an implicit affirmation of the Principle, which in relation to the world is "void" (*shûnya* in Sanskrit) and "not this" (*neti*). Suffering transposes the problem to the plane of what is most intimately human; it is for man like a fissure in his existential illusion.

There is no spirituality that is not founded, in one of its constituent elements, on the negation of this dream; there is no spirituality devoid of ascetic elements: even simple mental concentration implies sacrifice. When the concentration is continuous, it is the narrow path, the dark night: the soul itself, this living substance full of images and desires, is sacrificed.

Distress affirms the Principle by denying manifestation; but noble enjoyment affirms the Principle by direct analogy and becomes in this way a possible channel for intellection. The question of opportuneness arises only on the level of individual applications.

* * *

The cult of suffering or of what is disagreeable is a different thing from the spiritualizing of suffering: it is the error of believing that suffering is the only thing that brings one nearer to God. In a certain sense this is true when suffering, martyrdom, is given a universal meaning. In this case it is true that man draws nearer to God only through suffering—that is, through sacrifice, renunciation, poverty, extinction, loss of self.

Clearly what matters is not that man should suffer, but that he should think of God. Suffering has a value only to the extent that it provokes, deepens, and perpetuates this thought; now it plays this role for every man who believes in God and the immortality of the soul.

An enjoyment that brings man nearer to God—by virtue of its symbolism, its nobility, and the contemplative quality of the subject—is no less profound than suffering, and perhaps in some respects even more profound; but this possibility requires rare qualities of nobility and contemplative penetration, of intuition of the universal essences.

* * *

The fact that spiritual causes can engender darkness in no way signifies that darkness always has spiritual causes.

The criterion is in the nature of the darkness in question and in the way in which it is experienced. A spiritually necessary form of darkness is passive, and it never destroys continuity of judgment or humility; it gives rise to suffering but not to error; it could not tarnish the life of a saint. Man has a right to grief but never to sin: to lack light is a different thing from putting out the light one already has.

2

Fundamental Keys

Meditation, concentration, prayer: these three words epitomize the spiritual life, while at the same time indicating its principal modes. Meditation, from the standpoint here adopted, is an activity of the intelligence in view of understanding universal truths; concentration for its part is an activity of the will in view of assimilating these truths or realities existentially, as it were; and prayer in turn is an activity of the soul with respect to God.

We have spoken of universal truths; by this term we mean principles which determine everything that is. The first function of the intelligence, from the point of view considered here, is to distinguish between the Absolute and the relative; its second function will then be, on the one hand, to perceive relativity intellectually insofar as it seemingly enters into the domain of the Absolute[1] and, on the other hand, to perceive the Absolute as it is reflected in the relative.

Let it be said once again—since the context requires it—that the "pure Absolute" is "the Essence of Essences" or Beyond-Being; as for the relative, it includes both Being and its central reflection in the world, and then the world itself; Being—or the personal God, the Creator—is the "relative Absolute", if for want of a less problematical term one may thus speak of it.

We may therefore distinguish four degrees in the total Universe: Beyond-Being, God-Being, Heaven, and Earth, the last term designating symbolically and comprehensively all that is situated below the celestial Summit. Or again: Beyond-Being and Being taken together—if one may so express it—constitute the divine Principle, while Heaven and Earth constitute universal Manifestation, Heaven

---

[1] Or insofar as it appears mysteriously within that which, seen from the standpoint of contingency or manifestation, is still the Absolute—a paradox that can be explained despite the clumsiness of the language, though not in a few words.

being able to be conceived as including Being and Beyond-Being, as is suggested by the phrase "Our Father who art in Heaven".

But the total Universe is not only made up of degrees, for there are modes as well; the degrees are disposed in a "vertical" order, whereas the modes are in a "horizontal" order and situated in the appropriate manner at each of the four degrees. There is first of all a duality: an "active" and divinely "masculine" pole, and a "passive" and divinely "feminine" pole;[2] then there comes a trinity: Power, Consciousness, and Felicity.[3] Finally, we may distinguish a quaternity: Rigor, Gentleness, Activity, and Passivity; in other words, Purity or Sacrifice, Goodness or Life, Strength or Light—or victorious Act—and Beauty or Peace; herein is to be found the origin of all the Qualities, divine and cosmic.[4]

* * *

After meditation, which pertains to Truth and intelligence, comes concentration, which pertains to the Way and the will; there is no Truth that does not have its prolongation in the Way, and there is no intelligence that does not have its prolongation in the will; the authenticity and totality of the values in question require this.

Concentration in itself—apart from its possible contents—ultimately pertains to the "deiformity" of the planes constituting the human microcosm: man is like a tree whose root is the "heart" and whose crown is the "forehead". Now our mental space—the substance or energy containing or producing thought—is in itself consciousness of the divine Reality; the mind emptied of all coagulations "thinks God" by its very substance, in "holy silence", man being "made in the image of God".

The same is true of our bodily substance—or more precisely our consciousness of this substance—actualized in perfect immobility:

---

[2] *Purusha* and *Prakriti* at the level of Being, *Îshvara*; but these poles are also reflected at other levels, beginning with the supreme *Paramâtmâ*, in which they necessarily have their root.

[3] *Sat, Chit, Ânanda*, which enter into all existence, although in Vedantic parlance these terms designate only the "dimensions" of *Âtmâ* as such.

[4] Hindu mythology, like every other, designates these root Qualities by the names of numerous divinities, the quaternity being moreover an opening to indefinite differentiation. With the American Indians, the four universal Qualities are manifested mythically by the cardinal points.

the moment we do nothing but "exist" we are virtually identified with Being, beyond all cosmic coagulations. Concurrently with bodily consciousness, there is vital, energetical consciousness—in short, life and movement—which, as sacred dances testify, can be a vehicle for our participation in cosmic rhythms and universal life, at all the levels accessible to us by virtue of our nature and through Grace.

This leaves, in the human microcosm, the consciousness of self—namely, the "heart"—which can likewise be the support of an existential "remembrance of God" on the basis of intellectual, ritual, and moral conditions that guarantee the legitimacy and efficacy of such an alchemy. Whatever the case, the psychosomatic analogies we have just called to mind convey teachings that concern all men: every human being must, out of love for God, strive to "be what he is"—to disengage himself from the artificial superstructures which disfigure him and which are none other than traces of the fall—in order to become once again a tree whose root is made of liberating certitude and whose crown is made of beatific serenity. Human nature is predisposed toward the unitive knowledge of its divine Model; *Amore e'l cor gentil sono una cosa.*

We must now consider another aspect of the question, which is that of symbolic content. Mental activity is capable not only of thought but also of imagination, thus of visualizing a symbolic form; in like manner, the spirit is sensitive not only to concepts but also to evocative sounds, to auditory symbols; and in like manner again, the body is capable not only of movements that are necessary or useful, but also of symbolic gestures. All this enters into a psychosomatic alchemy of which the spiritual traditions of the East afford us many examples, and of which the Christian liturgies offer echoes. The visual image *a priori* addresses the mind, and thus pertains to the region of the forehead; sound is connected with our center, the heart; and symbolic movement, quite evidently, concerns the body. And this relates both to the deiform character of the planes constituting the microcosm and to the alchemy of non-discursive, existential symbols—namely, forms, sounds, and gestures.

Such is the alchemy of existential participation in the life of the spirit; the mental space participates in it by means of the image, the heart-root through sound, and the body—which is a projection or extension of the two poles—either through immobility and static gesture or through rhythm and dynamic gesture; and we have in mind here basic postures as well as ritual operations accompanied by an awareness of their profound nature.[5] It goes without saying that all this has its applications in the diverse forms of sacred art or traditional craftsmanship, and sometimes even in legitimate forms of secular art.

* * *

Man possesses a soul, and to have a soul is to pray. Like the soul itself, prayer comprises modes, and each mode contains a virtue; to pray, then, is to actualize a virtue and at the same time to sow the seed of it. First of all comes resignation to the Will of God: acceptance of our destiny insofar as we cannot and should not change it; this attitude has to become second nature with us, since there is always something from which we cannot escape. Correlative to this attitude or virtue there is the compensating attitude of trust: whoever puts his trust in God while conforming to the divine demands will find God altogether disposed to come to his aid; but what we expect from Heaven we must ourselves offer to others: whoever desires mercy for himself must himself be merciful.

Another compensatory attitude with respect to resignation is the petition for help: we have fundamentally the right, based on our acceptance of destiny, to ask God for this good or that favor; but it goes without saying that we can ask nothing of Heaven if we lack gratitude. Now to be thankful is to be conscious of all the good that Heaven has given us; it is to appreciate the value of even small things and to be content with little. Gratitude is the complement of supplication, just as generosity is the complement of trust in God. The great lesson of prayer is that our relationship with the world depends essentially on our relationship with Heaven.

[5] Of which Hinduism and Northern Buddhism especially, with their science of *mantra, yantra,* and *mudrâ,* possess the secret.

One Word

There is one Word, it is the saving key:
Dwell thou in God, and God will dwell in thee.
Out of compassion to our world He came;
His are two homes on earth: our heart, His Name.

Spiritual Perspectives

II

Metaphysical certainty is not God, though it contains something of Him. This is why Sufis accompany even their certainties with this formula: "And God is more wise" (*wa 'Llâhu a'lam*).

The cult of intelligence and mental passion distances man from truth: intelligence narrows as soon as man puts his trust in it alone; mental passion chases intellectual intuition away just as the wind blows out the light of a candle.

Monomania of the mind, with the unconscious pretension, prejudice, insatiability, and haste that are its concomitants, is incompatible with sanctity; indeed sanctity introduces into the flux of thought an element of humility and charity, and thus of calm and generosity—an element which, far from being prejudicial to the spiritual momentum or the sometimes violent force of truth, delivers the mind from the vexations of passions and thus guarantees both the integrity of thought and the purity of inspiration.

According to the Sufis mental passion must be ranked as one of the associations with Satan, like other forms of passional "idolatry"; it cannot directly have God for its object; if God were its direct object, it would lose its specifically negative characteristics. Furthermore it does not contain within itself any principle of repose, for it excludes all consciousness of its own destitution.

* * *

We must beware of two things: first of replacing God—in practice if not in theory—by the functions and products of the intellect, or of considering Him only in connection with this faculty; second of putting the "mechanical" factors of spirituality in place of human values—virtues—or of considering virtues only in relation to their "technical" utility, not their beauty.[1]

---

[1] According to Eckhart's conception, the sufficient reason for the virtues is not in the first place their extrinsic usefulness, but their beauty.

19

*   *   *

Intelligence has only one nature, luminosity; but it has diverse functions, different modes of working that appear as so many particular intelligences. Intelligence with a "logical", "mathematical", or one might say "abstract" quality is insufficient for reaching all aspects of the real; it would be impossible to insist too often on the importance of the "visual" or "aesthetic" function of the intellective faculty. We are faced in reality, on the one hand, with what is determined in advance—starting from principles—and, on the other hand, with that which is incalculable and in some way unforeseeable, and of which we must obtain knowledge by concrete "assimilation", not abstract "discernment".[2]

In reflecting upon formal elements, one would be at a serious disadvantage if one were deprived of this aesthetic function of the Intellect. A religion is revealed not only by its doctrine, but also by its general form, which has its own characteristic beauty and is reflected everywhere, from "mythology" to art. Sacred art expresses the Real in relation to a particular spiritual vision. Aesthetic intelligence sees manifestations of the Spirit in the same way that the eye sees flowers or jewels: for example, in order to understand Buddhism profoundly—if one is not born a Buddhist—it is not enough to study its doctrine; it is also necessary to penetrate the language of Buddhist beauty as it appears in the sacramental image of the Buddha or in such features as the "Flower Sermon".[3]

*   *   *

The aesthetic function of intelligence—if we may call it that for lack of a better term—enters not only into the form of every spiritual manifestation, but also into the process of its manifestation: truth must be enunciated not only with a sense of proportion, but also

---

[2] This is the perspective of Chaitanya and Ramakrishna. It happened to them to fall into ecstasy (*samâdhi*) on seeing a beautiful animal. In Sufism analogous examples of "spiritual aesthetics" are to be found in Omar ibn al-Farid and Jalal al-Din Rumi.

[3] Without saying a word the Buddha lifted a flower, and this gesture was the origin of Zen. Let us recall here that the Buddhas save not only by their teaching, but also by their superhuman beauty, which is perpetuated—in a manner half-concrete, half-abstract—in sacramental images.

according to a certain rhythm. One cannot speak of sacred things in just any manner, nor can one speak of them without measure.

Every manifestation has laws that intelligence must observe when manifesting itself, or otherwise truth will suffer.

*   *   *

The Intellect is not cerebral, nor is it specifically human or angelic; all beings "possess" it. If gold is not lead, this is because it better "knows" the Divine; its "knowledge" is in its very form, and this amounts to saying that its form does not belong to it in its own right, since matter cannot know. Nonetheless we can say that the rose differs from the water-lily by its intellectual particularity, by its "way of knowing", and thus by its mode of intelligence. Beings have intelligence in their form to the extent that they are "peripheral" or "passive" and in their essence to the extent that they are "central", "active", "conscious".

A noble animal or a lovely flower is "intellectually" superior to a base man.

God reveals Himself to the plant in the form of the light of the sun. The plant irresistibly turns itself toward the light; it could not be atheistic or impious.

*   *   *

The infallible "instinct" of animals is a lower "intellect"; man's Intellect may be called a higher "instinct". Between instinct and Intellect there stands in a certain sense the reason, which owes its poverty to the fact that it constitutes a sort of "Luciferian" duplication of the divine Intelligence, the only intelligence there is.

*   *   *

Knowledge of facts depends upon contingencies, which cannot enter into principial knowledge. The plane of facts is in certain respects opposed to that of principles in the sense that it includes modes and imponderables that are at the opposite extreme from the wholly mathematical rigor of universal laws; at least this is so in appearance, for it goes without saying that universal principles do not contradict themselves; even beneath the veil of the inexhaustible diversity of what is possible, their immutability can always be discerned, provided that the intelligence finds itself in suitable circumstances.

*   *   *

Although the Intellect is, so to speak, sovereign and infallible on its own ground, it cannot exercise discernment on the level of facts otherwise than conditionally; moreover God may intervene on this level with particular and at times unpredictable manifestations of His will, and this is something that principial knowledge can verify only *a posteriori*.

*   *   *

Hidden causes—whether cosmic or human—must be admitted where their intervention results from the nature of things, but not for the sake of satisfying a postulate whose metaphysical basis and practical bearing have been lost sight of. When we see a waterfall we have no reason for saying that it is moved by a magical force, even when a saint is drowned in it. The fact that there are some men who produce evil more consciously than others does not authorize us in saying that all human evil is a conscious production as regards its scope and repercussions, and still less that every work that has a negative aspect was undertaken for the sake of this aspect. Human evil is intentional as to its immediate object, but not as to its cosmic significance; were this not the case, the evil would end up being dissolved in knowledge. If Voltaire had foreseen the ills of the twentieth century, he would have become a Carthusian.

A true principle always corresponds to a necessity, and on the other hand it never excludes a possibility; every postulate is false if it does not refer to a necessity that is divine, natural, traditional, or spiritual—according to the case or point of view—or if it excludes some possibility inherent in the order with which it is concerned.

From another angle, the *de jure* truth of a postulate must not be confused with some particular factual application, even when this represents a relative norm. Reality is differentiated, comprising diverse combinations; one can never escape the necessity of a direct insight into the spiritual or cosmic factors whose nature one seeks to define.

*   *   *

What is better in principle does not always appear so in fact; the virtuous act of a simple and ignorant man may have a secret quality that makes it more pleasing to God—not more than metaphysics in itself, certainly, but more than the soul of some particular metaphysician.

In a general way the plane of facts has a tendency to escape from the determinism of principles, and this is because of the limitlessness of universal Possibility. This truth provides a safeguard against illusions and creates an atmosphere of circumspect humility, which alone allows us to concern ourselves with wisdom fruitfully and with impunity.

When a fact seems to contradict a principle, it is in reality manifesting another principle, which of necessity corroborates the first and is consequently an aspect of it.

To interpret facts with reference to principles is quite a different thing from distorting them in order to adjust them to preconceived conceptions.

* * *

The Biblical idea of "justice" sums up the fundamental qualities of a man centered on God. This justice is made of intelligence and generosity: the primordial object of intelligence is the Divinity, and the object of generosity is man, the neighbor.

Generosity may be a matter of sentiment, just as intelligence may be a matter of thought, but intelligence unaccompanied by generosity becomes fallible, and generosity lacking in intelligence becomes arbitrary. True knowledge does not dry up the soul, and true charity does not dissolve truth.

What is human must never be confused with what is spiritual: one who finds that he is the receptacle of the Spirit of truth should never forget that the receptacle is not the Spirit. It is true that the Spirit may burn and consume the recipient, but on condition that he is not closed to the influx of Light. "God alone is good."

* * *

In order to be forearmed against all unconscious presumption, a man may start from the idea that the human recipient is bad, the Spirit alone being good. But he may also start from the idea that the recipient is whatever he pleases—"good" or "bad" or both at once—and that the Spirit alone is real, or truly the "Self".

The unconscious presumption of an intelligent man often has its occasional cause in the unintelligence of other people, which he is bound to observe and from which he is bound to suffer. But he must never forget that the one-eyed man is king among the blind.

* * *

The spontaneous manifestation of truth implies an aspect of incorruptibility and an aspect of generosity: without the first, truth is engulfed and finally dissolved in some absurdity or other; and without the second, it loses the grace that nourishes it and ends by giving rise to error.

It could also be said that truth includes an aspect of self-respect and an aspect of humility.

* * *

Doctrine, in relation to which individuals are of no account, must not be confused with those doctrinal functions which, on the contrary, involve the individual substance. Light is colorless in itself, but it may be transmitted through a crystal that is more or less transparent or through a crystal that is either white or colored.

* * *

Strictly speaking, doctrinal knowledge is independent of the individual. But its actualization is not independent of the human capacity to act as a vehicle for it; he who possesses truth must nonetheless merit it, though it is a free gift. Truth is immutable in itself, but in us it lives because we live.

If we want truth to live in us, we must live in it.

* * *

Knowledge saves only on condition that it engages all that we are: only when it constitutes a path which works and transforms, and which wounds our nature as the plough wounds the soil.

This means that intelligence and metaphysical certainty alone do not save and do not of themselves prevent titanic falls. This explains the psychological and other precautions with which every tradition surrounds the gift of doctrine.

* * *

When metaphysical knowledge is effective it produces love and destroys presumption. It produces love: that is, the spontaneous directing of the will toward God and the perception of "myself"— and of God—in the neighbor. It destroys presumption: for knowledge does not allow man to overestimate himself or underestimate others; by reducing to ashes all that is not God, it orders all things.

Everything that Saint Paul says about charity concerns effective wisdom, for this wisdom is love; he opposes it to theory considered as a human concept. The Apostle desires that truth should be contemplated with our whole being, and he calls this totality of contemplation "love".

Metaphysical knowledge is sacred. It is the property of sacred things to require of man all that he is.

* * *

Intelligence, as soon as it distinguishes, perceives proportions, if one may put it this way. The spiritual man integrates these proportions into his will, into his soul, into his life.

All defects are disproportions; they are errors that are lived. To be spiritual means not to deny with one's "being" what is affirmed with one's "knowledge", that is, what is accepted by the intelligence.

Truth lived: incorruptibility and generosity.

* * *

Since ignorance is all that we are, and not merely our thinking, knowledge will also be all that we are to the extent that our existential modalities are by their nature able to participate in truth.

Human nature contains obscurities that no intellectual certainty could *ipso facto* eliminate.

* * *

The knowledge that man enjoys—or can enjoy—is at once animal, human, and divine: animal insofar as man knows through the senses; human when he knows by reason; and divine in the contemplative activity of the Intellect. Now man could not be divine without first being human; the Intellect, in the direct and higher meaning of the word—for the reason and senses are equally, though indirectly, derived from the Intellect—could not be actualized in a being that did not possess what, in the human domain, is supplied by the reason. In the same way, the uncreated Intellect, of which Meister Eckhart speaks, would not be accessible to man without the created Intellect, which, far from being identical with the rational faculty, is as it were its center and its secret, the fine point turned toward the infinite Light.

Man knows through the senses, the brain, and the heart, which correspond respectively to his animality, his humanity, and his divinity.

Reason is like air, without which fire—intellection—could not manifest itself discursively, but which can put out that same fire.

* * *

One must distinguish between intellectuality and intellectualism: intellectualism appears as an end in itself; it is an intelligence contented with its multiple visions of the true and forgetful that it is not alone in the world and that life is passing; it practically makes itself God. The intellectualist acts as if he had concluded a security pact with the Eternal.

Intellectualism cannot fail to engender errors. It confers self-complacency and abolishes fear of God; it introduces a sort of worldliness into the intellectual domain. Its good side is that it may speak of truth; its bad side is the manner in which it speaks of it. It replaces the virtues it lacks by sophistries; it lays claim to everything, but is in fact ineffectual.

In intellectualism a capacity to understand the most difficult things readily goes hand in hand with an inability to understand the simplest things.

* * *

Pure intellectuality is as serene as a summer sky—with a serenity that is at once infinitely incorruptible and infinitely generous.

Intellectualism, which "dries up the heart", has no connection with intellectuality.

The incorruptibility—or inviolability—of truth involves neither contempt nor avarice.

*   *   *

What is the certitude possessed by man? On the plane of ideas it may be perfect, but on the plane of life it rarely pierces through illusion.

Everything is ephemeral; every man must die. No one is unaware of this, and no one knows it.

*   *   *

A man may have a quite illusory interest in adopting the most transcendent ideas and may readily believe himself to be superior to someone else who, not having this interest—perhaps because he is too intelligent or too noble to have it—is sincere enough not to adopt them, though he may all the same be better able to understand them than the one who adopts them. Man does not always accept truth because he understands it; often he believes he understands it because he wants to accept it.

People often discuss truths, whereas they should limit themselves to discussing tastes and tendencies.

*   *   *

It is possible to speak of "intellectual pride"—although there is a contradiction in this expression[4] when a man attributes to his intelligence virtues and rights that are disproportionate, and also when acuteness of intelligence provokes in the mind a passional activity contrary to contemplation, in such a way that the spirit becomes separated from the remembrance of God.

Acuteness of intelligence is a blessing only when it is compensated by greatness and gentleness of soul; it should not manifest itself as a disruption of equilibrium, an excess that splits man in two. A gift of nature requires complementary qualities that permit its harmonious manifestation; otherwise there is a risk of the light becoming mingled with darkness.

---

[4] Strictly speaking, we should call this "intellectualist pride".

3

Prayer and the Integration of the Psychic Elements

Prayer in the most usual sense of the term is a practice that appears to imply an anthropomorphic and sentimental point of view: anthropomorphic because it seems to attribute to God a temporal nature and a human understanding, and sentimental because it expresses itself readily in forms pertaining to feeling. Now it is legitimate and even necessary to conceive of the Divinity in a more or less personified aspect, since it really includes such an aspect in relation to us; moreover, by virtue of this same point of view, the standpoint of man can be affirmed without difficulty in ways that are strictly human.

Thus conceived, prayer by no means implies by definition the conception of a God arbitrarily humanized and divested of His infinite transcendence, any more than it implies the presence in man of a purely sentimental disposition. In a general way it is too often forgotten that sentiment as such is not to be identified with its deviations but that it is on the contrary a normal psychic fact, which is capable of playing a positive role in spirituality; the mere fact that in praying man makes use of all his inward faculties in striving toward God, and consequently also of his natural sentimentality, which he cannot abolish or treat as non-existent, in no way means that feeling should be taken as an end in itself or that it thus should entail a more or less individualistic alteration of doctrinal truths. Prayer could never be contrary to the purest intellectuality;[1] without contradicting any transcendent truth, prayer has its reason for being in the existence of the human "I", which, since it exists, must be channeled toward its ultimate sufficient reason. In other words, the individual as such never ceases to be "I", and since prayer is the

[1] Hence the example of Shri Shankaracharya, who implores the mercy of Shiva and prays to the divine Mother. We are here very far from the naïve error according to which prayer is incompatible with "pure" *jnâna*; as for Shankara, either he was a *jnânin* or there never has been one. When the God-Man prays, his prayer is cosmic, whence the use in revealed prayers, such as the *Pater* or the *Fâtihah*, of the first person plural.

spiritual act of the "I", it must be practiced as long as the individual exists, that is, to the extent that he maintains the idea of the ego.[2] Man's attitude in prayer must in some sense remain egocentric by definition; in metaphysical meditation, on the contrary, man places himself symbolically at the "standpoint" of the nature of things.

On the other hand, when it is said that forms are supports, it must never be forgotten that a support, in order to be such, must be entirely what it is in itself, and that it must not and cannot be a "part" of what it must transmit, just as a light cannot be the means for reflecting another light; thus prayer must always remain a conversation with God or an appeal addressed to Him, and it is only on condition that prayer be first entirely what it is in its most immediate possibility—namely, the translation and expression of an individual intention—that it can serve as a support for intellections transcending the individual plane. By this we mean that prayer cannot be replaced by impersonal and abstract meditation, for the immediate objectives of the two are different; but this is not to say that meditation cannot be integrated, in suitable ways, into prayer, or that the formulas of revealed prayers do not include a universal meaning.

All that we have just said makes it easier to understand why there is no need to invoke at every turn the opposition between reason and sentiment; if the relatively lower psychic faculties can form an obstacle to the activity of reason, the seat of theoretical knowledge, reason itself constitutes no less an obstacle once effective knowledge is at issue; for it is then the whole mental faculty as such that can become an obstacle, reason being only the most direct reflection of the Intellect, which is beyond all cerebral contingencies.

* * *

The Intellect, since it is universal in essence, necessarily penetrates the entire being and embraces all its constituent elements; for to exist is to know, and every aspect of our existence is a state of knowing or—in relation to absolute Knowledge—a state of ignorance. If it is true that reason is the central mirror of the Intellect, whose organ is the subtle heart, the other faculties are nonetheless

---

[2] This is closely related to the theory of the two natures of Christ.

also planes of manifestation for the Intellect; the individual being cannot be reintegrated into the Absolute without all his faculties participating in due measure in the process. Spiritual knowledge, far from opposing any particular mode of conformity or participation, on the contrary brings into play all that we are, hence all the constituent elements, psychic and even physical, of our being, for nothing positive can be excluded from the process of transmutation; nothing can be destroyed, and therefore the psychic faculties or energies that form a part of our reality, and whose existence must have a meaning for us, have to be determined and channeled by the same governing Idea that determines and transforms thought. But this cannot be done without first placing oneself on the very level of the psychic faculties: it is not enough to consider these faculties by means of reason and in a theoretical light; one must realize the Idea, to the extent this is possible, on the plane of these faculties, by universalizing them as it were in virtue of the different symbolisms corresponding to them.[3] Man must transpose onto a higher plane all the positive reactions that the surrounding reality provokes in him, remembering divine Realities through sensible things; it could also be said that if spiritual things have to be humanized in some way, then conversely human things have to be spiritualized; the first symbolic mode envelops Truth, and the second reveals it.

We have seen that the very existence of individual or psychic elements is a sufficient reason for taking them into consideration and that we must necessarily do so in a way that is not purely negative, since these elements are none other than ourselves insofar as we are individuals; if we were able, such as we are, to be absolutely spiritual—an obviously contradictory supposition—we would be identical with the divine Principle, and we would not have to be delivered from anything. To be more precise, we may add that the man who through ignorance or theoretical preconceptions neglects to integrate the psychic elements of his personality into his spiritual attitude possesses these elements nonetheless, whether he allows them to wander about at will, side by side with theoretical conceptions and in contradiction to them, or represses them, so that they slumber in his subconscious as more or less latent obstacles. In any

---

[3] For instance, the passion of love becomes the love of God, and anger becomes "holy wrath"; or again, warlike passion finds its meaning and sufficient reason in "Holy War".

spiritual realization it is important that a man not be fixed, so to speak, within one restricted area of his ego; on the contrary, all his possibilities must be awakened, recapitulated, and channeled in accordance with their respective natures, for man is all that constitutes him; his faculties are interrelated. It is not possible to open the intelligence to the Divine without ennobling the psychic and even physical being; there is no spirituality without greatness and without beauty.

We shall illustrate the foregoing considerations by the following example: in too many cases the psychological potentiality of childhood never achieves its normal flowering; the necessary manifestation of this possibility is checked—most often by the misdeeds of school education—and subsists as though stifled or crushed, or like a shrunken and hardened kernel, throughout the further development of the individual; from this results a psychic imbalance, which will show itself on the one hand by the apparent absence of the childlike element, and on the other by childish reactions such as are not undergone by the balanced man, whose virile possibility will have integrated his childlike possibility, the latter being as it were the background of the former. Virility—*virtus*—is always an aspect and a fact of equilibrium; the person who is only adult, that is, adult to the exclusion of any childlike element, is so only imperfectly and as it were through an inability to remain a child; now an incapacity is never a superiority. The state of childhood must be transcended by integration, by "digestion" if one may so express it, and this necessity is already indicated by the fact that there is a perfect continuity between different ages; this means that the individual must at every age make use of all the positive contents of the preceding ages,[4] and that he will then respond to events not in a way strictly dependent on his age, but with complete balance, uniting for example the spontaneity of youth with the reflectiveness of maturity; in other words, he will possess his temporal "self" in its integral state; every positive attitude, be it childlike or other, is necessary and precious.[5]

---

[4] If childhood did not have a positive aspect peculiar to itself, what meaning could there be in the symbolism of the Child Jesus and in Christ's saying concerning holy childlikeness?

[5] These considerations are intended to show that the childlike element is not a residue but a necessary, and therefore legitimate, element in the adult, who never wholly ceases to be a child.

Reason, the seat of theoretical knowledge, is too abstract a substance to represent the "I" by itself alone; it is therefore necessary that feeling and desire, that is, what is most strictly "I", be transmuted by the Idea. But this transmutation introduces a most important principle that must never be lost sight of: the psychic faculty as such—which is a limitation—must be distinguished from its possible contents; these contents translate the Idea in their own way and are necessary to a man's psychological and physical equilibrium. Sentiment is more remote from pure knowledge than reason; however, the natural impulses of sentiment are less harmful to intellectuality—supposing they are such in themselves—than are rational conceptions; these, when taken too literally in the absence of intellectual intuition, can paralyze the possibilities of understanding, whereas sentiment is neutral in this respect.

Psychic conformity based on the symbolism of sentiment or desire is possible, however, only on condition of a rational conformity, that is, a sufficient theoretical knowledge on the one hand and a conformity of action on the other; and this must be so because the most clearly individual elements can have their sufficient reason and hence their ideal determination only through the Intellect, and also because these elements are substantially dependent on the physical world where action takes place. Through the Idea the natural emotions are, on the one hand, reduced to proportions that correspond to the individual's psychic equilibrium and, on the other hand, they are endowed with a spiritual essence; through action, or by the participation of action in the Idea—hence through action which is symbolic and which has become a ritual, so to speak—the emotions receive as it were a new substance.

*   *   *

For man as such, the question of the divine Reality can be stated thus: if other individuals—or objects such as food—possess an immediately tangible and empirically incontestable reality, so that it is perfectly natural to speak to someone else or to partake of food, then God, who is the ultimate Prototype of all things, possesses a reality that is incommensurable in relation to the reality that surrounds us and upon which we live. Now if it is logical to talk to people or to eat food because both of these are "real", it is all the more logical—or less illusory—to speak to God, who is the infinite

Cause of all good, and to live on His Word, which is the infinite Essence of all nourishment.

We said earlier that in prayer God is conceived, as it were automatically, as personal: indeed it is in the nature of things for God to reveal Himself under a more or less human aspect once He enters into contact with man, for otherwise there would be no possible meeting point between God and the individual; but this human aspect does not pertain to the Divinity in itself, any more than a color pertains to light. God hears our prayers and replies to them, while He Himself, needless to say, undergoes no change at all. Our prayers cannot penetrate God, since they are nothing before Him. The divine replies are so many effects of absolute Plenitude; it is we, the reflections, who are affected by the universal Cause, and not inversely. "Before" we formulated our prayers, the divine replies "were" in eternity; God is for us the eternal, omnipresent Response, and prayer can have no other function than to eliminate all that separates us from this Response, which is inexhaustible.

Prayer

"Grandfather, hear my words, I talk to Thee:
Look down, take pity, not alone on me
But on my people," prays a noble mind.
In this a deeper meaning thou wilt find.

When thou invokest God, His Grace is thine,
But like the living sunlight it will shine
For others too; the sacred, saving Sound
Will bless believing people all around.

A Sound that always in our heart should be;
A Wave of Bliss, Peace, Immortality.

———————————————

Spiritual Perspectives

III

There is something in man that is contrary to God and something that is conformable to Him: on the one hand the impassioned will, and on the other the pure Intellect. For those paths that are founded on the first aspect, the conversion of the will—asceticism—is everything, and doctrinal truth is a background. For the ways that are founded on the second element, it is the Intellect—thus intellection—that is all important; asceticism is an auxiliary.

But these two perspectives give rise to indefinitely varied combinations in keeping with the inexhaustible diversity of spiritual and human possibilities.

* * *

The excellence of *gnosis* results from the very nature of God, who is Light, and also from the primordial—and essential—nature of man: "The dignity of man", says Saint Gregory of Nyssa, "lies in his intelligence."[1]

* * *

In intellection it is God who is the "subject", for man as such cannot bring an activity to bear upon God, who alone is pure Act; the creature is always passive in relation to the Creator and His graces. It is impossible for God to be the object of a knowledge of which

[1] According to Saint Maximus the Confessor, "It is intuition that unites man to God." "You adore", he says, "in the inmost sanctuary—not in the *atrium* of sensory knowledge or in the temple of reason—when you give yourself up exclusively to the supernatural activity of the intelligence." Meister Eckhart said similarly that he would rather abandon God than Truth, and he adds: "But God is Truth." Again, Ramakrishna said one day that he could give back everything to Kali, even love—everything except the Truth.

He is not the subject; the answer to the objection that, in the final analysis, God is always the subject of all real knowledge is that God is the indirect subject to the extent that the knowledge is indirect and the direct subject to the extent that the knowledge is direct; now pure intellection is distinguished precisely by its directness, although here as well there are degrees.

* * *

Sometimes, though quite wrongly, the name "natural mysticism" is given to a spirituality not explicitly founded on the idea of grace, although presenting itself as a method that necessarily leads to the *fiat lux*; now grace and method are not antagonistic principles, but two poles as it were of the same reality, so that there is a predominance of one over the other depending upon the perspective, and not a reciprocal incompatibility.[2] A methodic perspective—yoga, for example—can easily conceive of grace, whereas a devotional perspective seems to be ignorant of the "supernatural" character implicit in method; this is all the more surprising in that sacraments also make the "supernatural" rest upon elements that are precise, necessary, and infallible.

Method itself is already a grace, freely given by the fact of its revelation, but necessarily efficacious in its modes of operation, like the sacraments—with this difference, however, that it requires more complex conditions. If one believes in absolute gratuitousness, is it not contradictory to speak of "means of grace"?

On the other hand, it is scarcely logical to insist on the importance of "gratuitousness" while also protesting on every occasion against "easy solutions", whether real or apparent; there are elements in *gnosis* that inevitably elude the devotional perspective.

---

[2] The spiritual line of Ramanuja is divided into two schools, one of which—the "Northern" (*Vadakalai*)—holds that grace is not given except to one who actively collaborates with it, whereas the other—the "Southern" school (*Tenkalai*)—starts from the idea that man is incapable of collaborating with grace and must therefore have trust in God, allowing himself to be carried along by His mercy. The first of these points of view is even more prominent in the school of Shankara; as for the second, it gave rise in the Christian world to the quietist deviation. In Japanese Buddhism, the school of "Pure Land" (*Jôdo*) distinguishes between a way of "individual power" (*jiriki*), thus of "effort", and a way of the "power of another" (*tariki*), that is, of grace.

Moreover, if "gratuitousness" is conceived as an exclusive dogma, this amounts to attributing arbitrariness to God and to denying Him the perfection of necessity: if God is perfect, He must be both free and necessary; this truth appears in all domains. Human activity is simultaneously free, since man is not under complete constraint, and predestined, since God is not ignorant of what, in human terms, is the future. Perfection is made of geometry and beauty, of rigor and radiation, of the absolute and the infinite; geometry is in the method, and beauty is in the grace.

The use that some people make of the term "supernatural" may appear to others as a negation of the metaphysical homogeneity of the cosmos, a negation that also explains the reduction of man to his volitive and rational aspects. It goes without saying that a distinction between the "natural" and the "supernatural" is fully valid on the plane of human experience, but this plane has itself only a quite relative validity.

* * *

By comparison with the element of absoluteness in intellection, the facts of our will amount strictly to nothing; it is therefore absurd to speak of "easiness" when it is a question of knowledge.

Since the will is essentially a relative thing, its necessity cannot be absolute in relation to intellection.

* * *

Grace is an intrinsic aspect of intellection; it is not something separate as it is on the moral plane; its gratuitousness is that of knowledge.

To "provoke grace": this is certainly an ill-sounding phrase; but it does not prevent grace from always being accessible in pure intellection, to the extent that intellection itself is accessible. What is perhaps most shocking to partisans of spiritual "difficulty" and "gratuitous grace" is that intellection, when it is in fact accessible, can be actualized through sensory supports by reason of the law of hierarchical analogies.

* * *

A philosopher has said that saints contemplate, not in order to know, but in order to love. This opinion is not only contrary to the teachings of the Fathers, but also self-contradictory, for contemplation is an act of knowledge.[3]

Polemics in the name of love against knowledge are like wanting to put out the light of one fire by the heat of another.

* * *

Love has man for its subject; it starts from man and converges toward God, and it becomes "enlightened" to the extent that it conforms to its divine Object. Knowledge—that is, the intellective identification of the subject with the object—has on the contrary the Self for its subject; it realizes love by ontological necessity as a result of returning to its own root, its essence: the Self, who is the divine Subject and who is Beatitude.

In the case of love, man is the subject, and God is the Object.

In the case of knowledge, it is God who is the Subject, and man is the object.

* * *

The follower of the affective or volitional way will say that love is more than knowledge because love engages the whole of man's being, all our "life", whereas knowledge concerns only the mind, thus only "thought"; he will make a connection between love and the heart, on the one hand, and between knowledge and the brain, on the other, in conformity with his individual starting point; the follower of the cognitive way will say, on the contrary, that the heart

---

[3] "Love is inseparable from knowledge, from *gnosis*. It provides an element of personal consciousness, without which the way toward union would be blind and without a certain goal, an 'illusory asceticism', according to Saint Macarius of Egypt. The ascetical life 'apart from *gnosis*' has no value, according to Saint Dorotheus. . . . This consciousness in spiritual life is called knowledge. . . . It is fully manifested in the higher stages of the mystical way as perfect knowledge of the Trinity. That is why Evagrius Ponticus identified the kingdom of God with knowledge of the Holy Trinity—consciousness of the object of union" (Vladimir Lossky, *Essai sur la théologie mystique de l'Église d'Orient*). According to Evagrius, "Everything that exists exists for the sake of the knowledge of God." "Christ himself is the Intellect of all intelligent beings." "Faith is the principle of charity, and the end of charity is the knowledge of God."

represents the Universal, knowledge,[4] and the brain represents what is human and "subjective", the ego. For the spiritual man of an affective temperament, to love is to be and to know is to think; the heart represents the totality, the very depths of the being, and the brain the fragment, the surface. But for the spiritual man of an intellective temperament, to know is to be and to love is to will or feel; the heart represents universality, the Self, and the brain individuality or the "I". Knowledge starts from the Universal, and love from the individual; it is the absolute Knower who knows, whereas it is the human subject, the "creature", who is called to love.

*   *   *

Knowledge is one and indivisible; the superimposed planes that proceed from sensory knowledge up to the infinite resplendence of the Self truly exist according to the "horizontal" degrees of cosmic reality—or unreality—but not according to the essential Reality, which is "vertical" and "continuous". This is why knowledge, intellective light, which is "uncreated" in its "created" reflection, reaches all things and is sufficient unto itself.[5]

---

[4] According to the Hesychasts, the essence of the Jesus Prayer is the "descent of the intelligence into the heart".

[5] "But God hath revealed them unto us by His Spirit: for the Spirit searcheth all things, yea, the deep things of God. For what man knoweth the things of a man, save the spirit of man which is in him? even so the things of God knoweth no man, but the Spirit of God" (1 Cor. 2:10-11). "And all such things as are either secret or manifest, them I know. For wisdom, which is the worker of all things, taught me: for in her is an understanding spirit, holy, one only, manifold, subtle, lively, clear, undefiled, plain, not subject to hurt, loving the thing that is good, quick, which cannot be letted, ready to do good, kind to man, steadfast, sure, free from care, having all power, overseeing all things, and going through all understanding, pure, and most subtle, spirits. For wisdom is more moving than any motion: she passeth and goeth through all things by reason of her pureness. For she is the breath of the power of God, and a pure influence flowing from the glory of the Almighty: therefore can no defiled thing fall into her. For she is the brightness of the everlasting light, the unspotted mirror of the power of God, and the image of his goodness. And being but one, she can do all things: and remaining in herself, she maketh all things new: and in all ages entering into holy souls, she maketh them friends of God, and prophets. For God loveth none but him who dwelleth in wisdom. For she is more beautiful than the sun, and above all the order of stars: being compared with the light, she is found before it. For after this cometh night: but vice shall not prevail against wisdom. Wisdom reacheth from one end to the other mightily: and sweetly doth she order all things" (Wisd. of Sol. 7:21-8:1).

* * *

Man is a state of hardening. The man of an affective temperament pulverizes this hardness with the help of noble errors—or half-truths—such as the idea of being the vilest of men; the intellective man dissolves this hardness with the help of objective and impersonal truths. Such at least are the extreme positions.

God comes to meet the affective man, who hammers at the ice of his hardness, just as the sun comes to melt ice and makes hammering superfluous. As for the intellective man, God is already in his method, one might say, for if God resides indirectly in virtue, He resides directly in knowledge. When a body is dissolved in a chemical solvent, the dissolving power is already in the solvent and does not have to come from outside.

In practice it is always necessary to take account of the indefinitely varied combinations of these two attitudes; it is rare, if not impossible, that they should appear in isolation. In principle the affective attitude concerns the man who has a passional disposition and the intellective attitude the man in whom pure intelligence predominates.

* * *

Why is the volitive perspective generally speaking also an affective perspective? It is because the will, if it is directed toward God, inevitably becomes negative in the sphere of its terrestrial ends; now this negative character must be compensated by a positive factor, an individual not being able to live on negations; and this factor is love. If this factor were knowledge, there would no longer be a volitive perspective; the will would simply find itself integrated into the intellectual perspective.

* * *

When man is reduced to his will, intellection can hardly be looked upon as something human.

The will can determine and vitiate reasoning, but not intellectual intuition, which it can at most only paralyze in certain cases. As for reason, it may be either humble or proud, since its domain is that of opinions; it is a kind of intelligence degraded by the initial Luciferian quality of the will. Reason can exaggerate and falsify, distorting proportions without being illogical in the actual mechanism of its working; Intellect on the other hand can only perceive, and if it acts it is not through restrictive movements, but through the principial activity of its very substance.

* * *

In doctrinal formulations, those of an affective temperament (the *bhaktas*) tend to adopt individual and rational modes of thought, and being more or less aware of the limitations that this implies, they attribute them to man as such.

For Shankara theory is an objectification of Reality, which is the Self; for Ramanuja theory is a dialectic—even an apologetic—destined to prepare the ground for the way of love.

For the affective man, knowledge results from love as a gift; for the intellective man, the gnostic (the *jnânin*), love results from knowledge as a necessity.

* * *

The way of love (*bhakti*), in order that it may escape all danger of deviation, needs an external protection that is impersonal in character, namely, the general traditional environment; *gnosis* (*jnâna*), on the other hand, requires an inner axis of a personal kind, namely, the effort of realization. In other words, if the affective way cannot subsist without the static, objective element that the traditional framework provides, the intellective way cannot subsist without the dynamic, subjective element provided by the personal will for actualization. Love possesses this element by definition, just as *gnosis* necessarily possesses the discernment of essential forms, to the extent at least that such forms may concern it.

The relationship often established between intelligence and pride, while absurd from the standpoint of principles or essences, has a certain human—one might say moral—justification, inasmuch as intelligence, if it turns aside from Truth and refuses to retrace the course of its ontological process, produces arrogance: the intelligent man who, when contemplating, does not realize that God alone contemplates makes himself God.[6] Pure intelligence implies by definition the realization of its single Essence and consequently the forgetting—or surpassing—of the cosmic accidentality that is the thinking ego: intelligence "serves God", one might say, by "becoming what it is"; it is "impious" when it deliberately remains an individualized vision that is committed to nothing, that constitutes an end in itself and dispenses man from any obligation. Although intelligence is in itself contemplation and thus "non-acting", it requires of man an inward act that is total, and this act is "love".

* * *

If, as Saint Thomas said, "love of God is better than knowledge of God", this is primarily for the following reason: in principle knowledge is more than love; but in fact—in the world—the relationship is the reverse because of the law of analogy between the principial and manifested planes, and love, the will, the individual tendency is in practice more important than knowledge, since for the individual as such knowledge can only be theoretical.

However, there is not only inverse analogy but also direct or parallel analogy, by virtue of which—and this is the "essential" or "vertical" perspective—knowledge always remains what it is by its metaphysical nature; this is the point of view of *gnosis*.

* * *

The saying in the Gospels: "Blessed are they that have not seen, and yet have believed", not only concerns "faith" in the usual meaning of that word, but also refers to a general human reality that is independent of the distinction charity-*gnosis*: in other words, individuality as such will always be a veil before the divine Reality; the individual as such cannot "know God". The Intellect, whether it is envisaged in its "created" aspect or in its "uncreated" reality, is not the individual;

---

[6] Theologically, one would say that man should always be aware that intelligence is a gift of God.

the individual experiences it as a fulgurating darkness; he grasps only the flashes that enlighten and transfigure him.

*   *   *

What is "love" at the outset will appear as "Knowledge" in the result; and what is "knowledge" at the outset will appear in the result as "Love".

Perfect Love is "luminous", and perfect Knowledge is "warm", or rather it implies "warmth" without being identified with it.

*   *   *

In God Love is Light, and Light is Love. It is irrelevant in this case to object that one divine quality is not another, for here it is not a question of qualities—or "names"—but of the divine Essence itself. God is Love, for by His Essence He is "union" and "gift of Self".

*   *   *

The spiritual man of an affective temperament knows God because he loves Him.

The spiritual man of an intellective temperament loves God because he knows Him, and in knowing Him.

The love of the affective man is that he loves God.

The love of the intellective man is that God loves him; that is, he realizes intellectively—but not simply in a theoretical way—that God is Love.

The intellective man sees beauty in truth, whereas the affective man does not see it *a priori.* The affective man leans upon truth; the intellective man lives in it.

*   *   *

To love God is to attach oneself to Him. The spiritual man of an affective temperament arrives at the *vacare Deo* through love; the intellective man arrives at love in the *vacare Deo*; and this emptiness is the fruit of his science, not of his fervor as with the affective man. True science is fervent in a secondary manner, however, since it involves the entire being, and true fervor is conscious, lucid, active in its very center, where it is attached to truth.

*   *   *

Christianity insists upon the aspect of "love"; Sufism for its part insists—though in a different way—upon the aspect of "beauty". The Arabic words denoting virtue (*ihsân*) and the virtuous (*muhsin*) contain the root *husn*, "beauty". According to Ibn Arabi, God loves the beauty of forms because form reflects the beauty of God, just as it reflects Being. A *hadîth* says, "God is beautiful, and He loves what is beautiful." Here beauty appears as the sufficient reason for love; in love of the neighbor, which for Sufis is charity in action, it is God who is loved through man; divine beauty, which the *muhsin* attains through the creature, is reflected in him in purity and generosity of soul. Virtue makes the soul a mirror of divine beauty.

*   *   *

Why is Christianity not able to speak about "knowledge" without meaning "love" when—in the *Vedânta* for example—knowledge seems sufficient in itself? It is because in Christianity—as also in Buddhism—everything *a priori* converges toward man's spiritual realization; *gnosis* is envisaged with reference to its "realization" by the human being, not in its divine essentiality.

Among Shivaite Vedantists knowledge is considered above all in itself, its subject being by definition the Self, not the human being; in this perspective there is no starting point, no springboard: its logical center is "everywhere and nowhere", and its doctrinal form is not anthropocentric.

For some men knowledge and love are complements, which means that each term is regarded from the standpoint of what distinguishes it from the opposite term; for others knowledge is unique; it is not the complement of anything, and it thus contains love; for still other men there is only love, and this contains wisdom, which is actualized to a degree corresponding to the "quality" the love attains.

*   *   *

"God is Light" (1 John 1:5)—and thus Knowledge—even as He is "Love" (1 John 4:8). To love God is to love also the knowledge of God.[7] Man cannot love God in His Essence, which is humanly unknowable, but only in what God "makes known" to him.

In a certain indirect sense God answers knowledge by Love and love by Knowledge,[8] although in another respect, direct in this case, God reveals Himself as Wise to the wise and as Lover to the lover.

* * *

Intellective contemplation is "contained" in the "peace" that Christ gave the Apostles: "It is thus"—says the *Century* of the monks Callistus and Ignatius—"that our merciful and beloved Lord Jesus Christ . . . bequeathed to his own these three things [his Name, his Peace, and his Love]." This "peace" is analogous to the Hindu *shânti*, spiritual ataraxia, and to *Shânta*, the Infinite conceived in its calm and profound nature, "non-agitated" because "non-exteriorized" (or "non-manifested"); and this *shânti*, this "peace" or "serenity", is closely related to pure, intellective contemplation;[9] "peace" therefore indicates, in Christian mysticism as well, an attitude of intellection.[10] This element of *gnosis* is likewise found in the apophatic and

---

[7] Evagrius Ponticus says that "charity is the higher state of the reasonable soul in which it is impossible to love anything in the world more than the knowledge of God" (*Centuries*). And the same Father calls charity the "gate of *gnosis*", which clearly points to the transcendence of knowledge in relation to love.

[8] If Saint Maximus the Confessor says that "charity brings about knowledge", it must be understood in this indirect sense, for it is clear that nothing "outside" knowledge can be the cause of knowledge.

[9] This ontological connection between knowledge and peace—or between contemplation and immobility—is expressed in many inspired writings: according to Saint James, "The wisdom that is from above is first pure, then peaceable" (James 3:17). Evagrius Ponticus says that "the divine Intellect is an Intellect calmed from all movement." Again, according to Nikitas Stithatos, "He [the Holy Spirit] gives them intelligence that is peaceful and sweet in order to understand the deep things of God."

[10] This is the *gnosis* of the Alexandrians. Besides, this term is scriptural and does not properly belong to any school. As for the "holy silence" of the Hesychasts, this fundamentally designates the same thing, though it puts the accent on the aspect of "peace". It is the state of *samprasâda*, the "serenity" in which the Truth shows itself without veils and which resembles, according to Shankara, a flame that does not flicker.

antinomian theology of the Fathers, a doctrine that is crystallized in the Palamite teaching.

From the affective point of view peace is connected with trust and hope, that is, with the "sentimental certitude" that must compensate for what is "obscure" in faith.

Peace implies satisfaction, possession, just as agitation implies privation, separation. The trace of intellective contemplation in the affective soul is reassurance and also, in a certain sense, trusting abandonment, hope.

* * *

Peace is the absence of dissipation. Love is the absence of hardness. Fallen man is hardness and dissipation; the hardness is manifested by indifference toward God, an attitude that is poles apart from spiritual impassibility, and the dissipation is manifested by curiosity, preoccupation, anxiety with regard to the world, an attitude that is the inverse of vigilance of mind. In the peace of the Lord the waves of this dissipation are calmed, and the soul is at rest in its primordial nature, in its center; through love the outer shell of the heart is melted like snow, and the heart awakens from its death; hard, opaque, and cold in the fallen state, it becomes liquid,[11] transparent, and aflame in the divine Life.

Peace is contemplation in opposition to action;[12] it is therefore also intellection. Love is the spiritual will in opposition to natural inertia; but it is also, in a higher sense, the content of contemplation, the immutable intoxication of union.

Peace is first of all the calm that truth confers, then its direct contemplation; when the mind is perfectly calm—or perfectly simple—Truth is mirrored in it, just as objects are reflected in calm

---

[11] This "liquefaction" of the heart is mentioned by the most various Christian writers: the Greek Fathers, Saint Thomas, Angelus Silesius, the Curé d'Ars, to name but a few examples; and it is closely related to the "gift of tears". According to Silesius, who was moreover also an alchemist, the tears of Saint Mary Magdalene at the Savior's feet represent her "melted heart" (*sind ihr zerschmolzen Herz*).

[12] Strictly speaking the relationship is the reverse: it is action that is in a certain manner opposed to contemplation, for contemplation, having no opposite, does not oppose anything.

water.[13] Love is first of all the will turned towards God, then the bliss that God gives us in return.

* * *

Every spiritual path begins with an inversion with regard to the preceding state: the profane soul finds itself in a state of "hardness", for it is closed to God, who shines "outside". This hardness reveals itself by indifference toward God, then by egoism, greed, anger, distraction; consequently spiritual conversion will involve fervor, goodness, renunciation, peace: the soul must "melt" before Truth, so that the divine presence may henceforth be felt as "inward" and "central". One can legitimately call this conversion "love", for where there is no longer any hardness, no longer a constricting coil around the ego, the distinction between "I" and "thou" is abolished; within there is bliss, and outwardly there is goodness; there is a gentle warmth like spring sunshine,[14] comparable to the joy of love. It is for this reason that there is no spirituality without love; no spirituality is possible in the heart that is hardened and at the same time dissipated.

This aspect of spirituality calls for another, apparently its opposite but in reality complementary: this is incorruptibility, the cold and hard purity of the diamond.

* * *

Charity has two meanings in the doctrine of the ante-Nicene Fathers and their spiritual heirs: first, it is "a good disposition of the soul, which makes it prefer the knowledge of God above all things" (Saint Maximus the Confessor);[15] and second, it is the beatitude

---

[13] A Chinese Buddhist master said to us in a letter: "Serenity leads to higher knowledge." This phrase enunciates not only the relationship between calm and contemplation, or peace and *gnosis*, but also that between virtue and intellection.

[14] "When man discovers in the intelligent soul a tender feeling, completely calm and pure as day, let him recognize that it is the quality of ascending perfection"—*sattva*, conformity with Being, *Sat* (*Mânava-Dharma-Shâstra*, 12).

[15] "If the life of the spirit is the illumination of knowledge and if it is the love of God that produces this illumination, then it is right to say: there is nothing higher than the love of God" (*Centuries on Charity*). According to Evagrius Ponticus, "Holy knowledge draws the purified spirit, even as a magnet, by the natural force it possesses, draws iron" (*Centuries*).

that inheres in this knowledge by virtue of its Object, for "God is Love"; in the first sense charity is in man, and in the second it is in God.[16] In principle love is as it were enveloped in knowledge, for God is Love "in being" Light, or "because He is" Light, if one may so express it; but on the level of facts, effective knowledge is as it were enveloped in love, for man as such is will[17] "before" he knows what surpasses him.

* * *

The will cannot act without the collaboration of the intelligence or sentiment, or both together; now to the extent that a mystical "voluntarism" is not bound up with a truly intellectual perspective, it is of necessity allied to an affective element.

It is this that allows us to see a form of "love" in every volitive attitude and consequently to realize love through will. It is in the will, in asceticism, that love and knowledge most visibly meet. All spiritual paths, from the most modest to the loftiest, converge upon one and the same act of will, the rejection of the world and the search for the Divine.

* * *

Intelligence is the noblest thing in the world precisely because it represents "something of God", being a ray of the "Self"; it is by

---

[16] These considerations show that the hymn of praise to charity in the First Epistle to the Corinthians should also be understood in a sense conformable to the intellectual perspective. In this connection we may quote the following passage from our book *L'oeil du coeur* ("Modes of Spiritual Realization"): "The use . . . of the term 'love' to designate an intellectual reality is explained by the fact that sentiment, while inferior to reason on account of its 'subjectivity', is nonetheless symbolically comparable to what is higher than reason, namely, the Intellect; this is so because sentiment is not discursive but direct, simple, spontaneous, limitless, like the Intellect, to which it is in a sense diametrically opposed; compared to reason sentiment appears free from form and fallibility, and that is why the divine Intelligence can be called 'Love', and even really is Love in a transposed sense, compared with the poor human intelligence; there is here a simultaneous application of direct and inverse analogies, which at one and the same time link and separate the divine and cosmic orders."

[17] An Upanishad says that "the essence of man is made of desire", thus of "will".

intelligence, even if it is only virtual[18]—not by reason, which is only its specifically human mode and which characterizes man insofar as he is a "thinking animal"—that man surpasses the other creatures on earth; and it is again by virtue of his intelligence that man, when he betrays it by turning it away from its proper object, falls to a lower level than that of other creatures, although this fall always retains a specifically human form, that is, a mental or rational form, which makes for an illusion that is even more satanic.

The "active" or "direct" intelligence of which mankind is the beneficiary is therefore a "nobility that imposes demands"; it may thus seem surprising that there are spiritual paths that appear to exclude it, or in any case to assign to it a secondary and indirect role. Nevertheless for these "voluntarist" paths it is still always intelligence that matters, though understood with regard to its volitive function, and it is then free choice that constitutes the nobility of the human being: it is by free will that man surpasses the animals, by it that he resembles God, and by it that he returns to Him.

* * *

Intelligence, in order to purify and save man, does not have to become something other than it is; it has only to conform to its own nature. The will, on the other hand, if it seeks to bring man back toward his origins, must contradict itself. The will has the freedom to do evil, but the intelligence does not have the freedom to err; in evil the will remains itself, whereas intelligence becomes stupidity when it is in error, whatever the appearances. When the will conforms to its true end and thus realizes its primordial movement, it is absorbed into the intelligence; it can then be called "love". Love is the will reintegrated into Truth.

Intelligence, having become "knowledge" by its application to the "object" inherent in it, which is its normal goal, in addition determines the will. The converse is true only indirectly: the will, though it inevitably carries with it a certain illumination, nonetheless acts on the intelligence only in a roundabout and quite relative

---

[18] This reservation is necessary because a noble animal has a more adequate knowledge of God—although eminently indirect and passive—than has a man whose spirit is blinded and paralyzed by error; but this man nonetheless retains the possibility of a relatively direct and active knowledge, which is lacking in the animal.

way; the will is incapable of producing knowledge; all that it can do is remove obstacles.

*   *   *

When the object of the intelligence is God, and to the extent this is so, intelligence becomes "love", and this is because of the essentially attractive nature of the Divinity; intelligence becomes purely "itself" only through the "object", God, which "qualifies" it. From this point of view the intelligence as such is without quality; it is a human fact. The Hindu—or Alexandrian—perspective is more direct: the intelligence is *a priori* envisaged in its universal Essence, not in its human modes, and it is for this reason that it is "knowledge" by definition; it is truth, not by virtue of an object imposed on it apparently *ab extra*, but thanks to the elimination of the microcosmic accidents that veil its true nature in an illusory manner. In other words the intelligence is "qualified" by its own supernatural essence, and its inherent object, which it involves by definition, is the divine Reality, even if microcosmic accidents reduce this object, by veiling it, to the appearances of the world.

Knowledge is holy when it is the knowledge of God; it then possesses love. Only that knowledge is holy which in this way is love, for it alone is the knowledge of God.[19]

*   *   *

Knowledge does not abolish faith, but gives it a more inward meaning. He who "knows" theoretically does indeed enjoy metaphysical certitude, but such certitude does not yet penetrate his whole being; it is as if, instead of believing a description, one saw the object described, but without the sight of it implying either a detailed knowledge or a possession of the object, for a single visual perspective does not of course teach us the whole nature of the thing seen; thus there is certitude regarding the object as such in this case, but uncertainty regarding its integral nature. To "know" an object perfectly means to "possess" it, to "become" it, to "be" it; if the sight of

---

[19] Al-Hallaj calls wisdom "that of which the tiniest atom surpasses in its beauty and extent the two worlds [the earthly and the heavenly]".

an object is very much more than an abstract belief in its existence, the realization of the object will likewise be infinitely more than the sight of it; metaphysical certitude thus stands in a sense between belief—"faith" in the ordinary meaning of the word—and the realization of union. As long as man is not delivered from the chains of existence, there is always an element of "faith" in his "knowledge"; otherwise there would be nothing separating him from the Reality "known" or "to be known".

"Blessed are they that have not seen, and yet have believed." Metaphysical truths, in their deepest sense, are never "visible" to the "soul-desire"; otherwise they would immediately perfect it. The soul-desire—the man who rejoices and suffers—must therefore "believe" the truths that are evident to the Intellect. In metaphysics faith is the assent of the whole being.

* * *

The difference between the affective and intellective ways can also be defined in the following manner: the first proceeds essentially in an "objective" or "dualistic" way whereas the second, though it does not lack an appropriate "objective" perspective, is able to proceed in a "subjective" way:[20] this means that in the first case God is objective, outward, and that in the second case He can be conceived as subjective, inward; He is the "Self".

Each of these perspectives must account for the reality of the other: the "lover" knows that God—from whom he is separated, since the Beloved is "other" in relation to the lover—is also "within" him; and the "gnostic" knows that the Self—which is his own essential Reality—appears as "objectivity" by reason of the fact that ego-centric objectification, the illusion of "I", is produced by existence itself, so that for man as such, whether *jnânin* or *bhakta*, God will always be "external", "objective", "other"—infinitely "other" in relation to human nothingness.

---

[20] In the current sense of the word, "subjective" means what is colored by the limitations of the ego; but in reality the ego is not a pure subject, but an objectification; only the divine Intellect is absolutely Subject. The "subjective" way spoken of here can base itself on the scriptural formula: "The kingdom of God is within you."

* * *

The renunciation of the contemplative does not at all have the aim of accumulating merits for the sake of individual bliss; it serves to put the soul, by what one might call radical measures, into the most favorable possible state for realizing its own infinite Essence.

Love of God, far from being essentially a sentiment, is what makes the wise man contemplate rather than do anything else.[21]

The virtue of the contemplative is that he makes of his virtues a grace for others; in the final analysis his positive virtue is that of God, which he realizes in his vision.

* * *

For certain people the intention of loving God brings with it an inability to love men; now the second of these things destroys the first. In an ordinary soul, concern for spiritual love and mortification may bring with it an icy egoism and sometimes also a curious hatred of animals as "useless" beings, not to speak of a no less curious aversion to beauty; beauty, with its breath of infinity and generosity, breaks down the fixed attitudes and closed systems of this supposedly spiritual egoism.

Beauty is an aspect of love, and conversely; it is utterly contradictory to seek to realize love in ugliness and avarice.

* * *

Charity is first of all the faculty of putting God before the world and then the faculty of putting oneself in the place of others. When Saint Louis urged his friends to thrust their swords into the body of anyone who made impious remarks in their presence, he was in no way forgetting that one must love one's neighbor as oneself; he

---

[21] For Shankara *bhakti* is what Muslims call *himmah*—spiritual fervor; for Ramanuja it is continuity or perpetuity of contemplation; for Chaitanya it is limitless love, though this is but the means and not yet the end: the goal is *prema*, divine Love, Beatitude. For Origen, "The whole life of a saint should be a single and continuous great prayer; what commonly bears this name is only a part of this great prayer, a part one should perform no fewer than three times a day" (*De Oratione*). "He who truly celebrates the feast does what he should and prays without ceasing, continually offering bloodless victims in his prayers to God" (*Contra Celsum*).

Place
Stamp
Here

World Wisdom

World Wisdom

World Wisdom
P.O. Box 2682
Bloomington, IN 47402-2682
U.S.A.

World Wisdom

Send us this card, or contact us at

www.worldwisdom.com

Please Print

Book in which this card was found

Name

Address

City _____ Zip or Postal Code

State

Country (if outside the USA)

E-mail

Please detach bookmark before mailing card

We must understand,
then, that even though
God doesn't always
give us what we want,
He gives us what we
need for salvation.

St. Augustine
of Hippo

World Wisdom

visit
www.worldwisdom.com

would have wished to be struck through with a sword himself had he pronounced a blasphemy; he loved his neighbor as he loved himself, neither more nor less; and since society is also—and even *a fortiori*—one's neighbor, charity impelled him to seek to rid it of a harmful virus. There are alternatives that no virtue can escape.[22] Love of the neighbor may sacrifice the individual to the collectivity; it should never sacrifice the qualitative collectivity to the individual as such any more than it should sacrifice the qualitative human person to the quantitative and crude collectivity.

For the mother who loves her child more than herself—by nature and not supernaturally, for otherwise she would have no reason for preferring her own child to those of others—the child is an extension of the "I"; it is only partly the "neighbor"; it is nature that loves through the mother even as it loves through lovers or spouses. This love is nature's egoism; but love of the neighbor—if one may put it this way—is the "egoism" of God.

Without charity it is not possible to see the total truth, or even the complexity of partial truths.

* * *

In the final analysis charity is to make a gift of God to God by means of the ego and through beings. It communicates a blessing whose source is God; and it communicates it to the neighbor, who, insofar as he is the object of love, is God's representative.

In giving God to our neighbor we give ourselves to God.

---

[22] "For it cannot be that he who loves God does not love himself. Indeed he alone knows how to love himself who loves God. Assuredly whoever is careful to do that good which is sovereign and true loves himself in sufficient measure" (Saint Augustine, *The Customs of the Church*). Origen notes that according to the Gospel it is God alone whom we must love "with all our heart"; and just as we must not love ourselves with all our heart, since we are not God, neither should we love our neighbor in a manner suiting God alone. As for our enemies, Origen adds, we should love them by abstaining from hating them. According to Richard of Saint Victor, only God should be loved without measure; the neighbor should be loved with measure, as we should love ourselves; and the enemy should not be hated.

4

Modes of Prayer

The most elementary mode of orison—of contact between man and God—is no doubt prayer in the most ordinary sense of the word, that is, the direct expression of the individual, of his desires and fears, his hopes and gratitude. This prayer, however, is less perfect than canonical prayer, which has a universal character by virtue of the fact that God is its author and that the reciting subject is not a particular individual, but man as such, the human species; thus canonical prayer contains nothing that does not concern man, every man, and this is as much as to say that it includes "eminently" or in addition all possible individual prayers; it can even render them unnecessary, and in fact the Revelations permit or recommend individual prayer, but do not impose it. Canonical prayer shows its universality and timeless value by being expressed very often in the first person plural and also by its preference for using a sacred or liturgical and therefore symbolically universal language, so that it is impossible for whoever recites it not to pray for all and in all.

As to individual prayer, the reason for its existence is incontestably to be found in our nature, since individuals do in fact differ from one another and have different destinies and desires.[1] The aim of this prayer is not only the securing of particular favors, but also the purification of the soul: it loosens psychic knots or, in other words, dissolves subconscious coagulations and drains away many secret poisons; it sets forth before God the difficulties, failures, and tensions of the soul, which presupposes that the soul be humble and truthful, and this disclosure, carried out in the face of the Absolute,

---

[1] With the *Avatâras* every personal prayer becomes polyvalent and canonical, as is shown by the Psalms, for example; but these great Messengers give us at the same time the example of spontaneous prayer, since they seldom repeat the prayers of others, and they show us in any case that canonical prayer must be said with spontaneity, as if it were the first or last prayer of our life.

has the virtue of reestablishing equilibrium and restoring peace—in a word, of opening us to grace.[2] All this is offered us as well and *a fortiori* by canonical prayer, but the human spirit is in general too weak to extract from it all the remedies it contains.

The personal character of non-canonical prayer does not imply that it is free from rules, for the human soul—as the Psalms admirably show—is always the same in its miseries and joys, and therefore in its duties towards God; it is not enough for a man to formulate his petition: he must also express his gratitude, resignation, regret, resolution, praise. In petition man is seeking some favor, provided that it is of a nature agreeable to God, thus to the universal Norm; thankfulness is the consciousness that every favor of destiny is a grace that might not have been given; and while it is true that man always has something to ask, it is just as true, to say the least, that he always has reasons for gratitude, without which no prayer is possible. Resignation is the anticipated acceptance of the non-fulfillment of some request; regret or contrition—the asking of pardon—implies consciousness of what puts us in opposition to the divine Will; resolution is the desire to remedy some particular transgression, for our weakness must not make us forget we are free;[3] finally, praise means not only that we relate every value to its ultimate Source, but also that we look upon every trial in light of its necessity or usefulness, or in its aspect of fatality and grace. Petition is a capital element of prayer because we can do nothing without the help of God; a resolution offers no guarantee—as the example of Saint Peter shows—if we do not ask for this help.

---

[2] The sacrament of penance is founded upon these facts, adding to them the particular, compensatory power of celestial grace. Psychoanalysis offers an analogous process, but in a satanic form, for it replaces the supernatural by the infra-natural: in place of God it puts the blind, dark, and inhuman aspects of nature. Evil for psychoanalysts is not what is contrary to God and the final ends of man, but what troubles the soul, even if the cause of disquiet is beneficial; thus the equilibrium resulting from psychoanalysis is basically of an animal order, and this is entirely contrary to the requirements of our immortality. In man imbalances can and must be resolved for the sake of a higher equilibrium that conforms to a spiritual hierarchy of values, and not in some quasi-vegetative state of bliss; a human evil cannot be cured outside of God.

[3] Logically, regret and resolution are inseparable, but regret can be conceived without resolution, and this is lukewarmness or despair, as also resolution without regret, and this is pride, unless it is based upon wisdom. It is not a question here primarily of sentimentality, but of attitudes of the will, whether or not these are accompanied by feelings.

*   *   *

Another mode of orison is meditation; contact between man and God here becomes contact between intelligence and Truth, or relative truths contemplated in view of the Absolute. There is a certain outward analogy between meditation and individual prayer in that man formulates his thought spontaneously in both cases; the difference, which is infinitely more important, is that meditation is objective and intellectual—unless it is a question of imaginative, even sentimental, reflections, which are not what we have in mind here—whereas prayer is subjective and volitive. In meditation, the aim is knowledge, hence a reality that in principle goes beyond the ego as such; the thinking subject is then, strictly speaking, the impersonal intelligence, thus man and God at the same time, pure intelligence being the point of intersection between human reason and the divine Intellect.

Meditation acts on the one hand upon the intelligence, in which it "awakens" certain consubstantial "memories", and on the other hand upon the subconscious imagination, which ends up incorporating into itself the truths meditated upon, resulting in a fundamental and quasi-organic process of persuasion. Experience proves that a man can do great things even in unfavorable circumstances provided that he believes himself capable of accomplishing them, whereas another, more gifted perhaps but doubting himself, will do nothing even in favorable conditions; man walks fearlessly on flat ground, but imagination may prevent his taking a single step when he has to pass between two chasms. By this one can see the importance of meditation even simply from the point of view of autosuggestion; in the spiritual life as in other domains, it is a precious help to be deeply convinced both as to the things toward which we are tending and of our capacity to attain them, with the help of God.

Meditation—as defined in Vedantic terms—is essentially "investigation" (*vichâra*), which leads to the assimilation of theoretical truth and then to "discernment" (*viveka*) between the Real and the unreal; there are two levels here, one ontological and dualist and the other centered on Beyond-Being or the Self, and consequently non-dualist; this is the entire difference between *bhakti* and *jnâna*.

Pure concentration is also orison if it has a traditional basis and is centered on the Divine; this concentration is none other than silence,[4] which itself has been called a "Name of the Buddha" because of its connection with the idea of emptiness.[5]

* * *

We have distinguished canonical prayer from individual prayer by saying that it is a particular individual who is the subject in the second, whereas the subject is man as such in the first; now there is a form of orison wherein God Himself is the subject in a certain way, and this is the pronouncing of a revealed divine Name.[6] The foundation of this mystery is, on the one hand, that "God and His Name are identical" (Ramakrishna) and, on the other hand, that God Himself pronounces His Name in Himself, thus in eternity and outside all creation, so that His unique and uncreated Word is the prototype of ejaculatory prayer and even, in a less direct sense, of all orison. The first distinction that the Intellect conceives in the divine nature is that of Beyond-Being and Being; now since Being is as it were the "crystallization" of Beyond-Being, it is like the "Word" of the Absolute, through which the Absolute expresses itself, determines itself, or names itself.[7] Another distinction that is essential

---

[4] "The Father spoke one word, and this Word was his Son, and this Word He utters without end in an eternal silence, and in this silence the soul hears it" (Saint John of the Cross, *Spiritual Maxims and Counsels*, 307).

[5] *Shûnyamûrti*, "Manifestation of the Void", is one of the Names of the Buddha. The silent prayer of the North American Indians, which presupposes a symbolist outlook and the framework of virgin Nature, offers striking analogies with Zen.

[6] In his *Cudgel for Illusion*, Shankara sings: "Control thy soul, restrain thy breathing, distinguish the transitory from the True, repeat the holy Name of God, and thus calm the agitated mind. To this universal rule apply thyself with all thy heart and all thy soul." The connection between metaphysical discrimination and the practice of invocation is one of capital importance. We find the same connection in this *Stanza on the Ochre Robe* (of *sannyâsins*), also by Shankara: "Singing *Brahma*, the word of Deliverance, meditating uniquely on 'I am *Brahma*', living on alms and wandering freely, blessed certainly is the wearer of the ochre robe."

[7] In the Torah, God says to Moses: "I am that I am" (*Ehyeh asher Ehyeh*); this refers to God as Being, for it is only as Being that God creates, speaks, and legislates, since the world exists only in relation to Being. In the Koran, this same utterance is rendered as follows: "I am God" (*Anâ 'Llâh*); this means that Being (*Anâ*, "I") is derived from Beyond-Being (*Allâh*, this Name designating the Divinity in all its aspects without any restriction); thus the Koranic formula refers to the divine Prototype of the pronunciation of the Name of God. *Anâ 'Llâh* signifies implicitly that "God and His Name are identical"—since Being "is" Beyond-Being inasmuch as it is its "Name"—and for the same reason the "Son" is God while not being the

here, one which is derived from the preceding by principial succession,[8] is that between God and the world, the Creator and creation: just as Being is the Word or Name of Beyond-Being, so too the world—or Existence—is the Word of Being, of the "personal God"; the effect is always the "name" of the cause.[9]

But whereas God, in naming Himself, first determines Himself as Being and second, starting from Being, manifests Himself as Creation—that is, He manifests Himself "within the framework of nothingness" or "outside Himself", thus "in illusory mode"[10]—man for his part follows the opposite movement when pronouncing the same Name, for this Name is not only Being and Creation, but also Mercy and Redemption; in man it does not create, but on the contrary "unmakes", and it does this in a divine manner inasmuch as it brings man back to the Principle. The divine Name is a metaphysical "isthmus"—in the sense of the Arabic word *barzakh*: "seen by God" it is determination, limitation, "sacrifice"; seen by man, it is liberation, limitlessness, plenitude. We have said that this Name, invoked by man, is nonetheless always pronounced by God; human invocation is only the "outward" effect of an eternal and "inward" invocation by the Divinity. The same holds true for every other Revelation: it is sacrificial for the divine Spirit and liberating for man; Revelation, whatever its form or mode, is "descent" or "incarnation" for the Creator and "ascent" or "ex-carnation" for the creature.[11]

"Father". What gives metaphysical force to the Hebraic formula is the return of "being" to itself; and what gives force to the Arabic formula is the juxtaposition, without copula, of "subject" and "object".

[8] By "descent" (*tanazzulah*) as Sufis would say.

[9] This relationship is repeated on the plane of Being itself, where it is necessary to distinguish between the "Father" and the "Son"—or between "Power" and "Wisdom"—the "Holy Spirit" being intrinsically "Beatitude-Love" and extrinsically "Goodness" or "Radiation". This is the "horizontal" or ontological perspective of the Trinity; according to the "vertical" or gnostic perspective—ante-Nicene one might say—it would be said that the Holy Spirit "proceeds" from Beyond-Being as All-Possibility and "dwells" in Being as the totality of creative possibilities, while "radiating" forth into Existence, which is related to the concept of "creation by love".

[10] It is absurd to reproach Creation for not being perfect, that is, for not being divine, hence uncreated. God cannot will that the world should be and at the same time that it should not be the world.

[11] In Japanese Amidism, there have been controversies over the question of whether invocations of the Buddha must be innumerable or whether on the contrary one single invocation suffices for salvation, the sole condition in both cases being

The sufficient reason for the invocation of the Name is the "remembering of God"; in the final analysis this is nothing other than consciousness of the Absolute. The Name actualizes this consciousness and, in the end, perpetuates it in the soul and fixes it in the heart, so that it penetrates the whole being and at the same time transmutes and absorbs it. Consciousness of the Absolute is the prerogative of human intelligence and also its aim.

Or again: we are united to the One by our being, by our pure consciousness, and by the symbol. It is by the symbol—the Word—that man, in central and quintessential prayer, realizes both Being and Consciousness, Consciousness in Being and conversely. The perfection of Being, which is Extinction, is prefigured by deep sleep and also, in other ways, by beauty and virtue; the perfection of Consciousness, which is Identity—or Union, if one prefers—is prefigured by concentration, and also *a priori* by intelligence and contemplation. Beauty does not produce virtue, of course, but it favors in a certain way a pre-existing virtue; likewise intelligence does not produce contemplation, but it broadens or deepens a contemplation that is natural. Being is passive perfection and Consciousness active perfection. "I sleep, but my heart waketh."

* * *

Why is Being "Word" or "Name"[12] rather than "Thought", "Act", "Sacrifice", and why is ejaculatory prayer not thought, act, sacrifice, and so forth? In the first place it is quite true that Being has all these aspects, and many others as well; these aspects are to be found in every Revelation. Nonetheless, speech realizes all possible aspects of affirmation, and it has a kind of pre-eminence in that it is the feature most notably distinguishing man from animal. Speech implies

---

a perfect faith and—as a function of that faith—abstention from evil or the sincere intention to abstain. In the first case invocation is viewed from the human side, that is, from the standpoint of duration, whereas in the second case it is conceived in its principial, hence divine and therefore timeless, reality; *Jôdo-Shinshû*, like Hindu *japa-yoga*, combines both perspectives.

[12] Meister Eckhart says in his commentary on the Gospel of John, "The Father neither sees, nor hears, nor speaks, nor wishes anything but His own Name. It is by means of His Name that the Father sees, hears, and manifests Himself. The Name contains all things. Essence of Divinity, it is the Father Himself. . . . The Father gives thee His eternal Name, and it is His own life, His being, and His divinity that He gives thee in one single instant by His Name."

thought since it is an exteriorization, but thought does not imply speech; in an analogous fashion speech, which itself is an act, adds to action a new dimension of intelligibility. Similarly, speech has a sacrificial side in that it limits what it expresses; and as for ejaculatory prayer—which, being speech, is at the same time thought, act, and sacrifice—it includes yet another sacrificial or ascetical aspect in that it excludes every other preoccupation of the heart and is thereby a form of "poverty" or *vacare Deo*. Or again: man, in being born, manifests his voice before any other faculty, and though this cry is undoubtedly unconscious, it is already a prayer insofar as it is a prefiguration or symbol; the same is true for the last gasp of the dying man or his last breath, since voice and breath refer to the same symbolism.

It goes without saying that every normal activity reflects in its way the eternal Act of God: thus a weaver could say that Being is the first divine "fabric" in the sense that Beyond-Being weaves into it the principial possibilities—the "divine Names"—and that Being in its turn weaves the existential manifestations, hence Angels, worlds, beings;[13] not every man is a weaver, but every man speaks, which clearly shows that speech has priority over secondary and more or less "accidental" activities; such activities are too outward to be assimilated into "prayers", and yet they can be the vehicle of prayer by virtue of their symbolic quality.[14] In other words, any kind of occupation, whether a craft or otherwise—provided it is "natural"—can be a spiritual support, thanks not only to the symbolism inherent in it, which would not suffice by itself, but above all to the contemplative orison that is superimposed on it, which actualizes the value of the symbol.

* * *

The principle according to which "prayer of the heart" is able to replace all other rites—on condition of sufficient spiritual matu-

[13] It is this second proposition that the artisan will adopt in fact, the first belonging to the province of pure metaphysics and not necessarily entering into the outlook of a craft initiation, the basis of which is cosmological.

[14] It is thus that one ought to understand every fundamental and naturally "ritual" activity, the gesture of the sower, for example, or the work of the mason; is it not God who sows cosmic possibilities in the *Materia prima* and truths and graces in the soul, and is He not the "Great Architect of the Universe"?

rity—is to be found in Hesychasm, but it is emphasized much more in Hindu and Buddhist paths, where the abandonment of general ritual prayers and practices is considered normal and sometimes even a *conditio sine qua non*. The profound reason for this is that it is necessary to distinguish between the realm of the "divine Will" and that of the "divine Nature"; the latter "is what it is" and is expressed by the Name alone, whereas the former projects into the human world differentiated—and necessarily relative—wills and is expressed by complex prayers corresponding to the complexity of human nature.[15] Rites, however—especially those having a purifying or sacramental character—can be looked upon as necessary aids for prayer of the heart; this belongs to a point of view deriving from a perspective differing from the one just envisaged and better suited to certain temperaments.

We would doubtless hesitate to speak of these things if others—Europeans as well as Asians—did not speak of them, and if we were not living at a time when all sorts of testimonies are demanded and when the compensating Mercy simplifies many things, though this cannot mean that everything will become easily accessible. It is obvious that a spiritual means has significance only within the rules assigned to it by the tradition that offers it, whether it is a question of outward or inward rules; nothing is more dangerous than to undertake "improvisations" in this field. This reservation will not fail to surprise those who hold that man is free in all respects before God, and who will ask by what right we seek to subject prayer to conditions and to enclose it in frameworks; the response is simple, and it is the Bible itself that gives it: "Thou shalt not take the name of the Lord thy God in vain; for the Lord will not hold him guiltless that taketh His name in vain" (Exod. 20:7; Deut. 5:11). Now man is *a priori* "vain" according to certain spiritual criteria, those precisely that apply when it is a question of direct and "mystagogical" methods; man is thus not absolutely free, even apart from the fact that absolute Freedom belongs to God alone. Only what is given by Him has value for salvation, not what is taken by man; now it

---

[15] Here is the whole difference between form and essence, which penetrates every domain. If "in the resurrection they neither marry, nor are given in marriage", this relates to mode or form, not essence; if on the other hand Paradise shelters the houris, this relates to essence and not to mode; and it is in relation to essence that Saint Bernard could speak of "torrents of voluptuous delight".

is God who has revealed His Names, and it is He who determines their usage; and if, according to the Apostle, "whosoever shall eat this [divine] bread unworthily eateth damnation to himself" (1 Cor. 11:27-29), the same holds true for the presumptuous use of ejaculatory prayers.

This being acknowledged, we can return to the positive side of the question: in whatever degree it may be opportune, according to circumstances and surroundings, ejaculatory prayer results finally from these two requirements: perfection and continuity. "Pray without ceasing," says the Apostle (1 Thess. 5:17),[16] and again: "Likewise the Spirit also helpeth our infirmities: for we know not what we should pray for as we ought: but the Spirit itself maketh intercession for us with groanings which cannot be uttered" (Rom. 8:26).[17]

---

[16] Basing himself on the Gospel: "And he spake a parable unto them to this end, that men ought always to pray, and not to faint" (Luke 18:1); "Watch ye therefore, and pray always, that ye may be accounted worthy to escape all these things" (Luke 21:36). Saint Bernardino of Siena says in a sermon that "the name [of Jesus] is origin without origin" and that it is "as worthy of praise as God Himself"; and again: "Everything that God has created for the salvation of the world is hidden in this Name of Jesus" (Saint Bernardino of Siena, *Le Prediche Volgari*, ed. P. Ciro Cannarozzi). It is not by chance that Bernardino gave to his monogram of the Name of Jesus the appearance of a monstrance: the divine Name, carried in thought and in the heart, through the world and through life, is like the Holy Sacrament carried in procession. This monogram—I H S, signifying *Iesous*, but interpreted in Latin as *In Hoc Signo* or as *Jesus Hominum Salvator* and often written in Gothic letters—can be broken down in its primitive form into three elements: a vertical straight line, two vertical lines linked together, and a curved line; and thus it contains a symbolism at once metaphysical, cosmological, and mystical; there is in it a remarkable analogy, not only with the name *Allâh* written in Arabic, which also comprises the three lines of which we have just spoken (in the form of the *alif*, the two *lams*, and the *hâ*), but also with the Sanskrit monosyllable *Aum*, which is composed of three *mâtrâs* (A U M), indicating a "rolling up" and thereby a return to the Center. All these symbols mark, in a certain sense, the passage from "coagulation" to "solution".

[17] "At all times let us invoke Him, the object of our meditations, in order that our mind may always be absorbed in Him and our attention concentrated on Him daily" (Nicholas Cabasilas, *Life in Christ*). What invocation of the divine Name is for other prayers, the Eucharist is for the other sacraments: "One receives the Eucharist last precisely because one can go no further, add nothing to it: for clearly the first term implies the next, and this in turn the last. Now after the Eucharist there is nothing further toward which one could tend: a stop must be made there and thought given to the means of keeping, to the end, the good acquired" (*Life in Christ*).

*   *   *

Divine Names have meanings that are at once particular, since they belong to a revealed language, and universal, since they refer to the supreme Principle. To invoke a Divinity is to enunciate a doctrine: he who says "Jesus" says implicitly that "Christ is God",[18] which means that God "descended" in order that man might "ascend";[19] moreover, to say that "God became man" means at the same time that man is fallen, since the sufficient reason for the divine descent is the fact that man exists "below"; God is "made flesh" because man is "flesh", and flesh signifies fall, passion, and destitution. Christianity takes its starting point in the volitive aspect of man; it grafts itself so to speak, not upon the fundamentally theomorphic properties of our nature, but upon the "accident" of our fall, which in practice is decisive for most believers; but starting from this point of view—and this is of capital importance—the Christian tradition can open the door to *gnosis* and thus rejoin perspectives that are founded on the intellectual theomorphism of the human being, and this is because of the evident—and dazzling—analogy between Christ and the Intellect, as well as the idea of "deification" that is derived from it.

To say that "God became man that man might become God"[20] means in the final analysis—if we wish to pursue this reciprocity to

---

[18] That is to say, "Christ alone is God"—not "God is Christ"—just as the sun alone is "our sun", the sun of our planetary system. We need not here return to the question—non-existent in practice for the vast majority of ancient, and even modern, Christians—of knowing where the boundaries of that "planetary system" which is Christianity are drawn; this involves the whole problem of the refraction of the celestial in the terrestrial or, more precisely, the concordance between the divine Light and different human receptacles.

[19] And because the Absolute has entered into man, into space, into time, the world and history have become as if absolute, whence the danger of an anti-metaphysical conception of the "real" or the temptation of involving God—the Absolute insofar as it has become in a sense human or historical—in the "current of forms"; this is not unconnected with a theological "personalism" that would seek to substitute the humanized divine for the Divine in itself, which is revealed to the pure Intellect. When we say "absolute" in speaking about the Word or Being, it is not through failing to recognize that these aspects belong metaphysically to the relative domain, whose summit *in divinis* they mark, but because, in relation to the cosmos, every aspect of God is absolute.

[20] Saint Irenaeus: "Because of His boundless love, God made Himself what we are in order to make us what He is."

its ultimate foundations—that Reality has entered into nothingness that nothingness might become real. If it is objected here that nothingness, being nothing, can play no part, we would respond with two questions: how is the existence of the very idea of nothingness to be explained? How is there a "nothing" on the level of relativities and in everyday experience? Nothingness has neither being nor existence, certainly, but it is nonetheless a kind of metaphysical "direction", something we are able to conceive and pursue, though never attain; "evil" is none other than "nothingness manifested" or "the impossible made possible". Evil never lives from its own substance, which is non-existent, but it corrodes or perverts the good, just as disease could not exist without the body that it tends to destroy; according to Saint Thomas, evil is there to allow the coming of a greater good, and in fact qualities need corresponding privations to enable them to be affirmed distinctively and separately.

But the Christic reciprocity has above all a meaning of love, considering its emphasis on saving effectiveness: the Name of Christ signifies that God loved the world in order that the world might love God; and since God loves the world, man must love his neighbor, thus repeating God's love on the human plane. Likewise, man must "lose his life" because God sacrificed Himself for him;[21] the cross is the instrument and symbol of this sacrificial meeting, the point of intersection as it were between the human and the Divine. Christianity presents itself above all as a volitive reciprocity between Heaven and Earth, not as an intellective distinction between the Absolute and the relative; but this distinction is nonetheless implicit in the reciprocity as such, so that the Christian perspective cannot exclude it: the Subject makes itself object that the object might become Subject, which is the very definition of the mystery of knowledge. *Gnosis* is based—"organically" and not artificially—on the polyvalent symbolism of the Incarnation and the Redemption, which implies that such a "symbiosis" is in the nature of things and consequently within the "divine intention".

The Name of Christ is "Truth" and "Mercy"; however, this second quality is crystallized in a particular fashion in the Name of

---

[21] In the Eucharistic rite, man eats or drinks God in order to be eaten or drunk by Him; the "elect of the elect" are those who drink and are consumed in a divine wine where there is no longer either "Thee" or "Me".

the Virgin, so that the two Names appear like a polarization of the divine Light. Christ is "Truth and Power" and the Virgin, "Mercy and Purity".[22]

* * *

Before going further, we must insert a parenthesis: in one of our previous works we said that a Christian can only be either a child of his times or a saint, while a Muslim—or a Jew—can be either an exoterist or an esoterist, and that it is only by virtue of this second quality that he realizes sanctity; in Islam, we said, there is no sanctity outside esoterism, and in Christianity there is no esoterism outside sanctity.[23] To understand this properly, it is necessary to recall that the exoterism transcended by Christ, logically and in principle, is the Mosaic Law; now this Law, like every exoterism properly so called—and consequently like the Muslim *sharî'ah*—requires essentially the sincere[24] observance of a body of prescriptions, whereas Christianity aims at replacing the "external" Law or the "letter" by a "personal" and qualitative attitude, while becoming dogmatist in its turn.[25] This partial and conditional "coagulation" is due,

---

[22] In many icons the Blessed Virgin expresses mercy by the inclined and spiral-like movement of her posture, whereas the severity of her facial expression indicates purity in its aspect of inviolability; other icons express solely this purity, emphasizing the severity of the features by a very upright position; others again express mercy alone, combining the inclination of the body with sweetness of expression.

[23] "Contours of the Spirit", *Spiritual Perspectives and Human Facts.*

[24] Without this element of sincerity, which results from faith, the observance of these prescriptions would be of no use.

[25] It is doubtless this dogmatization or "crystallization" of an initiatic "wine" that causes Muslims, who like the Jews are guardians of an exoterism *de jure*, to say that the Christian message (*risâlah*) became "corrupted"—a quite exoteric definition to be sure, but instructive from the point of view that interests us here. Let us recall that for the Sufis, Christ brought only a *haqîqah* (an "inward" truth), an idea that is in any case proper to Islam as such, since to the saying of Christ: "My kingdom is not of this world", the Prophet in a sense "replies" when he says: "I bring you not only the goods of the other world; I bring you those of this world as well", namely, definite rules for individual and social behavior. As we wrote in one of our previous works: "If esoterism does not concern everyone, it is for the reason, analogically speaking, that light penetrates some substances and not others; but on the other hand, if esoterism must manifest itself openly from time to time, as happened in the case of Christ, and at a lesser degree of universality in the case of al-Hallaj, it is, still by analogy, because the sun illuminates everything without distinction. Thus, if the 'Light shineth in darkness' in the principial or universal sense we are concerned with here, this is because in so doing it manifests one of its possibilities,

not to unforeseen circumstances—which are excluded in such a case—but to the original intention of the divine Founder, who sent the Apostles to "teach all nations"; now sanctity brings this *de facto* exoterism back to its essence, which is an esoterism "by right"—on the plane of love and in opposition to the outwardness of the Jewish Law[26]—and this is what allowed us to write that there is no Christian, "bhaktic" esoterism outside sanctity. But there is yet another dimension to be considered: Christianity also includes an esoterism in the absolute sense, and this is precisely *gnosis* or "theosophy";[27] thus it is not only sanctity with a volitive and emotional basis, but also sapiential doctrine, and with all the more reason the sanctity connected to it, which we may describe as "esoterism"—if we have a reason for using this term, which in itself is irreproachable; and let us recall in this context the correlation between the "Peace" of Christ and pure contemplation.[28] *Gnosis,* while in a certain way transcending "faith" and "love"—since knowledge finally goes beyond thought and will—represents in another respect a mode of faith and love that is virtually divine.

*   *   *

In Islam, the implicit doctrine of the Name of God is Unity; by "Unity" one must understand that God is the Absolute and that there is only one Absolute; it is this aspect of overwhelming obvi-

---

and a possibility, by definition, is something that cannot not be, being an aspect of the absolute necessity of the divine Principle" ("The Particular Nature and Universality of the Christian Tradition", *The Transcendent Unity of Religions*). This exotericization of an esoterism was for the West the last hope of salvation, other traditional structures being for it either outworn or completely inapplicable; but this "anomaly"—although quite providential—was at the same time indirectly, and through a kind of "rebound", the cause of the "offence which must needs come", and this alone can explain the multitude and extent of errors in the West, or such paradoxical features as the habit of swearing and blaspheming, which is singularly widespread in Christian lands, but unknown in the East. This was what Islam, which seeks to be a normative totality and a timeless equilibrium, implicitly foresaw.

[26] What is in question here is not the Cabala, which, in being what *Moysi doctrina velat,* is a kind of "Christianity before its time", at least in certain respects.

[27] Genuine "theosophy" is to theology what *gnosis* is to faith, although from another point of view *gnosis* and theosophy cannot be situated outside faith and theology respectively.

[28] We have treated all these questions in the chapter "Knowledge and Love" in *Spiritual Perspectives and Human Facts.*

ousness or absoluteness which "unifies", that is, transmutes and delivers. He who says *Allâh* says, "There is no Truth or Absolute but the one Truth, the one Absolute"—to paraphrase the *Shahâdah*: *lâ ilâha illâ 'Llâh*—or in Vedantic terms: "The world is false; *Brahma* is real"; or again: "Nothing is evident except the Absolute." And this amounts to saying that Islam takes its starting point not in our fallen and passional nature, but in the theomorphic and inalterable character of our humanity, thus in what distinguishes us from the animal, namely, an objective and in principle limitless intelligence; now the normal content of the intelligence—that for which it is made—is the Absolute-Infinite; in a word, man is intelligence at once integral and transcendent, "horizontal" and "vertical", and the essential content of this intelligence is at the same time our deliverance: man is delivered by consciousness of the Absolute, his salvation being the remembrance of God.

Consequently, the simple fact that we are men obliges us to "become One"; we have no choice, for we cannot demand that destiny turn us into birds or flowers; we are condemned to the Infinite. A receptacle necessitates a content: if there were no water, milk, or wine, then jugs and waterskins would have no right to exist; likewise for our spirit, which is made in order that it might know the Evidence that delivers. The human state calls for a "knowing", and this knowing calls for a "being": to believe "sincerely" what the Name *Allâh* implies—that *lâ ilâha illâ 'Llâh*—is at the same time to assume the consequences of this conviction and to profess, by practicing it, Unity on all planes, social as well as spiritual; that which is normative, on whatever plane—namely, an element of equilibrium or union[29]—reveals itself by that very fact as a manifestation of Unity or a participation in it. There is no *îmân* (unitary "faith") without *islâm* ("submission" to the Law), and there is neither one nor the other without *ihsân* (spiritual "virtue"), that is, without profound understanding or realization; whoever accepts the One has already given himself (*aslama*) to Him, unless he is to lose himself in a

---

[29] Equilibrium as regards the collectivity and union as regards the individual; but there is no radical division here, for the individual also needs equilibrium, and the collectivity participates in its way, by religion, in union. To say that the collectivity is something other than the individual does not mean that there is a radical incompatibility, or that these two poles of the human condition do not influence each other. Morals are the asceticism of the collectivity, just as asceticism constitutes the morals of the individual.

mortal hypocrisy (*nifâq*).[30] To admit the existence of some relativity may obligate one to nothing or may obligate one to a merely relative position; to admit the Absolute obligates a man totally.

But the Name *Allâh*, besides its aspect of Truth or Evidence, also includes an aspect of Mercy, and it is then equivalent to the formula of consecration: "In the Name of God (the Unique), the infinitely Good or Blessed (in Himself) and the infinitely Merciful (as regards the world)": *bismi 'Llâhi 'r-Rahmâni 'r-Rahîm.*[31] This Mercy God manifests by His Revelations as well as by the symbols and gifts of nature, the word "sign" (*âyah*) referring to both categories, the one supernatural and the other natural; the meaning of the formula of consecration is thus very close to that of the second testimony of faith: "Muhammad is the Messenger of God."[32] The testimony that God is One expresses the absorption of the human or the terrestrial by the "Truth", whereas the testimony that Muhammad—and with him all the Revealers[33]—is the Messenger of the One God marks the outpouring of virtues and graces into the world or the soul, and thus compensates for the negative character that the first testimony has in relation to the cosmos. If the first testimony bears witness that "the world is false; *Brahma* is true", the second does not allow us to forget that "everything is *Âtmâ*".[34]

---

[30] The Mosaic revelation—"Judaism" properly so called—puts all its emphasis on the element *islâm*, or more exactly on the formal—or formalist—aspect of this element, so that the saving quality here is the "Israeliteness" of man, his attachment to a divine framework, and not *a priori* a character pre-existing in human nature.

[31] In this formula, the *Basmalah*, the first phrase—"in the Name of God"— indicates the divine causality, whereas the first of the two divine Names that follow expresses the "divine Substance"—or the "underlying Bliss"—of the cosmos, and the second expresses the divine Mercy insofar as it enters into the cosmos by discontinuous influences and nourishes it "successively" with its gifts and graces.

[32] The difference between the *Basmalah* and the second *Shahâdah* lies in the fact that the former proceeds "from above downward", and the latter proceeds "from below upward": the *Basmalah* is the formula of divine manifestation, creation, revelation, whereas the second *Shahâdah* indicates ascent, realization, the path.

[33] According to Saint Thomas, faith in the existence—the reality—of God and faith in Providence are indispensable to salvation: "In the existence of God are contained all the things that we believe to exist [to be real] in God eternally; and in faith in Providence are included all the dispensations of God in time that are concerned with the salvation of men" (*Summa Theologica*, Pt. II-II, Q.1, Art. 7).

[34] On the Christian side and from the point of view of *gnosis*, the assertion that Christ alone is God combines in its way the two testimonies of Islam, or rather two angles of vision corresponding to them metaphysically.

The Koran indicates the conditions—and outlines the frame-work—for the orison of the "solitary" (*mufrad*) or "supreme" (*a'zam*) Name in enjoining the invocation of *Allâh* "with humility and in secret" and also "through fear and through desire" (*Sûrah* "The Heights" [7]:55, 56); it says moreover: "Be steadfast and remember God often" (*Sûrah* "The Spoils of War" [8]:45), nor does it neglect the aspect of quietude: "Is it not through remembrance of God that hearts repose in security?" (*Sûrah* "The Thunder" [13]:28). From this is derived the following doctrine: we must fear God—and in fact it is Him alone we fear, without knowing it—and we must not "take His Name in vain" (*cf.* Exod. 20:7), that is, with an impure intention aimed at the approval of men or glory, or even at magic; we must desire God—and in fact it is Him alone we desire, without knowing it[35]—and we must pronounce His Name "with all our heart, with all our soul, and with all our might" (*cf.* Deut. 6:5);[36] as for humility, it is indispensable, for it is the consciousness of our nothingness, which is determined by consciousness of the All-Reality; and as for secrecy, the divine Name demands it, for this Name is not suited for collective devotion, its domain being in no way that of the communal Law. But secrecy also has a quite inward meaning, and then it refers to the "heart" as the symbolical seat of the Self; finally, the resoluteness and frequency of "remembering" vanquish space and time, the world and life; and as for the "repose of hearts", it is in God alone that we find Peace.

The Name *Allâh* contains all of these meanings. *Allâh*, who is the Unique, is thereby the great Peace: being pure Reality, there is in Him no disequilibrium, no narrowness. His Name is the Peace that silences all the sounds of the world, whether around us or within us, in accordance with this verse: "Say: *Allâh!* then leave them to their vain discourse" (*Sûrah* "Cattle" [6]:92).[37] Thus the Name casts as it were an immense blanket of snow over the things of this world or

---

[35] The love of God implies love of the neighbor just as the fear of God implies flight from sin, hence fear of its consequences.

[36] This is equivalent, despite the diversity of possible applications, to the Hindu ternary *jnâna*, *bhakti*, and *karma*.

[37] "The most noble of words is the utterance of *Allâh*," says the Prophet, which means that this Name contains all words and makes all words superfluous. "Every creature"—sings Mahmud Shabistari—"has its existence from the unique Name, out of which it comes and to which it returns with endless praises." "God has cursed everything on earth except the remembrance [the invocation] of God" (*hadîth*).

of our soul, extinguishing all and uniting all in one and the same purity and in one and the same overflowing and eternal silence.

* * *

The Hindu who invokes Shri Rama abandons his own existence for that of his Lord: it is as if he were asleep and Rama were watching and acting for him; he sleeps in Shri Rama, in the divine form of him who is invoked, who takes on all the burdens of the life of the devotee and in the end brings him back into this divine and immutable form itself. The doctrine of Rama is contained in the *Râmâyana*: the myth retraces the destiny of the soul (Sita) ravished by passion and ignorance (Ravana) and exiled in matter, at the confines of the cosmos (Lanka). Every soul devoted to Shri Rama is identified with Sita, the heroine who is carried off, then rescued.[38] Radha, the eternal spouse of Krishna, gives rise to the same symbolism; and he who says *Krishna* expresses the wisdom hidden in the *Mahâbhârata* and expounded in the *Bhagavad Gîtâ*, which is its synthesis and flower.

* * *

The invocation of the Buddha Amitabha—the *Logos* inasmuch as he "transmigrates", accumulating "merits" and returning "with full right", being the *Logos*, to his original and nirvanic plenitude—is founded upon a doctrine of redemption, that of the "original Vow". Amitabha—the Japanese Amida—is the Light and the Life of the Buddha Shakyamuni; by invoking Amitabha the devotee enters into a golden halo of Mercy; he finds security in the blessed light of that Name; he withdraws into it with perfect surrender and also perfect gratitude.[39] The whole of Amidism is contained in these words: purity, invocation, faith: abstaining from evil, invoking the Name, having trust.[40] Amida is Light and Life;[41] his Name carries the devotee toward the "Western Paradise" (*Sukhâvatî*): the devotee follows the solar Name through to its consummation, "to the West"[42];

---

[38] The ordeal of Sita—Rama doubting her fidelity—refers to the discontinuity between the "I" and the "Self", to the hiatus in the incommensurable dialogue between the soul and the Lord; the repudiation of Sita and her return to her mother, the Earth, means that the ego as such remains always the ego. But the eternal Sita is none other than Lakshmi, spouse of Rama-Vishnu, and she it is who is the prototype of the soul *in divinis*.

[39] In Amidism gratitude is what we could call the "moral stimulus".

he follows it right into the hereafter, leaving the world behind him, in the night—following this sun which, having traversed the "round of Existence", is "thus gone" (*tathâgata*), "gone, gone not to return, gone to the other shore" (*gâte, pâragâte, pârasamgâte*).

* * *

Prayer implies an inward alternative, a choice between an imperfection arising from our nature and the "remembrance of God", which is perfection by reason of its prime mover as well as its object. If this alternative is above all an inward one—otherwise we would have no right to any outward action—it is because prayer can be superimposed on any legitimate action; likewise, if the alternative is relative and not absolute—otherwise we would have no right to any thought outside of prayer—it is because prayer, though it cannot be superimposed on every beautiful or useful thought, can at least continue to vibrate during the course of such thought; and then the mental articulation, while in practice excluding prayer—to the

---

[40] This trinity belongs to every path founded on the power of divine Names. Abstention from evil is the passive condition; faith or trust is the active condition.

[41] It is the aspect Amitayus—issued from the forehead of Amitabha—that relates more particularly to "infinite Life". When the historical Buddha speaks of "previous Buddhas", it is as if he spoke of himself, in the sense that they incarnate aspects of his nature and are of his essence, or of the essence of the unique and universal Buddha, the *Âdi*-Buddha, who is the "celestial body"—the *Dharmakâya*—of all Buddhas. In Amidism it is Amitabha who is identified with the universal Buddha; from another point of view, as we have just said, the "mystical" Buddhas personify aspects of Shakyamuni, in the sense that Amitabha, Vairochana, Akshobhya, Ratnasambhava, and Amoghasiddhi—the five *Dhyâni*-Buddhas—each relate to one of the great moments in the life of the historical Buddha, but also *a priori* to one of the great cosmic cycles, as well as to the cosmic "regions" and to the aspects or functions of the universal Intellect, the regions being represented by the directions of space and the aspects or functions by the mental faculties. Outside the specifically Amidist perspective, it is Vairochana—inasmuch as he is Mahavairochana (Dainichi in Japanese)—who is identified with the *Âdi*-Buddha and who, remaining "at the center", produces by his radiance the four other *Dhyâni*-Buddhas. In Hindu terms, the *Âdi*-Buddha or Vairochana—and Amitabha or Shakyamuni insofar as they are identified with them—correspond to *Chit* (the enlightening, but not creating, *Purusha*) and its cosmic reflection, *Buddhi* or Sarasvati.

[42] As for the East, it indicates the Paradise of the Buddha Akshobhya (Ashuku in Japanese), conqueror of the demon (Mara); the East is attributed also—outside the sphere of the five *Dhyâni* Buddhas—to the Buddha Bhaishajyaguru (Yakushi), who drives away maladies just as the rising sun drives away darkness, and whose mercy more particularly concerns this terrestrial world, whereas that of Amitabha is manifested in the other world.

extent that the mind cannot do two things at once—nevertheless does not interrupt the "remembrance" in the eyes of God. In other words, just as prayer cannot be superimposed on a base or illicit action, so the fragrance of prayer cannot subsist during a thought that is opposed to the virtues; of course it goes without saying that the vibration of prayer in the absence of its articulation—when the mind is engaged elsewhere—presupposes a habit of prayer in the subject, for there is no perfume without a flower; it presupposes as well the intention to persevere in prayer and to intensify it; it is thus that the "past" and the "future", the acquired and the intended, participate in the unarticulated continuity of prayer.

Life is not a sort of space filled with possibilities offering themselves to our good pleasure, as children and worldly people believe; it is a road that becomes more and more narrow, from the present moment to death. At the end of this road there is death and the encounter with God, then eternity; all these realities are already present in prayer, in the timeless actuality of the divine Presence.

What matters for a man is not the diversity of the events he may experience as they stretch out along the magic thread we call duration, but perseverance in the "remembrance", which takes us outside time and raises us above our hopes and our fears. This remembrance already dwells in eternity; in it the succession of actions is only illusory, prayer being one; prayer is thereby already a death, a meeting with God, an eternity of bliss.

What is the world if not a flow of forms, and what is life if not a cup that is seemingly emptied from one night to the next? And what is prayer if not the sole stable point—made of peace and light—in this dream universe and the narrow gate leading to all that the world and life have sought in vain? In the life of man, these four certitudes are everything: the present moment, death, the meeting with God, eternity. Death is an exit, a world that closes down; the meeting with God is like an opening toward a fulgurating and immutable infinitude; eternity is a fullness of being in pure light; and the present moment is an almost ungraspable "place" in our duration where we are already eternal—a drop of eternity amid the to and fro of forms and melodies. Prayer gives to the terrestrial instant its full weight of eternity and its divine value; it is a sacred ship that bears its load, through life and death, toward the further shore, toward the silence of light. And yet at a deeper level it is not prayer that passes through time by repeating itself; it is time that halts, so to speak, before the already celestial unicity of prayer.

The Name

Thy Name is wine and honey, melody
That shapes our sacred way and destiny.
Who is the Speaker and who is the Word?
Where is the song Eternity has heard?

The liberating Word comes from the sky
Of Grace and Mercy; and we wonder why
Such gift can be; the truth is not so far:
Thy Name is That Which is, and what we are.

Spiritual Perspectives

IV

The infinity of God requires His affirmation: the Word. The affirmation requires manifestation: the world, the apparent "going forth" of the Divine "outside" itself. Manifestation requires limitation or diversification, without which it could not subsist "outside" God, at least from the point of view of its own illusion. Manifestation requires negation, since it is not God: hence imperfections and destructions on the one hand and spiritual liberation on the other.

A perspective which holds that the world "necessarily emanates" from God will also hold that beings "return" to God; but a perspective which would have it that the world is "freely created" out of "nothing" cannot accept the opposite and correlative process, for that would require that the immortal person should again become "nothing". And yet there is here only a difference of words: the first perspective starts from the idea that the world is in God, whence a certain spiritual continuity, and the second starts from the idea that God is not in the world, whence the dogma of exclusive discontinuity.

* * *

"God does what He wills": this does not at all mean that He displays the capriciousness of a tyrant, but that universal Possibility is limitless and incalculable, of such complexity that human understanding cannot analyze it, any more than one glance can take in the extent and complexity of a virgin forest or a star-spangled sky. If there are men apparently of limited intelligence who are saints and men who are apparently saints who are really of limited intelligence, and if there are fish that fly and birds that swim—if God loves in His creation this interplay of compensations and surprises, this game of hide-and-seek, in which anything can be anything—this is by virtue of His infinity, which cannot stop at any limits.

If God is the Absolute, there is nothing that could be He: God is continually shattering whatever in creation appears to assume an absolute or infinite character. Were it not so, the relative would itself be God.

* * *

That we are conformed to God—"made in His image"—this is certain; otherwise we would not exist.

That we are contrary to God, this also is certain; otherwise we would not be different from God.

Apart from analogy with God, we would be nothing.

Apart from opposition to God, we would be God.

* * *

The separation between man and God is at one and the same time absolute and relative: were it not absolute, man as such would be God; were it not relative, there would be no possible contact between the human and the Divine, and man would be an atheist by ontological definition, thus irremediably so. The separation is absolute because God alone is real, and no continuity is possible between nothingness and Reality; but the separation is relative—or rather "non-absolute"—because nothing is outside of God.

In a sense it might be said that this separation is absolute from man to God and relative from God to man.

* * *

God as such does not have the possibility of not being God: He has this possibility only in the world and through the world. But the world is not in reality outside of God, or else it would limit Him.

One of the mysteries of the "Word made flesh" is that "God made nothingness": the world. To say that God made the world "from nothing" is to say that He made Himself "nothing"—and also that the world "is" not.

* * *

78

The notion of the radical otherness of creation in relation to the Creator—or of manifestation in relation to the Principle—does not do justice to the total nature of this manifestation; from the point of view of absolute Truth it is not enough to define the created, in an exclusive manner, as "infinitely other", although it is obviously so with regard to its existential separation.

The Infinite is that which is absolutely without limits, but the finite cannot be that which is "absolutely limited", for there is no absolute limitation. The world is not an inverted God; God is without a second.

*   *   *

A mere "resemblance" is nothing in relation to God. If the finite is absolutely distinct from the Infinite—and it is so with regard to the limitation that defines it, its "nothingness", though not with regard to its "qualitative content"—then it cannot draw near the Infinite; the disparity will always remain incommensurable.[1]

The human substance is only a veil. Nothing "returns" to God except what "pre-exists" in Him.

*   *   *

If the only thing that distinguished man, supremely beatified, from God were the "human substance"—in other words, if the "resemblance" were such that only the "human substance" prevented there being "identity"—then man would have something more than God has, namely, this very substance; he would then be more than God. Now, since "God alone is good", the said substance is necessarily privative. Now if the human substance is less than God, it cannot subsist, we do not say in man, but in absolute Reality.[2] If

---

[1] It goes without saying that, from the standpoint of its existence, qualitative content—beauty, for instance—is itself also "absolutely other" than God. Words cannot adequately express these things; they cannot simultaneously grasp all aspects of the real.

[2] According to Saint Basil, "Man has received the order to become God." Saint Cyril of Alexandria expresses it thus: "If God has become man, man has become God." According to Meister Eckhart, "We are wholly transformed into God and changed into Him, in the same manner as the bread is changed into the body of Christ in the sacrament. Thus I am changed into Him because He makes me one with His Being,

the "content" is God alone, what does the "container" matter? If the "container" is privative, how can the "content" be God? Only the doctrine of the degrees of Reality can account for this mystery.

Apophatic and antinomian theology is in conformity with the inward incommensurability of dogma. Thus it acknowledges simultaneously the imparticipability and the participability of the divine Nature: the soul is not God, and according to Saint Macarius of Egypt, "there is nothing in common between their natures"; in another respect, however, there is a "transmutation of the soul into the divine Nature". If theology never makes use of direct expressions of the doctrines of identity—such as those of the Shankarian *Vedânta*—it is because it looks at everything in relation to man; for theology, identity comes under the heading of the inexpressible.[3]

* * *

The most explicit metaphysical doctrine will always take it as axiomatic that every doctrine is only error when confronted with the divine Reality in itself, but a provisional, indispensable, salutary "error", containing and communicating the virtuality of Truth.

The Divinity is beyond "knowledge" insofar as this implies a subject and object; for this reason the divine Essence is "unknowable".

* * *

The human "I" reflects the divine "I"; however, the human "I" represents an inverse principle in relation to the "I" of God. All exoterism stops at this aspect of inversion and ignores the aspect of essential identity; exoterism, which is by definition formal, does not have the capacity—nor the duty, of course—to combine antinomic aspects of the Real in a direct and non-formal vision of things.

---

and not simply like it. By the living God it is true that there no longer remains any distinction." Angelus Silesius says, "Man has not perfect bliss before Unity has swallowed up alterity." And again: "The blissful soul no longer knows alterity; it is one single Light with God and one single Glory."

[3] According to the Sufi Hasan al-Shadhili, "The desire for union with God is one of the things that most surely separate us from Him"; in this case it is a question of the desire—understood as something individual—to be united to God as an individual. On the other hand, desire for "deliverance" is permissible, since this is liberation from a privation.

To say, "He alone is real, the ego is not" and to say, "I am not other than 'I' (the Self)" amount to exactly the same thing.[4]

* * *

In Monotheism religious dogmatism excludes non-dualistic formulations of union; no formulation can go against dogma, which is of necessity dualistic. Now this dualism, like that of the Vishnuites moreover, says that human nature is human nature and the divine Nature is the divine Nature, and nothing else. From the point of view of dogmatic language, non-dual union belongs to the domain of the inexpressible; it is as though, being unable to say that a plant is green, one said that it was at the same time yellow and blue, and neither one nor the other. Created nature assuredly remains what it is: no one has ever maintained that the created as such is transformed into the Uncreated.

* * *

The man still undelivered is in truth a delivered man who does not know it.

The bridge from the finite to the Infinite is this: that the finite is infinite in its center and essence—that the finite as such is not.

When the sun rises, the night has never been.

* * *

Spiritual doctrines allow for "union" or "identity" according to whether they consider a being from the point of view of creation or from that of the divine Reality. From the standpoint of creation nothing can "become God" or "become nothing"; in the divine Reality the world has never been, and therefore the creature could never cease to be. Now the intelligence that is plunged in God sees according to the divine Reality; otherwise it would not truly see God. In the final analysis everything is reduced to a question

[4] According to an expressive phrase of the Shaykh Ahmad al-Alawi, "The invocation of God is like a movement to and fro, which affirms an increasingly complete communication until there is an identity between the glimmer of consciousness and the dazzling fulguration of the Infinite."

of terminology: the unconditional affirmation of identity by Shan-kara—not by all Vedantists—necessarily results from the perspec-tive of the absolute Subject. For Ibn Arabi it is not a question of "becoming one" with God: the contemplative "becomes conscious" that he "is one" with Him; he "realizes" true unity. In Christianity "deification", the necessary complement of "incarnation", does not imply any "identification" on the same plane of reality; that man as such should literally "become" God would imply that there was between God and man a common measure and a symmetrical con-frontation; no doubt it was this reservation Shankara had in view when he affirmed that the delivered one (*mukta*) is without the creative power of *Brahma*. Be that as it may, there is no more reason to reject the expression "to become God" than to reject Shankara's formula of "identity", for they retain all their antinomic and ellip-tical value.

* * *

Inevitably, a dialectic conforming to transcendent wisdom is not only apophatic and antinomic, but also elliptical.

"He (the delivered one) is *Brahma*" is an elliptical formula, and the same is true of the most controversial of Eckhart's formulations, such as his teaching about the uncreated and deifying character of the Intellect "in the soul". Retraction was easy, since the formula in question—*aliquid est in anima quod est increatum et increabile . . . et hoc est Intellectus*—when not regarded as elliptical, is erroneous by reason of the fact that it seems to affirm immanentism pure and simple; in reality it implicitly affirms the created intellect as the vehicle of the uncreated Intellect, but it does not put this into words, since spiritual vision is "vertical" and "essential", not "hori-zontal" and "analogical".

* * *

The opposition of Creator and creature, of Lord and servant, is irreducible because man cannot be God.

The essential identity of manifested intelligence and principial Intelligence is necessary and metaphysically clear because the microcosmic subject cannot be of another essence than the absolute Subject, the Subject as such, the Self. There is only one single Subject; the rest is blindness.

We may thus differentiate between perspectives that are objective and outward, where the divine Objectivity confronts the individual subject, and a perspective that is subjective and inward, where the universal Subject is considered without regard to possible degrees of objectification.

The monotheistic religions are objective perspectives; now it is not possible to set forth directly, in "objective" terms, the "subjective" truth[5] of the essential identity between the objectivized subject and the pure Subject; the extinction of the microcosmic subject in the metacosmic Object[6] is not strictly speaking a formula of identity, although the reality thus expressed is the same.

Objective perspectives start from the irreducible distinction between the subject and the Object; subjective perspectives do not see the object except as a function of the one and exclusive reality of the Subject.

* * *

There are three great, divine mysteries: the world, Being, Non-Being.

In the world no quality is another quality, and no quality is God. In Being no quality is another quality, but each of them is God. In Non-Being—Beyond-Being—there are no qualities; but since Non-Being is transcendence and not privation, having no qualities because it is beyond all diversity, it can be said that in it every quality is every other and that their non-distinction—or their transcending—is God.

---

[5] It goes without saying that the terms "subject" and "object" are used here only with the strictly logical and universal meaning that they have in themselves, and not in the least "psychologically".

[6] Al-Ghazzali speaks of "those who are consumed by the splendors of the sublime Face (the Essence) and who are submerged by the majesty of the divine Glory to such an extent that they are effaced and brought to nothing, and there is no longer any room for contemplation of themselves, since they no longer have anything to do with the soul. Nothing remains except the One, the Real" (*Mishkât al-Anwâr*). Monotheistic dogmas do not exclude formulations that are "subjective" in their mode, however, and the Hallajian *Anâ' l-Haqq* is an example of this.

What reason cannot comprehend is how the world can be metaphysically reducible to God and how God can be Non-Being, or better yet Beyond-Being. The world exists, but it "is" not. When the divine Reality is envisaged in its totality, God "is" not, but He "possesses Being": God-Being is in reality only the Being of God. Nonetheless it is not false to say, in relation to the world, that God "is"; humanly speaking, it can even be said—though the expression is incorrect—that God "exists" in order to specify that He is not "non-existent", that is, that He is "real", "positive", "concrete".

* * *

Analogy is a mode of identity; otherwise there would be only an absolute difference, an irreducible opposition, between the two terms of comparison: now such an opposition would reduce one of the terms to nothing. Man is "nothing" in the context of his separation, but not from the standpoint of analogy.

Man is made "in the image" of God. This is what allows him to "become" what he "is".[7] The word "become" is here entirely approximate and provisional, for there is no real continuity between "what should be" and "what has never been".

* * *

Creatures are good or bad; in created things there are qualities and defects, perfections and imperfections. Everything that is good in one way or another "pre-exists" in God; otherwise there would be perfections whose source or cause was other than divine. Everything that is good is good because God is good; hence no quality, no perfection, can be lost; God can never be something "less" in relation to the world. For this reason one may say that what is "lost" before God is "found again" in Him.

* * *

God is said to have created the world "by an absolutely gratuitous act"; He was not "obliged" to create it. This amounts to saying that

---

[7] Meister Eckhart said that the image—the Son—expresses "identity" (*Gleichheit*) with the Father.

necessity is an imperfection and arbitrariness a perfection; one might as well say that God is perfect by caprice, since He is not "obliged" to be so. Is it not its necessity that constitutes the perfection of a geometrical figure? God possesses in an absolute fashion two complementary perfections, liberty and necessity, each in a different way: liberty refers to the Infinite, necessity to the Absolute. The absolute character of God is not an imperfection any more than His justice. God creates because He is God—there is no place here for arbitrariness—but in His creation He gives free rein to all the imponderables of His infinite liberty. The creative act is derived from divine necessity, the created content from divine liberty. God could refrain from creating a particular being, but He cannot not create at all, since He cannot not be God.

* * *

Human liberty is necessary, since it is determined by God, the cause of all.

Divine necessity is free, since it has no cause outside itself.

Human necessity is doubly necessary: first of all divinely and then humanly; the impossibility of man's changing his form has a metaphysical cause and, secondarily, a physical cause. As for the divine liberty it is doubly free, above all in itself and then with regard to the world.

But the divine necessity is not free with regard to the world; otherwise it would contradict itself and create the impossible. And inversely: human liberty is not necessary with regard to God, because in this respect it participates in the absolute, divine liberty.

Man's freedom to choose God is already something of the freedom of God.

* * *

Between the human microcosm and the divine Metacosm there stands the macrocosm, which represents "the Principle manifested" or "the manifestation of the Principle" in relation to the human subject. There is no common measure between man and God, the "I" and the "Self": in order to become conscious of the "Self" the "I" has need of the Intellect, which is its direct manifestation in man. In an analogous fashion, what necessarily stands between the formal creation and the Uncreated is the supra-formal or non-formal creation, the world of the Spirit.

There is no common measure between manifestation and the Principle, and consequently there cannot be an intermediate point situated as it were "mathematically" at the center; this center exists only in relation to the world, in a purely symbolic manner. It appears either as "the Principle manifested" or as "the manifestation of the Principle"; it has no existence apart from these two "poles", but may be reduced to either one: it is either "Principle" or "manifestation". Between God and the world stands the "avataric", Christic, prophetic mystery: the mystery of the human God or the divine man.

Man cannot know or meet God if he has not known or met Him in the world; he is separated from God if he denies revelation or if he does not see God in his neighbor. In a certain sense everything that comes into contact with man acts as "neighbor"—and thus indirectly as God—in an appropriate manner. In the neighbor God wishes to be loved and heard: He wishes to be loved through the charity we practice toward men and to be heard in the teachings they give us either directly or indirectly; He is hidden in the neighbor, either in the perfections that teach the truth or in the misfortunes that call forth charity.

If a man does not trample on a flower without reason, it is because the flower is something of God, a distant effect of the infinite Cause; whoever despises a flower indirectly despises God. If a good man had the power to destroy a stone, he would nevertheless not do so without a motive, for the existence of the stone—that quasi-absolute something that distinguishes it from nothingness—is a manifestation of the Principle; it is therefore sacred. In every neutral contact with matter—and this is all the more true of contact with one's fellow-men—a man should either not leave any trace or else leave a beneficent trace; he should either enrich or pass unperceived. Even when there is a need to destroy—in which case the destruction is divinely willed—a man should destroy in conformity with the nature of the object, which then objectifies human nothingness to the extent that the man is the agent of a celestial will. The life of man being sacred, the destructions it inevitably requires are also sacred.

The ternary "ego-world-God" or "I-Intellect-Self", or again "form-spirit-Cause", is found analogically in the ternary "humility-charity-truth" as well as in the three great stages of the spiritual life: purification, perfection, union.

* * *

Life is the passage of an individual dream, a consciousness, an ego through a cosmic and collective dream. Death withdraws the particular dream from the general dream and tears out the roots that the former has thrust into the latter. The universe is a dream woven of dreams; the Self alone is awake.

The objective homogeneity of the world does not prove its absolute reality, but rather the collective nature of the illusion, or a particular illusion, a particular world.

For the ego the world is not a subjective state; it is an objective and polyvalent reality; but for the divine Self the world—or a particular world—is a subjective unity like a particular soul. When the Intellect, which is as it were hidden within us and in which we can participate under certain conditions of realization and grace, has seen the Self and has penetrated us with this vision, then the world will appear to us a precarious and fugitive substance—thus a dream—and it is our spiritual consciousness that will be revealed as polyvalent and stable, whether one calls this realization grace, knowledge, or something else.

5

Trials and Happiness

Since evil is inevitable in the world, it is inevitable also in one's destiny; being necessary in the economy of the objective reality surrounding us, it is no less necessary in the experience of the subject-witness; the imperfections of the world are coupled with the trials of life.

First of all one has to answer the question of why the painful experiences man must undergo are called "trials". We would reply that these are trials in relation to our faith, which indicates that with regard to such troubling experiences, we have duties resulting from our human vocation. In other words, we must prove our faith in relation to God and in relation to ourselves: in relation to God by our intelligence, our sense of the absolute, and thus our sense of relativities and proportions; and in relation to ourselves by our character, our resignation to destiny, our gratitude. There are in fact two ways to overcome the traces that evil, or more precisely suffering, leaves in the soul: the first is our awareness of the Sovereign Good, which coincides with our hope to the extent that this awareness penetrates us; and the second is our acceptance of what, in religious language, is called the "will of God". And assuredly it is a great victory over oneself to accept a destiny because it is God's will and for no other reason.

Life is a succession of moments, and we can—and must—at every moment say "yes" to the divine will, that is, to what God wills for us at this very moment. Doubtless this does not deliver us from the evils we must face in the outward world, but it does deliver us from our passional reactions to these evils; without our knowing or willing it, these reactions—made of bitterness or even despair—are revolts against divine decrees, and that is why very often God is slow to save us from our tribulations. The error here is, on the one hand, wishing the world to be other than what it is, and on the other hand, wishing that what happens to us were not our destiny.

The golden rule is first to resign oneself to the will of God as it is manifested in the inevitable, although we are obviously free—and even obliged, depending on the case—to abolish avoidable evil if we can do so justly; and second to trust in the Justice and Goodness of God and place our cares in His hands while accomplishing with equity what we can or must accomplish, for "Heaven helps those who help themselves."

A trial is not necessarily a chastisement; it can also be a grace, and the one does not preclude the other. In any case, a trial in itself not only tests what we are, but also purifies us of what we are not.

But there is also holy gratitude; by this we mean our awareness of the divine gifts which enable us to live and which, out of simple habit, we have forgotten. Gratitude—the capacity to appreciate even little things—is part of nobility of soul as is generosity; both virtues, together with faith, help us to bear the burdens that destiny imposes on us; God helps us to bear our burdens when we bear them with faith and magnanimity.

We must beware of becoming hypnotized by the world which surrounds us, and which reinforces our feeling of being exposed to a thousand dangers. It is as if one were walking along a narrow path between two abysses: when looking to either side one risks losing one's balance; one must on the contrary look straight ahead and let the world be the world. The whole purpose of our life lies before us, and that is one of the meanings of the injunction not to look back when one has put one's hand to the plow. It is necessary to look towards God, in relation to whom all the chasms of the world are nothing.

*   *   *

Apart from the trials of life, which concern our faith and moral perfection, there are ritual and initiatic trials, which refer to our higher spiritual qualifications; they are met with in the Egyptian and Greco-Roman mysteries of antiquity, and later in the craft initiations of Christian Europe. On the one hand, these are symbolic actions representing various aspects of cosmic *Mâyâ*, which the neophyte is supposed to vanquish within himself; on the other hand, they are "touchstones" intended to provoke reactions in the neophyte that test his qualification, or his disqualification, for surpassing himself. Because the initiatic way by definition implies operations that risk bringing about disequilibriums and falls, it is therefore necessary to prevent those who do not fulfill the required conditions from committing themselves. But this does not mean that these ritual trials are found wherever there is an initiation and a corresponding method, for there are other means to try our capacities or cushion psychic shocks, as the case may be; these means are above all of the moral order, whereas in the ancient mysteries and those of the crafts they are rather of the "alchemical" order, so to speak.

The most important or characteristic initiatic trials are perhaps the "trial by water" and the "trial by fire". The first seems to refer to gentle and seductive *Mâyâ* and the second to terrible and destructive *Mâyâ*; in other words, it is necessary to brave not only the "sirens' song" but also the "dragons". Both powers sleep within ourselves and awaken as soon as we seek to go beyond their level; but they exist *a priori* in the macrocosm, of which we are part and which we realize in an individual and subjective mode. In spiritual combat, both *Mâyâs*, the outward and the inward, combine to create obstacles; but there is also celestial *Mâyâ*, most often represented by a goddess—in Christianity by the Blessed Virgin—who comes to the aid of the combatant, on condition that he has taken the measures, or fulfilled the conditions, that allow celestial *Mâyâ* to intervene.

* * *

One of the first conditions of happiness is the renunciation of the superficial and habitual need to feel happy. But this renunciation cannot spring from the void; it must have a meaning, and this meaning cannot but come from above, from what constitutes our reason for being. In fact, for too many men, the criterion of the value of life is a passive feeling of happiness, which is determined *a priori* by the outer world; when this feeling does not occur or when it fades—which may have subjective as well as objective causes—they become alarmed and are as if possessed by the question: "Why am I not happy as I was before?" and by the awaiting of something that could restore their feeling of being happy. All this, it is unnecessary to stress, is a perfectly worldly attitude, hence incompatible with the least of spiritual perspectives. To become enclosed in an earthly happiness is to create a barrier between man and Heaven, and it is to forget that on earth man is in exile, as the very fact of death proves.

The first response to the profane expectation of the feeling of happiness—or to the bad habit of imprisoning oneself in this expectation, as if there were not above us a serene and boundless sky—is remembrance of the Sovereign Good or awareness of its Reality and Beatitude. It is this awareness that allows us to perceive the relativity and pettiness of our "complex" of happiness and to notice that in this expectation there are two fundamental vices, namely, concupiscence and idolatry: two things, therefore, that take us away from God and consequently from Felicity as such, the source of all happiness.

But there is something else: to the renunciation of which we have spoken there should be joined what can be most simply called the "life of prayer". One must be able to find happiness in the spiritual act, the gift of self, rather than in the passive and narcissistic enjoyment of a well-being that the world is supposed to offer us. "It is more blessed to give than to receive," said Christ.[1]

However, the completion of the negative attitude of renunciation by the positive attitude of affirmation or gift could not by itself constitute the sole alchemy of spiritual contentment; we also need a state of soul that corresponds more directly to happiness properly so called, and this is in the first place and quite obviously the love of God: the sense of the sacred and thus recollection before the Divinity or before a given sacramental expression of its presence. This is contemplative beatitude within the sanctuary, a sanctuary that is above all in our heart, for "the kingdom of God is within you".

Another pole of spiritual happiness—complementary to the preceding one—is hope: our conditional certitude of salvation, resulting from our certitude of God and from the sincerity of this certitude. For being truly certain of the Absolute means drawing the operative consequences of this conviction, since the Absolute involves all that we are. Faith demands works; it is not works in themselves that bring about salvation, but they are part of faith, and faith opens our immortal soul to saving Mercy. Works, or simply work: this is above all dialogue with Heaven; the moral aura of this

---

[1] Acts 20:35. Similarly, Artaxerxes, according to Plutarch: "To give is more regal than to receive."

alchemy is beauty of soul, hence also the outward activity that manifests it.

Happiness is religion and character; faith and virtue. It is a fact that man cannot find happiness within his own limits; his very nature condemns him to surpass himself, and in surpassing himself to free himself.

* * *

"I love because I love," said Saint Bernard;[2] this saying indicates the highest reason for our happiness, namely—to repeat—our awareness of the Sovereign Good and our unshakeable attachment to Him who has given us intelligence and immortality.

But there is still more in the saying we have quoted. Its deepest meaning is: I love because I am Love; that is, it refers to the mystery of immanence and union; we would even say to the mystery of "identity". From this point of view, our happiness stems from what we are; and we are happy to the extent that we are really and fully ourselves, beyond the husks which, in our ignorance and egoism, we take for our true being. To know oneself is to remember That which is.

---

[2] An expression that remotely pertains to the "logic" of the Burning Bush: "I am that I am."

93

Remembrance

O Thou whose Name is sweetest remedy
And whose remembrance heals our soul's disease:
With Thee each moment is Eternity —
A drop from Heaven that consoles and frees.

Spiritual Perspectives

V

If we leave aside the purely formal factors of the contemplative life, which do not directly engage the intellectual and moral worth of man, we can say that spirituality stands in a sense between metaphysical truth and human virtue, or rather that it has an absolute need of these two, though it can be reduced to neither. The presence in our mind of metaphysical truth is by itself inoperative as far as our final ends are concerned. Similarly, virtues cut off from truth do not have the power to raise us above ourselves—if indeed they can still subsist—for only the truth can surpass the level of our nature.

Truths make us understand the virtues, giving them all their cosmic amplitude and their spiritual efficacy. The virtues for their part lead us to truths and transform them for us into realities that are concrete, seen, and lived.

* * *

Everything revolves around truth and the will; the one must penetrate the other. Truth illumines the will, which, when illuminated, vivifies the truth. From the point of view of fallen man, truth is dead, and the will is blind. Truth is life, but in human consciousness it appears *a priori* as a dead letter.

Intelligence is nothing without truth; moreover without virtue it is unable to contain truth in a way that is really adequate and absolutely stable. As for the will it is nothing without virtue, and it cannot realize virtue in a profound and total manner without truth.

Truth is what we must know: the Absolute and the relative and, at their points of contact—if one may speak in this way—the divine will in all its complexity. As for virtue, it is humility[1] and charity.

---

[1] This word is taken in its etymological sense, which is independent of the sentimental flavor it has in fact acquired. In itself the word "humility" expresses a fundamental attitude independent of any particular sentimentality; and this amounts to saying that the emotive concomitants of this attitude may differ according to the point of view.

Truth includes something of both humility and charity in its manifestation; humility is false if it has neither truth nor charity, and charity is false if it has neither truth nor humility. The virtues condition one another.

Truth, when it appears on the level of our will, becomes virtue, and it is then veracity and sincerity.

* * *

The three fundamental virtues—veracity, charity, humility—must penetrate even into our thinking, since this is an act. There is no plane of activity in which the virtues should not intervene. When pure truth manifests itself, it cannot do so without the virtues, for manifestation is an act.

Humility means to look at oneself in the limiting state of individuation; it means to turn one's gaze on the ego, on limitation, on nothingness. Charity means looking round about one: it means seeing God in one's neighbor and also seeing oneself there, but this time not as pure limitation, but as a creature of God made in His image. Veracity means to look toward Truth, to submit and attach oneself to it, and to become penetrated by its implacable light. Each of the three virtues must be found again in the others; they are criteria of one another.

* * *

Charitable humility will avoid causing scandal and thus injuring one's neighbor; it must not be contrary to self-effacement, which is its sufficient reason.

Veracious humility will avoid overestimation: virtue must not run counter to truth. But it can be more "true" than some outward and sterile truth; in this case it is virtue that is truth, and the contradiction is only apparent.

Humble charity will avoid exhibiting itself without any useful purpose; man must not pride himself on his generosity: "Let not thy left hand know what thy right hand doeth." The gift of oneself should above all be inward; without this gift, outward well-doing is devoid of spiritual value and blessing.

Veracious charity is conscious of the nature of things: I am not less than my neighbor, since I too exist and have an immortal soul.

On the other hand, it may be that some higher interest takes precedence over some particular interest of the neighbor; in a general way, spiritual interest takes precedence over temporal interest, whether it is a question of the "neighbor" or "oneself".

Humble veracity will not hide our ignorance; to pretend to a knowledge we do not possess is harmful to the knowledge we do possess.

Charitable veracity will neglect nothing in order to make the truth understood; if truth is a good, it should also be a gift.

Effacement of the ego, gift of oneself, realization of truth. It could be said that these attitudes correspond respectively to the stages—or states—of purification, expansion, and union. They are the three "dimensions" of perfect *gnosis*.

* * *

A spiritual virtue is nothing other than consciousness of a reality; it is natural—but immaterial—if it is accompanied by feeling. When virtue is purely sentimental, in the sense of being ignorant of the reality to which it relates, it may have a relative utility, but it is nonetheless a spiritual obstacle and a source of errors.

* * *

If metaphysics is sacred, this means that it cannot be presented as though it were only a profane philosophy sufficient unto itself, that is, not surpassing the sphere of mental operations. It is illogical and dangerous to talk of metaphysics without concerning oneself with its moral concomitants, the criteria of which are, for man, his behavior in relation to God and his neighbor.

* * *

The key to understanding the spiritual necessity of the virtues lies in the fact that metaphysical truths are reflected in the will and not only in the Intellect and the reason. To a given principial truth there corresponds a particular volitional attitude; this is a necessary aspect—or a consequence—of the principle that "to know is to be".

*   *   *

To meditate on the divine qualities is at the same time to meditate on the virtues—and consequently on the vices—of human beings. Spirituality includes both concentric circles and radii, modes of analogy and modes of identity: virtues and intellections. When intellections are replaced by rational operations, it is the virtues in their turn that appear as modes of identity, as "relatively direct" participations in the divine Being.

*   *   *

We must clearly distinguish between natural qualities and spiritual virtues, although the appearances may be the same and although, in principle, the first constitute qualifications for the second; we say "in principle" because in fact natural qualities may give rise to a moral idolatry that prevents the passage to a higher plane and can even provoke spiritual falls. In other words natural qualities do not necessarily keep their efficacy on the spiritual level; this is also true of a purely mental—or "worldly"—intelligence, though not of metaphysical intuition when it is predominant, for metaphysical intuition by definition belongs to the domain of the spirit and therefore to the domain of the immutable.

There are vices which, in the case of certain men, appear only on the spiritual, or so-called spiritual, level; and there results from this the paradox of men who are naturally intelligent and spiritually stupid, or modest on the surface and at bottom proud. As soon as a man tries to go beyond himself, those qualities which are strictly linked to his terrestrial nature, and which are not anchored in his spiritual essence, become more or less inoperative.

In some cases mental intelligence is the normal expression of the Intellect, but in others it is the opposition between the natural and the supernatural intelligence that manifests itself.

*   *   *

If qualities may be only apparent and not real, the same must be true as well of certain defects.

False qualities are always superficial and fragmentary, and thus inoperative outside certain limits; they are not false on their own

level of manifestation but in relation to the sum of the characteristics that make up the individual. The same thing is true *mutatis
mutandis* of superficial defects: these are situated on the surface
of the soul and cannot indefinitely resist the contrary—and fundamental—tendencies of the soul itself, and this implies that such
defects—like the qualities of which we have just spoken—always
remain within certain limits.

It is the global nature of man that decides his intrinsic worth: if
there is incompatibility between a quality and a defect, this means
that they are not situated on the same level and that one of the
two characteristics is only superficial; thus the criterion lies in their
respective scope, so that some essential aspect of the soul—one that
is decisive by its nature—will be the key for evaluating all the other
aspects. It goes without saying that there are qualities and defects
that are too important to be merely accidental; it is also evident that
a great good excludes a great evil of the same order, and inversely;
consequently they cannot both be found in the same individual.

* * *

Strictly social morality does not allow of psychological or spiritual
complications, and in this it is right in view of its practical bearing;
on the other hand, it is improper to attach an absolute value to this
point of view and to apply it to the intrinsic nature of man. Narrow-
minded moralists do not like complications, and they think this is
due to their own "straightforwardness", thus absolving themselves
of the need for reflection. Nonetheless, complexity is to be met with
everywhere in the world: there are mammals that live like fish and
others that live like birds, just as there are winged creatures adapted
to the water and others adapted to the land. There are men whose
qualities are real only at the level of profane life, and others whose
defects are due only to ephemeral conditions obtaining at this same
level.

Normally a man's evident qualities should manifest his fundamental worth, but it may happen that such qualities merely compensate for latent defects that are themselves fundamental; where
there is analogy there may also be opposition. Every human quality
may either express or contradict a divine perfection: it expresses it
thanks to its analogy with that perfection, and it contradicts it by
reason of its own relativity, which then, despite its positive content,

opposes it to its celestial prototype. To speak of expression is to speak at the same time of analogy, relativity, opposition.

A quality has a definitive value only through its inner humility, through its standing before God. False virtues are those that man alone enjoys without God being able to delight in them.

* * *

The world is woven of analogies and oppositions in relation to God; either of these can be real or merely apparent. This is why the world is full of paradoxes, both for good and for ill.

* * *

The disproportion between the natural virtues and those having a supernatural essence, or between those tainted by a secret vanity and those that are pure and deep, implies that virtues of the second category may be at times less apparent than those of the first, and that a certain spiritual modesty may even conceal them. It may also be that some inner reality, misunderstood from without, may seem to contradict them.

In an analogous manner, *gnosis* sometimes gives rise to paradoxical expressions, which in reality indicate the qualitative separation between the profane and spiritual planes; but this discontinuity is only one aspect beside another that is more important, that of analogy and essential continuity.

* * *

A virtue is a token of immortality only on condition that it is founded on God, which gives it a character at once impersonal and generous. A purely natural quality which has not been harnessed to a spiritual attitude infusing it with divine life has no more importance for God than "sounding brass".

* * *

There are men who are virtuous in a conventional way, on the surface of their being and for the sole reason that their habitual environment imposes certain styles of action on them; this does not at all mean that such virtues are without merit at a particular level, however small. There are other men who are incapable of being virtuous simply out of convention and without a deep understanding of the nature of things, but whose virtue would on the contrary be unshakeable given such an understanding.

A purely natural virtue, that is, a virtue independent of any acceptance of truth and any movement toward God, is like a crystal with which a man might try to light up a dark place. The crystal is by its nature luminous, but its properties of purity, transparency, and the power to condense luminous rays are inoperative without the presence of light, which in our example is nothing else than humility, or in other words perfect objectivity toward the ego and its infirmities. Or likewise: the color white is certainly luminous when set beside black, but nonetheless cannot light up a dark place; similarly a quality is certainly good when set beside a vice, but if it is not accompanied by a true, inner effacement before God and before the merit of our neighbor, it will be drowned in the blackness of hidden vanity, just as the color white is drowned in darkness. One other example: beyond question a horse in itself represents a force; but when two elephants, pulling in the opposite direction, are harnessed to the other end of a vehicle, the strength of the horse becomes inoperative, though it does not for a moment cease to exist. It is the same with the force or merit possessed by a strictly human virtue, one not illumined or transfigured by a spiritual development, by a real victory over our nature, by a gift of our being to God.

Virtue in itself is necessary, for light does not pass through an opaque stone and barely illuminates a black wall; man must therefore become like crystal or snow, but without maintaining that snow is light.

On the other hand, even fire loses its brilliance before the sun; it is thus that in knowledge—or in perfect love—the virtues lose their separate existence and their human conditioning.

* * *

God at times permits weaknesses in order to be able—by means of the contrast between these accidental infirmities and the essential being—to awaken virtues that are all the more profound. Qualities that have burgeoned in the compost of some affliction are as it were endowed with consciousness; in a concrete way they know the vanity of error.

At times God reinforces the appearance of the natural in order the better to be able to reveal the supernatural, or He permits weakness in order the better to be able to bring out the radiance and transcendence—or the gratuitous nature—of grace. This is without prejudice to the fact that in a general way God brings the receptacle into conformity with the supernatural gift, for these two possibilities are combined in different ways.

Too great an indulgence towards others is often caused, not by an innate weakness of character, but by an actual inability to conceive the frailty of men and the malice of the devil. Human beings have a tendency really to believe only what they see; now there are men who *a priori* see God rather than the secret evil of creatures.

*   *   *

Scandal mongering is an evil because one who is absent cannot defend himself and because the divulging of an unfavorable fact may injure him, and also because by his nature man tends to overestimate his own power of judgment. From the point of view of simple logic it is normal that a man should report facts that surprise him or make him suffer, since in principle he always has the right to ask for advice and to assure himself of the correctness of his own feeling; but this is conditional upon the accuracy of the facts and the impartiality of the witness, and also the moral dignity of the interlocutor, quite apart from the safeguarding of those who are absent. Now in practice there is no means of guaranteeing that these conditions are always completely fulfilled, and indeed in nine cases out of ten they will not be; consequently the moral law, insofar as it concerns the collectivity, is obliged to sacrifice the exception to the rule and the particular truth to the general expediency.

As for calumny, it consists in peddling inaccurate and unfavorable facts and in interpreting unfavorably things that are susceptible to a favorable interpretation, making no distinction between what is certain, probable, possible, doubtful, improbable, and impossible. Calumny is not a matter of accidental mistakes, but of systematic passion.

*   *   *

In psychology as elsewhere we must differentiate between accidental essences and essences as such. Thus the fact that a human
being is young or is a woman constitutes for that being a kind of
essence—the will cannot change it in any way—but its character is
accidental, for age is fleeting and a person's sex neither adds nor
takes away any fundamental human value. On the other hand, there
are also accidents which are essential, that is, accidents which manifest an essence: for example, a very unusual destiny that would be
incompatible with a different essence, the mortal sin of a man who
is damned, the sudden conversion of a dying man, or a crucial fact
determining the life of a saint.

Experience can teach us that a man who is apparently very
imperfect may, with time, reveal very solid virtues, or inversely. The
supernatural alone guarantees the stability of human values.

*   *   *

A thought that is in itself passionate and self-interested, and "jurid-
ical" instead of "just" in its external functioning—its logic lacking
a sense of proportion and consequently what one might call "the
aesthetic dimension" of intelligence—cannot encompass all aspects
of truth; it is a thought that "argues" and does not "listen".

Pure intellectuality depends upon thought which in itself is contemplative and as completely disinterested as the act of seeing, and
which in its external functioning employs a logic that is not artificial
and as it were mechanical, but consonant with the real nature of
things.

We could almost speak of a "moral dimension" of intelligence:
moral elevation, which has nothing to do with external laws but
depends upon beauty of soul, excludes an arbitrary functioning
of the mind; if "beauty is the splendor of the true", it is also in
a sense its criterion and guarantee, though in a subtle manner,
which cannot be comprehended by means of a purely theoretical
knowledge; otherwise the idea of beauty would automatically confer
beauty on the soul. It is true that every man has a tendency to attribute to himself what he is merely able to conceive: there is no proud
man who does not deem himself humble, assuming he admits that
humility is a virtue.

If truth is a constituent element of beauty, beauty is in its turn
a necessary factor of intellectual manifestation. There is no error

without some ugliness: like every form, thought is made up of conformities and proportions.

*   *   *

There are men who believe themselves to be without passions because they have transferred their whole passional life to the mental plane, which becomes "egoistic".

"Wisdom after the flesh" is, among other things, mental passion with its compensating complement—petrifaction; it is the thought of a "hardened heart".

The sage, since he transcends the mind, loses his concepts in contemplation; he is always being reborn anew. Charity means to lose oneself.

*   *   *

To take fallen man as the human norm ends in idealizing not man but the human animal, the thinking beast.

Men who spiritually speaking are "fools" are often more cunning than wise men; hence their conviction, which is sustained by a certain practical experience, that they are more intelligent than such men. But this experience is limited by their very ignorance and therefore furnishes only a quite illusory argument.

There are modes of intelligence that are more or less mutually exclusive as to their development; this becomes very apparent when a comparison is made between the Middle Ages and the modern era or between the traditional East and the "progressive" West.

*   *   *

In the normal state of the world the intelligent man possesses intelligence, and the fool is without it, but in our period of the "realization of impossibilities"—if one may venture such an elliptical definition—we see everywhere fools who are accidentally intelligent and intelligent men who are accidentally fools.

Among our ancestors intelligence had a sort of artlessness because, being both contemplative and practical, it was not projected in its entirety onto the plane of discursive thought and hardly had need of external complications. In our day the opposite occurs:

what characterizes our period is not so much stupidity in itself as intelligent stupidity.

In former times the devil could have had every reason for showing himself in his characteristic guise, for in this form he fascinated and intimidated the weak and the perverse; he was even obliged to reveal himself in this manner, because faith in God was everywhere. But today it is the devil who is everywhere, and he therefore no longer has any reason for showing himself as he is, nor does anything any longer oblige him to do so; on the contrary, he has every reason to make people deny him, since, in order to be able to make them forget God, the devil must himself be forgotten.

* * *

"Be ye therefore wise as serpents", says the Gospel, not "be ye therefore cunning as foxes". Wisdom, or prudence, is defensive and has a basis of generosity; cunning is on the contrary aggressive, and its basis is a glacial egoism.

True intelligence has no need of cunning, for it has a sense of proportion. With cunning, man falls "intelligently" into error, but with a sense of proportion he remains "naïvely" in truth.

Every man must resign himself to the thought that he is of necessity a little foolish; humility is not a luxury.

Most of our contemporaries would rather appear bad than naïve; and yet God is indulgent towards a sincere naïveté, and even has a tenderness for it, but always hates pretentious cleverness and spitefulness, or arrogance.

* * *

A tendency to suspicion is no more a normal mode of intelligence[2] than is guile. If suspicion is legitimate when it arises incidentally—and exceptionally—from an accurate impression, it is illegitimate as soon as it becomes a tendency and a kind of principle, for it then

---

[2] A *hadîth* says: "Keep yourselves from suspicion, for suspicion is the most deceitful thing the soul can hold out as an enticement to man." Another says: "Do not make investigations and do not spy." The police mentality is in fact closely linked with a suspicious and corrosive moralism, and even with a certain mania of persecution.

engenders a sickness of the soul that is incompatible with virtue and hence with sanctity.

But suspicion not only feeds on subjective illusions: it also lives on objective appearances, which are just as illusory but nonetheless rooted in facts. Indeed suspicion, which essentially ignores the laws of coincidence and paradox, often finds itself corroborated by appearances that the environment seems to create quite wantonly, and this is by no means the least of the aspects of cosmic illusion; these possibilities—accumulations of coincidences, of appearances contrary to a reality they hide—are necessary applications of the principle of contradiction, which is included in universal Possibility. Sometimes the paradox is intentional on man's part, as is shown by the classic example of Omar Khayyam, whose wisdom clothed in frivolity is opposed to a Phariseeism clothed in piety; if religious hypocrisy is possible, the contrary paradox must be equally so.

It is necessary for the good to show itself from time to time under the accidental appearance of evil, and inversely—a superficial illusion, which would always be discernible if self-interest did not prevent man from perceiving the truth.

*   *   *

In certain respects every human manifestation, every thought, is an "evil" before God, since every manifestation of oneself is an affirmation "alongside" of God and in "opposition" to Him; in other respects every thought is inevitably a form of egoism because it does not confer a blessing on one's neighbor; finally, every thought indicates a sort of illusion insofar as it does not act as a vehicle of Reality. Our nature lives on forgetfulness.

To efface oneself, to bless one's neighbor, to contemplate Truth: three ways of remembering.

There are evils which are inevitable, which are inherent in existence and in individuation, and which are consequently capable of being the vehicles of a good; in this case they lose, if not their limitative character, at least their poison; but as soon as they become the vehicles of an evil, their own wretchedness reappears before God; they again become evils.

6

What Sincerity Is and Is Not

How often one reads or hears it said that someone is gravely mistaken or vicious or criminal, but that he is "sincere" and is therefore "seeking God in his own way"—and other euphemisms of the sort—when what is really meant is this: there need be no fear of his making the slightest effort either for truth or for virtue. The opinion in question, which is strictly perverse, is one manifestation among others of modern subjectivism, according to which the subjective, however contingent it may be, takes precedence over what is objective, even in cases where the objective is the very reason for the subjective and thus determines its worth. In other words, the now fashionable cult of sincerity, far from being moral or spiritual, is simply a more or less cynical individualism: an individualism moreover with democratic overtones, since it believes that to wish to master and transcend oneself is to wish to be more than other people—as if the effort to perfect oneself somehow prevented others from doing the same.

Both cynicism and hypocrisy are forms of pride: cynicism is the caricature of sincerity or frankness, whereas hypocrisy is the caricature of scrupulousness or self-discipline, or of virtue in general. Cynics believe that sincerity consists in exhibiting shortcomings and passions and that to hide them is to be a hypocrite; they do not exercise self-control and still less do they seek to transcend themselves; and the fact that they take their fault for a virtue is clear proof of their pride. Hypocrites believe, on the contrary, that it is virtuous to make a display of virtuous attitudes or that the appearances of faith suffice for faith itself; their vice lies not in manifesting forms of virtue—which is a rule that must apply to everyone—but in believing that the manifestation is virtue itself and above all in mimicking virtue in the hope of being admired: this is pride, because it is individualism and ostentation. Pride is overestimating oneself and underestimating others, and this is what the cynic does just as much as the hypocrite, in a blatant or subtle way as the case may be.

All this amounts to saying that in cynicism as in hypocrisy the autocratic and therefore tenebrous ego takes the place of the spirit and light; the two vices are acts of theft by which the passional and egoistic soul appropriates what belongs to the spiritual soul. Moreover, to present a vice as a virtue and, correspondingly, to accuse virtues of being vices, as is done by cynicism posing as sincerity, is nothing but hypocrisy, and it is a particularly perverse hypocrisy.

As for pride, it was defined very well by Boethius: "All the other vices flee from God; only pride sets itself up against Him"; and by Saint Augustine: "Other vices attach themselves to evil that evil may be accomplished; pride alone attaches itself to good that good may perish." When God is absent, pride necessarily fills the void: it cannot fail to appear in the soul when there is nothing there to relate to the Sovereign Good. Without doubt the virtues of worldly men or unbelievers have their own relative worth, but the same is true of physical qualities at their own level; the only qualities that contribute to the soul's salvation are those that are quickened by the Truth and the Way; no virtue cut off from these foundations has the power to save, and this proves the relativity, and the indirect importance, of purely natural virtues. A spiritual man does not sense that he owns his virtues; he renounces vices and extinguishes himself—actively and passively—in the divine Virtues, Virtues as such. Virtue is that which is.

* * *

A virtuous man conceals his faults for the following reasons: first because he does not concede them any right to exist and because, after each failing, he hopes it will be the last; a man cannot really be reproached for concealing his faults because he is striving not to sin and to behave correctly. A second reason is conformity to the norm: in order to be rid of a fault, one must not only have the intention of eliminating it for the sake of God and not just to please men, but one must also enter actively into the mold of perfection; and if it is clear that this must not be done just to please men, it is no less clear that it must be done to avoid scandalizing them and setting a bad example; this is a charity that God demands of us, since love of God requires us to love our neighbor.

When so-called sincerity breaks the framework of traditional—or simply normal—rules of behavior, it thereby betrays its prideful nature; for the rules are venerable, and we have no right to disdain them or put our subjectivity above them. It is true that saints sometimes break these rules, but they do so from above not below: by virtue of a divine truth not a human sentiment. In any case, if a man of tradition effaces himself behind a rule of behavior, this is certainly not out of hypocrisy, but out of humility and charity: humility because he realizes that the traditional rule is right and better than he is; charity because he does not wish to thrust on his neighbors the scandal of his own shortcomings: quite the contrary, he intends to manifest a salutary norm even if he has not yet himself attained its level.

* * *

The noble man is one who masters himself and loves to master himself; the base man is one who does not master himself and shrinks in horror from mastering himself.[1] The spiritual man is one who transcends himself and loves to transcend himself; the worldly man remains horizontal and hates the vertical dimension. And this is important: one cannot subject oneself to a constraining ideal—or seek to transcend oneself for the sake of God—without bearing in one's soul what psychoanalysts call "complexes"; this means in fact that there are complexes which are normal for a spiritual man or simply for a decent man and that, conversely, the absence of "complexes" is not necessarily a virtue, to say the least. Undoubtedly primordial man or man deified has no complexes, but to have no complexes is not enough to make a man deified or primordial.

The root of all true sincerity is sincerity toward God, not toward our own good pleasure; this means that it is not enough to believe in God, but that all the consequences of belief must be drawn in our outward and inward comportment; and when we aspire to a perfection—since God is perfect and wills for us to be perfect—we seek to manifest it even before we realize it, and in order to realize it.

A man who submits to outward and inward norms, and who is thus striving along the way of perfection or in eliminating imperfections, knows very well that among those who do not make this effort

---

[1] It may be added that the noble man looks at what is essential in phenomena, not at what is accidental; he sees the overall worth in a creature and the intention of the Creator—not some more or less humiliating accident—and he thereby anticipates the perception of divine Qualities through forms. This is what is expressed by the words of the Apostle: "Unto the pure all things are pure."

there are some who surpass him in natural qualities; but endowed as he is with intelligence, without which he would not be a man, he cannot fail to realize that he is, whether he likes it or not, necessarily better than worldly men with respect to metaphysical truth and spiritual effort, and that any effort made for the sake of God infinitely outweighs a merely natural quality that is never turned to spiritual account. Besides, worldly people are always looking for accomplices in their dissipation and ruin, and for this reason spiritual people keep their distance from them as far as possible, unless they have an apostolic mission; but in this case they will be most wary of imitating the bad behavior of the worldly, thus being the opposite of what they preach.

* * *

By way of summary, we may say that the content of sincerity is our tendency toward God and our consequent adherence to the rules that this tendency imposes upon us, and not our nature pure and simple with all its shortcomings; to be sincere is not to indulge in vice before men, but to be virtuous before God and to enter accordingly into the mold of virtues as yet unassimilated, whatever may be the opinions of men. It is true that certain saints—the "people of blame" in Sufism—have sought to create scandal in order to be despised, which really amounts to despising others, but moral or mystical egoism is unaware of this; this attitude is nevertheless a two-edged sword, at least in extreme cases—those precisely that make it legitimate to speak of egoism—though not when it is simply a question of neutral attitudes intended to veil a perfection or desire for perfection. However, the imperatives of a particular mystical subjectivity cannot prevent the normal attitude, which is to practice the virtues in equilibrium and dignity; and it is important not to confuse equilibrium with mediocrity, which arises out of lukewarmness, whereas equilibrium arises out of wisdom. The essence of dignity is not only our deiformity but humility joined to charity; these two virtues compensate for the risks that come from being made in the image of God, while at the same time they participate in divine Virtues, which integrate them into our theomorphism. This quality could well make us arrogant and egotistical, but when we grasp its true nature we see that it binds us, on the contrary, to the perfections not only of the Lord but also of the servant; the whole mystery of the human *pontifex* lies in this complementarity.

It may be added, by way of supplement to these considerations of principle, that rules of behavior are at times subtle and complex, even paradoxical: for an old man to play with children involves no loss of dignity if he holds fast to the dignity of man as such; for a litigant to plead his right is not contrary to charity, provided he does not become unjust in his turn and is not motivated simply by meanness.[2] Charity does not preclude holy anger, any more than humility precludes a holy self-respect or dignity holy joy.

* * *

We have seen that hypocrisy consists, not in adopting a superior mode of behavior with the intention of actualizing and affirming it, but in adopting it with the intention of seeming to be more than one is. It therefore lies not in behavior that may well be above the level of our present state, but in the intention to appear to be above others, even in the absence of witnesses and for the sake of private satisfaction; the virulence of the error of sincerism moves us to make this self-evident *distinguo* once more. If the mere fact of adopting a form of model behavior were hypocrisy, it would be impossible to make any effort in the direction of goodness, and man would not be man.

Sincerity is the absence of falsehood in inward and outward behavior; to lie is deliberately to mislead; one can lie to one's neighbor, to oneself, to God. Now a pious man who wraps his weakness in a veil of rectitude does not mean to lie, and *ipso facto* he is not lying; he does not mean to manifest what in fact he is, but he cannot help manifesting what he wishes to be. And it is in the nature of things that he ends up being perfectly truthful; for what we wish to be is in a certain sense what we are.

Veil of hypocrisy, veil of rectitude: in the first case the veil is opaque and dissimulating; in the second it is transparent and transmitting. The "lowering of the veil" (*zawâl al-hijâb*) in the first case is a rejection of hypocrisy; in the second it is a relinquishing of effort, or rather a forgetting of the symbol, thanks to the liberating presence of the Real.

---

[2] The basis of charity is not only to understand that other men are ourselves—every man being "I"—but also to desire our own good; for if our immortal personality were not worthy of love, then neither would be that of our neighbor. "Hate thy soul" means: hate in yourself what harms your ultimate interests.

War

No peace with weakness: with our selfish soul
And idle dreams; the worldly powers might
Seduce and poison us. We have no choice;
Our weapon is God's Name. We have to fight.

Truth gives no strength without humility.
Darkness means war; Light's war means victory.

Spiritual Perspectives

VI

The spiritual necessity of the virtues is founded, not only on the analogy between the human and the Divine, but also on the complementary relationship—in the microcosm—between the center and the totality; this is so because it is not possible for man to realize in his heart-Intellect what he conceives in his mind without making the whole of his being participate in this realization. The intellective center of a being is not reached without involving his volitional circumference: he who wants the center must realize the whole; in other words he who wants to know with the heart-Intellect must "know" with the whole soul, and this implies the purification of the soul and therefore the virtues. When the mind is purified by doctrinal truth and the whole being is purified by virtue, Truth can reveal itself in the heart with the help of God.

Virtue is "moral"—and therefore volitive—"truth"; it concerns not only action but the whole of life. The center of man cannot see as long as his periphery is blind.

Virtue is the abolition of egoism. Why? Because the ego is error: it is a principle of illusion, which falsifies the proportions of things, with regard to both God and one's neighbor.

* * *

The spiritual importance of the virtues appears from the fact that there are inner obstacles that come only from the falsity—or what amounts to the same thing, from the ugliness—of certain human attitudes. At the moment man wants to draw near to God, the ugliness of his attitude toward others turns against him.

To know God with all that we are: the very infinity of the object of knowledge requires the totality of the act of knowing, and this totality requires the essential virtues.

It is always these essential virtues we have in view, and not the qualities required by secondary human functions, such as courage and diligence. Qualities such as these obviously combine, in appropriate circumstances, with the fundamental virtues, upon which they depend in principle. But this in no way concerns a moralism that sees in the most contingent quality an end in itself.

* * *

It is abundantly clear that virtue, in the general and ordinary sense of the term, is in no way a guarantee of spiritual knowledge, for the thinking of a man who is "normally" virtuous may—barring pure and simple ignorance—be plunged in mental passion and unconscious presumption. In order to awaken intellection, virtue must penetrate even into thought, just as knowledge, to be complete, should penetrate into inward and outward actions.

When virtue reaches the innermost regions of the soul, it gives rise to illumination; when the wall of a darkened room is broken, light cannot fail to enter. Complete virtue is the elimination of everything that constitutes an obstacle to *gnosis* and love.

Actions are not only superficial manifestations of the individual, but also criteria of his heart, and thus of his essence and of his knowledge or ignorance. Consequently, to watch over one's actions is not only an individual preoccupation; in some cases it is also a pursuit of purity of heart with a view to the knowledge of God.

This confers on the theory of sin, on the examination of conscience, and on penitence a significance that goes further than any religious individualism and makes them compatible with pure spirituality: in Muslim esoterism as in Christian mysticism, this strictly alchemical way of regarding actions, whether good or bad, goes hand in hand with selfless contemplation of God.

* * *

On the plane of activity everything is a matter of proportion and equilibrium: individualist or sentimental deviations are always possible, but cannot discredit action as such. If action directly or indirectly exteriorizes what the heart contains and what the individual "knows"—or does not know—of God, it may also and inversely act on the heart: it purifies the heart with a view to knowledge or else hardens and darkens it; it may be either virtuous or sinful.

It is in this sense that there exists a necessary connection between action and virtue.

* * *

If "beauty is the splendor of the true", then it can be said that moralism consists in cutting beauty off from truth. Without truth beauty cannot exist, and this explains the ugliness associated with moralism. It replaces knowledge of the true by idolatry of a "good" that is often arbitrary and cramped.

In the very nature of things moralism is ignorant of both truth and beauty: it cannot avoid being hypocritical in relation to the former and a mockery in relation to the latter.

One of the most salient criteria of moralism is calumny of the object on account of the corruptibility of the subject.

The inverse error—that of intellectualism—consists in cutting truth off from beauty—not truth as such, which is sufficient unto itself, but truth as it is reflected in us and transmitted by us. The question of beauty does not arise for pure truth; but it does arise for the human receptacle, for the substance it lends to the lightning flashes of the spirit.

* * *

Spirituality has for its object not man but God; this is something that a certain moral absolutism seems to forget.

Spirituality has a negative condition: the absence of error and vice, and it has a positive object: contemplation of the Divine. Vice—passion—clouds the organ that should contemplate God, and this organ is the whole man.

* * *

In esoteric doctrines it always comes about that things "worshiped" on one plane are "consigned to the flames" on another; hence the apparent rejection of the virtues, for example, by the Sufi Ibn al-Arif or by Buddhists.

"God alone is good." All that is not God can in principle be rejected on one ground or another. The setting of the sun is only an appearance, but an appearance that imposes itself on all men and consequently has nothing fortuitous about it: the sun must set because it is not God, or again, as the Prophet said, "It must prostrate itself every evening before the Throne of Allah."

*　*　*

If it is true that virtue is the absence of vice, it is even truer that vice is the absence of virtue. Virtue exists before vice because God is before the world; vice is the privation of virtue since the world is in a certain sense the privation of God. If one starts from the fallen nature of man, it is legitimate to say that virtue is in practice the absence of a vice, although in reality the relationship is the inverse; but the realization of God is the negation of the world only insofar as the world is the negation of God. It is evident that virtue, considered independently of human imperfection, reflects a divine perfection by its intrinsic quality.

*　*　*

The vulgarization of spirituality—inevitable within certain limits—carries with it a predominance of moral injunctions over considerations of spiritual alchemy: the dynamism of the will is preached, and the good residing in the very nature of things is neglected; the "duty of doing" is insisted on, and "being" is forgotten.

Intellective contemplation goes straight to the existential roots of the virtues; it finds the virtues again, beyond moral effort, in the nature of things.[1]

But since man is not pure contemplation, effort is also required of him.

*　*　*

Intellection and virtue: everything is there.

---

[1] The *Philokalia* says: "When the wise soul is in the state that is natural to it, virtue is necessarily found in it. The soul finds itself in its natural state when it remains as it has been created. . . . The soul is just when its knowledge remains in the state that is natural to it. . . . This is why virtue is not a difficult thing; when we remain as we have been created, we are in a state of virtue. . . . If we had to seek for virtue outside ourselves, this would certainly be difficult; but since it is within us, it is enough to avoid evil thoughts and to keep our soul [as it is *a priori*] turned toward the Lord."

Intellection refers to the divine "I", to the pure and absolute Subject, to "Consciousness" that is absolutely non-objectified, to God-Intellect. Divine Knowledge.

Virtue refers to divine "Being", to pure and infinite Objectivity, to Reality free of all individuation, to God-Being. Divine Qualities.

The way of intellection, the way of virtue; one does not go without the other, but one or the other predominates in accordance with human dispositions.

If "the soul is all that it knows", one may also say that, in another respect, "the soul knows all that it is".

7

Dimensions of the Human Vocation

Injustice is a trial, but a trial is not an injustice. Injustices come from men, whereas trials come from God; what is injustice and consequently evil on the part of man is trial and destiny on the part of God. One has the right, or in some cases even the duty, to fight a particular evil, but one must resign oneself to a trial and accept destiny; in other words, it is necessary to combine the two attitudes, since every injustice we undergo at the hands of men is at the same time a trial that comes to us from God.

In the horizontal or terrestrial dimension, one can escape from evil by fighting it and overcoming it; in the vertical or spiritual dimension, on the contrary, one can escape—if not from the trial as such, at least from its heaviness—by accepting evil insofar as it is the divine will while transcending it inwardly insofar as it is cosmic play, just as one can transcend spiritually any other manifestation of *Mâyâ*. For the din of the world does not enter the divine Silence, which we carry in our own depths and in which, like accidents in substance, both the world and the "I" are extinguished and reabsorbed.

Man has the duty to resign himself to the will of God, but by the same token he has the right to transcend spiritually the suffering of the soul to the extent that this is possible for him; and this is not possible, precisely, without a prior attitude of acceptance and resignation, which alone fully releases the serenity of the intelligence and which alone opens the soul to aid from Heaven.

It is plausible that God could send us sufferings in order that we might grasp all the better the worth of His liberating Grace and that we might force ourselves with all the more fervor to respond to the requirements of His Mercy. When a man is unaware that he is drowning, he does not take the trouble to call for help; now salvation depends on our call, and there is finally nothing more consoling than this cry of trust or certitude.

*　*　*

It is important not to confuse the two dimensions of which we have just spoken: that God would send us a trial does not prevent it from being a possible injustice on the human plane, and that men would treat us unjustly does not prevent this from being justice on the part of God. We must therefore avoid two errors: believing that an evil, on its own level, is something good because God sends it to us, or because God permits it, or because everything comes from God; and believing that a trial as such is an evil because it is so in its form and because we suffer from it. It would be equally false to believe that we directly deserve an injustice because God permits it, for if this were the case, there would be no injustice and the unjust would be just; it would be equally false to imagine that we do not deserve a trial because we have done nothing which, logically, has provoked it.

In reality the cause of a trial is inscribed in our very relativity and thus in the fact that we are contingent beings or individuals; there is no need to have recourse to the transmigrationist theory of good or bad *karma* to know that contingency implies fissures and that it does so in succession as well as in simultaneity. The cosmic possibility that constitutes individuality is what it must be, in its limitation as well as in its positive content, and in its opportunities for transcending itself: finite and passible in its contours, it is infinite and impassible in its substance, and this is why trials carry within themselves the virtuality of liberation. They are thus the messengers of a liberty which, in our immutable and immanent reality, has never ceased to be, but which is obscured by the clouds of moving contingency, with which the intelligent soul in a certain fashion mistakenly identifies itself.

It is correct to say that no one escapes his destiny; but it is useful to add a conditional reservation, namely, that fatality involves degrees because our nature does so. Our destiny is a function of the personal level—high or low—at which we halt or in which we enclose ourselves; for we are what we want to be, and we undergo what we are. Concretely, this means that destiny may change, if not as to style at least as to mode or intensity, depending on the change of level that spiritual ascension brings about in us.[1]

---

[1] For example, a slight accident may replace a serious accident; spiritual death may replace physical death; an initiatic pact may intervene in place of a marriage pact, or inversely.

This explains why Muslims, who are fully aware of predestination (*qadar*), can nevertheless on certain occasions pray that God may efface the evil that is inscribed on the tablet of their destinies. In a general manner, they could not pray—logically and reasonably—for anything whatever if there were not in predestination certain margins, modes, or degrees of application: in short, a kind of internal life, required by divine Freedom, which compensates for the implacable crystallinity of "what is written". This also explains why astrological data remain fixed only to the extent that man neglects or refuses to transcend himself; these things are difficult to grasp with the reason, perhaps, but they are no more mysterious than the illimitation of space and time or the empirical uniqueness of our ego, and other paradoxes of nature that we have no choice but to accept.

*　　*　　*

To transcend oneself: this is the great imperative of the human condition; and there is another that anticipates it and at the same time prolongs it: to dominate oneself. The noble man is one who dominates himself; the holy man is one who transcends himself. These are the two dimensions—the horizontal and the vertical—to which we alluded when speaking of injustices and trials: the first dimension is that of earthly and outward man, and the second that of celestial or inward man. The obligation to dominate oneself, and with all the more reason to transcend oneself, is inscribed in the intelligence and the will of man, for this intelligence is total, and this will is free: being total and free, the human soul has no other positive choice than to dominate itself in order to be able to transcend itself. Our intelligence and our will are proportioned to the Absolute, so that our vocation as man is determined existentially by this relationship; without this man would not be man. Nobility and holiness are the imperatives of the human state.

Man must dominate himself because, as center, he is called upon to dominate the periphery; if in Genesis God conferred on man dominion over all other earthly creatures, this means that man, being responsible and free, must above all dominate himself, for he also possesses in his soul a periphery and a center; no one can govern others without being able to govern himself. Man is by definition a total, although reduced, cosmos, and this is expressed by the very term "microcosm"; now the spirit must dominate the passional powers of the soul and hold in check its darksome elements in order that the microcosm may realize the perfection of the macrocosm.[2] On the level of everyday experience, it is only too obvious that reason must dominate sentiment and imagination and that it must in turn obey the Intellect or faith; faith plays the role of the Intellect in the non-metaphysician, which does not at all mean that it is absent in the metaphysician; in his case faith is the psychic prolongation or *shakti* of knowledge, and not a simple *credo quia absurdum est.*[3]

But dominion over oneself also depends on an extrinsic reality, namely, the fact that the individual exists in society; human intelligence being capable of transcendence and hence of objectivity, man escapes from animal solipsism and realizes that he is not the only one who is "I"; the result, normally or vocationally, is the virtue of generosity, by which man proves that his will is really free. Freedom of the will results directly from the totality of the intelligence: since the intelligence is capable of objectivity and transcendence, the will is necessarily capable of freedom.

If our intelligence obliges us to dominate ourselves, since the higher must dominate the lower and since the spirit within us is threatened by passions and vices, intelligence obliges us *a fortiori* to transcend ourselves: for intelligence, as we have defined it, necessarily realizes that man does not have his end in himself and that consequently he can find his meaning and his plenitude only in that which constitutes his reason for being. Transcendence is not simply the result of human reasoning; it is clearly the opposite that is true: if man is capable of reasoning according to the data of transcendence and if this reasoning imposes itself on his mind to the extent it is faithful to its vocation, this is because transcendence is inscribed in the very substance of human intelligence or—one might even say—because our intelligence is made of transcendence.

---

[2] Or of "Universal Man", as the Sufis would say. The Universe, in perfect hierarchy and equilibrium, is personified in the Prophet.

[3] We cite this phrase of Tertullian's in its elementary meaning, but it is capable of a more subtle interpretation, which relates it to the *credo ut intelligam* of Saint Anselm. In fact, the line of demarcation between discernment and faith is a complex matter and is repeated at different levels.

Our deiformity implies that our mind is made of absoluteness, our will of freedom, and our soul of generosity; to dominate oneself and to transcend oneself is to remove the layer of ice or of darkness that imprisons the true nature of man.

Tell Me

Tell me why thou hast loved the mountain top,
Its serene silence and its purity,
And I will tell thee that our spirit's rest
Is solitude with God: serenity
Above the noise of thoughts. And tell me why
Thou lov'st the secret of the whispering wood,
Its sacredness and dark security,
And I will tell thee that our lasting joy
Is union, love within our deepest heart,
Diving into our being's Mystery:
Union with what I am, and what thou art.

Spiritual Perspectives

VII

In Hindu morals—*yama* and *niyama*—humility appears as "modesty" (*hrî*); spiritual, or one might say esoteric, humility is "childlikeness" (*bâlya*) or, in its highest sense, "extinction" (*nirvâna*). An attitude that is in a sense intermediate—between *hrî* and *bâlya*—is that of devotion toward the master (*guru*).

Among Asians sentimentality is certainly not absent, but it lies less deep in them than it does in most Europeans.

Divine revelation always conforms to the human receptacle. Thus it is said that the angels speak to each man in the appropriate tongue.

*   *   *

The acceptance of injustice may have a spiritual meaning: humility then consists in having recourse to divine justice alone at the price of earthly rights; human justice may in fact become a pretext for egocentrism or, in Vedantic terms, for the superimposition of an "I" on the "Self".

*   *   *

Man is "made in the image of God"; to humiliate this image may be a profanation. Likewise, the intelligence cannot humble itself in its impersonal essence or its transcendent principle; one must not seek to humiliate the Holy Spirit along with man.

One thing remains intact in our fall, and this is the Intellect. Moral requirements do not account for the whole of man; if the difference between primordial man and fallen man were absolute, they would not be the same being; only one would be human. But there is something unalterable in man, and this can be a spiritual starting point, just as can the abyss of the fall.

That element in man which becomes aware that he is despicable cannot itself be what is to be despised; that which judges cannot be that which is judged.

* * *

Ramakrishna, when speaking of a certain show of humility—an unbalanced humility one might say—rightly remarks that people who are forever comparing themselves to the lowest animals end by becoming as feeble-minded as they. A purely moralistic humility blindly imitates a virtue that is in itself lucid, and it paralyses not only the knowledge but even the love of God; false humility never has its roots in truth. Virtue can be an idolatry like anything else.

Man has need of humility to the extent that he does not think of God—to the extent that he does not forget himself in thinking of God.

* * *

It is possible for a man not to know that he is nothing and yet cultivate a feeling of humility. He may believe he is far more than he is in reality and cultivate a sentimental humility.[1]

It is possible not to know that the "neighbor" is "myself" and yet cultivate a feeling of charity. One may be an egoist and at the same time cultivate a sentimental charity.

To know that "I am nothing" is perfect humility; to know that the "neighbor is myself" is perfect charity. That is perfect which is rooted in existence, not that which depends upon action.

* * *

When humility assumes a quasi-unique form, in the sense that it obliges a man to believe himself to be literally and individually the worst of sinners, it has something in common with what the same individualistic perspective calls "pride"; the opposite of such "pride" does not in fact consist in believing oneself to be for one reason

[1] Certain suspicions on the part of theologians regarding a Saint Bernadette or a Saint Teresa of the Child Jesus show to what confusions the purely moralistic conception of humility can give rise.

or another a unique being, but rather in knowing oneself to be an insignificant accident amid an indefinite number of such accidents. The Word humbled itself not by becoming Jesus but by becoming man.

Nirvâna, extinction; extinction of the "sin" of existence. He who literally believes himself to be the worst of sinners is not close to being extinguished.

* * *

If it is illogical to believe oneself to be "the worst of men", this is not only because the worst of men would not take himself to be such— for if he did he would not be the worst—but because such a unique individual does not exist, any more than does "the most beautiful of women"; if beauty has by definition an infinity of equivalent modes, which are reciprocally incomparable, the same is true of every other quality and also of every vice.

The most perfect—or the least imperfect—of ascetics can realize humility only in certain respects; otherwise he would end by sinning from humility.[2] This proves that humility, in the exclusively ascetic meaning of the word, is of value only in a quite conditional way, that it is relative, like all penitence. It is not on the ascetic level that humility can be total.

The exclusive moralist, instead of seeking the Absolute beyond himself, projects a kind of absolute into his own relativity by concerning himself indefinitely with the perfection—metaphysically impossible moreover—of what is only an instrument or support: the individual, the human. It is as if, instead of accomplishing a work with a usable instrument, a man devoted his whole life to making that instrument better.

It will be said that all our apparent qualities come from God and not from ourselves. That is perfectly true, but by the same token it removes from our neighbor all merit and from ourselves the possibility of being worse than he; in other words, it takes from us the possibility of believing ourselves to be the vilest of men, or at least of suffering from such a conviction.

---

[2] The concept of a "sin from humility", or of achieving humility through sin, did indeed exist among certain Russian heretics; the notion of humility, detached from its sufficient reason, is then reduced to absurdity.

*   *   *

The conviction of being the basest of men may determine a movement towards God; it may open a fissure in our darkness and thus allow grace to flow in.

But from a more profound point of view, the question of knowing whether a man is "high" or "low" is a matter of complete indifference. What is important to know is that every being, every relativity, is a limitation and thus a "nothingness".

Even on the terrestrial plane the nothingness of the "creature" is tangible in a quite immediate way: in space as in time we are nothing; the two "infinities" crush us on every hand. If the earth is a speck of dust in the measureless gulf of space, and if life is an instant between two incalculable abysses of time, what remains of man? Man cannot add one inch to his stature nor one instant to his life; he cannot be in more than one place at a time; he can live only in the moment destiny has prescribed for him, unable to turn backwards or to fly forwards; and with all his vain glories, man is physically only an animal, who with great difficulty hides his wretchedness.

*   *   *

We should never lose sight of the fact that a quality may be either the opposite of a defect on the same plane where this defect manifests itself, or the absence of a defect through the elimination of this plane; pride is not the most deep-seated root of evil, but egocentrism—whether "proud" or "humble"—which is itself the cause of all pride. It is true that in Christian terms this egocentrism is called "pride" and the spiritual elimination of this illusion "humility".

An affected and so to say expansive humility is not the same thing as an absence of pride. In the case of such humility, which disregards intelligence, one never knows whether one is required to be stupid or virtuous; in other words, one never knows whether stupidity is a virtue or whether virtue is a form of stupidity.

*   *   *

Individualistic, sentimental, and penitential humility is opposed to pride as the color green is opposed to the color red; it is always an affectation, either useful or harmful according to the case, and it is incompatible with a path that does not admit of subjective positions contrary to objective truth.

Humility, insofar as it is a spontaneous expression of virtue, is distinguished from pride as white is distinguished from red; it is not an affectation, but a natural, or more exactly a primordial, state. It is in no way opposed to a sane affirmation of oneself or to an objective knowledge a man may have of his own worth;[3] on the other hand, it does not constitute a path, but is to be found in every good man.

Humility, insofar as it is knowledge, is distinguished from pride as pure light is distinguished from every color; it belongs to paths that exclude individualistic sentimentalities or to states that have passed beyond such a level.

* * *

Men are very often prone to deem themselves exempt from the obligation of humility because they know their own qualities; they form an opinion of themselves according to their consciousness of some particular personal merit, and not according to the balance of their nature as a whole. What they forget is that this merit may be diminished or even reduced to nothing by a flaw of which they are unaware or to which they attach no importance.

No knowledge is ever illegitimate in itself; what is illegitimate is the improper conclusions drawn from it by human egocentrism, and it is for this reason that the qualities of which a man is conscious hardly constitute, by themselves and for him, a guarantee of overall worth. The good resides in the qualities themselves, and the evil comes from the consciousness we have of them; this consciousness is an evil, however, only when the good is drowned in it.

* * *

The possibility of our becoming aware with impunity of our personal merits is connected with our effective capacity for knowing

---

[3] Dante knew he was the greatest poet after Virgil, and even the last great poet of that line; no moral reasoning forced him to be mistaken about himself, and history has confirmed his judgment.

our limitations and our destitution, for man must be immunized against himself: he cannot really know himself without being penetrated by lights that wound him, the price of which is consequently high. Nonetheless, although our nature always obliges us to take account of the danger of illusion, it would not be possible to legislate about knowledge, the rights of which remain by definition imprescriptible.

* * *

Man sees in himself alternatives and efforts, abysses and conflicting possibilities, which another does not see and which he himself does not see in another; the will, which to an outside witness is something already set and intelligible, is itself in a state of constant fermentation even if the agent is able in large measure to assume the point of view of the spectator.

This is why, subjectively, no one can be good. Or again: while knowing that we are not evil in one respect, relatively speaking, we are in another respect ignorant of what we are, at least to the extent that "we are", that is, to the extent the individuality finds itself in act.

Spiritually speaking, to know oneself is to be conscious of one's limitations and to attribute every quality to God.

* * *

Habitual readiness to criticize other people presupposes a certain blindness in man as to his own state, but at the same time it induces such blindness by the effects of an inevitable concordant reaction.

He who is obliged to criticize through force of circumstances, that is, for the sake of truth, should show himself all the more humble and charitable, and capable of penetrating the secret good in creatures.

* * *

Humility towards men may be an aspect of humility towards God, but it may also be the opposite insofar as there is an antinomy between the human order and the divine Order; it will then be said that a man must humble himself before God, not before men, while being free from all pride. One must distinguish moreover between humility and humiliation.[4]

If "he that humbleth himself shall be exalted" and inversely, this cannot be taken to imply a purely sentimental attitude that tends to exclude more serene and more profound applications. If humility is an essential attitude, it cannot be limited to sentimentality, ascetic or otherwise. Humility is profound insofar as it is lucid; the more intelligent it is, the greater will be its detachment from forms.

Besides, is humbling oneself in order to be exalted, with zeal but without intelligence, truly being "humble"?

* * *

From the psychological point of view, humility is essential because it is logically impossible to be at the same time and in the same connection in potency and in act, or to be simultaneously subject and object, and therefore to be judge in one's own cause. Man cannot at one and the same time "be" good and "define himself" as good: he cannot bring his mind to bear at one and the same time on a particular content of his knowledge and on the act of knowing; the eye cannot see itself. "Let not thy left hand know what thy right hand doeth."

Virtue implies a kind of incessant movement since it involves our will; there is no life—and consequently no virtue—without continual renewal. Now to attribute to oneself a particular quality amounts to a fixation—or crystallization—of the inner flux that makes that quality live; the result is to make it sterile. In an analogous fashion, praise is unhealthy for the one who receives it and is not above it, for then it kills the good—which is never perfected since it must continue to live and renew itself—by a sort of anticipation calculated to exhaust its possibility, exactly as too much talk before an action compromises its realization in an almost magical way.

If we nonetheless say that knowledge remains always imprescriptible, this means that God can make known to us what we are, by the Intellect or by grace. God knows the qualities—the "talents" of

---

[4] Ibn Arabi says that the loftiest of the virtues, humility, is too noble to have to manifest itself as humiliation before men.

the parable—that He has entrusted to us, and insofar as we know that "God alone is good", we can participate in that knowledge, the real subject of which can only be God Himself. This is an instance of the reciprocity between God and man: what man, being logical "subject", cannot know about himself, he can know through God, for whom man is "object"—on condition that he gives up making himself God on the human plane.

* * *

We can understand without difficulty the meaning of humility before God; but what is the objective value of humility with regard to our neighbor? It resides in the fact that our neighbor can always teach us something, even if only in a quite indirect way; in this respect he assumes a function that is quasi-divine.

Since every man has limitations, either fundamental or accidental, and since men are by definition different, there is every chance that our neighbor will not be limited in exactly the same fashion as ourselves, and that he will consequently be free of limitations at the point where we are limited; in this respect he is our master.

In a certain sense the neighbor is the criterion of our sincerity towards God.

* * *

Pride consists in taking ourselves for what we are not and disparaging others; self-respect is knowing what one is and not allowing oneself to be humiliated. Self-respect does not prevent a man from humbling himself before what surpasses him; it is far from being the opposite of true humility, whatever the more superficial moralists may say.[5]

---

[5] To the question "Do you believe in God?" Joan of Arc replied: "Better than you!" Another instance of humble self-respect is this reply of a Hindu *guru* to a worldly traveler: "I am not worthy to be your master, and you are not worthy to be my disciple."

Modesty may be a quality or a defect according to whether it springs from veracity or weakness; but even in the latter case it is nearer virtue than vice, for weakness is preferable to presumption.

*   *   *

According to Saint Augustine, "The other vices attach themselves to evil in order that it may be done; pride alone attaches itself to the good in order that it may perish."

According to Boethius, "All the other vices flee from God; pride alone rises up against Him."[6]

*   *   *

Spiritually speaking, pride consists in attributing to oneself what is due to God. It poisons and kills every value, for as soon as a good is claimed in its cause and in its essence by man, it is transmuted into evil: it embraces the limitations of the creature and engenders limitations in its turn; pride appropriates the divine gift and then strangles it. A good vivifies insofar as it comes from God, not insofar as it is handed on by man, nor above all insofar as it is usurped by him.

Man deems himself good even before God, who is Perfection, and when he endeavors to recognize his wretchedness, he again deems himself good on account of this effort.

*   *   *

The existential drama has as it were three movements: adoration of God, adoration of the world, and adoration of self; the last is "pride", whereas all other vices belong to the second category.

Adoration of the world inevitably brings with it in some degree adoration of self, so that it is legitimate to attribute "pride", even if only as a virtuality, to every man. In its universal sense "humility" is

---

[6] The Hasidim Cabalists relate the following saying of their master, Baal Shem: "Pride is more serious than any sin. For it is in relation to sinners that God designates Himself [in the *Torah*] as 'He who dwelleth amid their impurities'. But as the wise men [of the *Talmud*] teach, God says of the proud man: 'I and he cannot dwell together in the world.'"

thus a *sine qua non* of all spirituality, all the more so because, as soon as man tears himself away from adoration of the world, he must pass through the temptations of "pride" in order to approach God; for the "I" wants to appropriate this approach and to glory in it to the detriment of what is its sufficient reason.

When the proud man learns that humility is a virtue, he wants to claim it for himself, because he cannot bear to be inferior to others. If humility is the concealing of the virtues one has, hypocrisy is the counterfeiting of the virtues one does not have.

In a general way, men readily believe they possess virtues simply because they are able to conceive of them.

*   *   *

In all manifestation there is an element capable of leading one away from the Principle, and it is upon this element that "pride", which is the error that subjectively brings about this remotion, is grafted.

This "demiurgic"—and virtually "luciferian"—element enters into the very definition of the created.

Pride: that "something" which prevents man from "losing his life" for God.

To be humble, then, is to "lose" oneself in the way, to forget oneself with a holy heedlessness that has God in view, to squander oneself in a gesture of final generosity.

*   *   *

The spiritual man does not rejoice at his progress, but at the disappearance of the old self; human perfection is the norm, not a peak.

After purifying oneself from one's defects one must purify oneself from one's virtues, say the Buddhists. Everything must be brought back to the divine Cause; this is the perfection of humility.

To think "I have" such and such a virtue is almost as false as to think "I am" God.

*   *   *

In a sense knowledge does not have, and cannot have, any direct relationship with strictly human attitudes, but in another sense—

that of manifestation—it is inseparable from them: in the first case, it shows its absolute transcendence by the fact that it appears as a "free" gift or "grace"; in the second case, on the contrary, it appears as a function of the receptivity—thus the "simplicity" or "humility"—of the individual. These two aspects are always linked in some degree.

* * *

The loftiest *gnosis* and the most perfect humility go together: the one is knowledge of the Divine and the other knowledge of the human.[7] Pride is to treat the human as the Divine, and inversely; it is therefore to be ignorant of both the one and the other.

What the proud man readily forgets is that human virtue could never overtake either Unicity or creative Power.

* * *

Humility is a state of emptiness in which our thoughts and actions appear as foreign to ourselves, so that we judge them as we judge the thoughts and actions of others.

Pride is a blind plenitude, which monopolizes everything.

* * *

Basilian spirituality includes four principal elements: separation from the world, purification, meditation on the sacred Scriptures, and continual prayer. The first element cuts man off from the current of profane life; the second empties the soul of illusory contents; the third infuses the discursive intelligence with divine Light; the fourth essentially brings about deification. This could be formulated as follows: in renunciation the soul leaves the world; in purification the world leaves the soul; in meditation God enters the soul; in continual prayer the soul enters God.

---

[7] Diadochos of Photike distinguishes two humilities: the first comes from earthly troubles and "most often includes grief and despondency"; the second comes from illumination of the Intellect, in which "the soul possesses humility as by nature" and "judges itself beneath everything because it participates in the divine equity"; this humility includes "joy with a wise reserve".

Here humility is not conceived as a "ladder"; it does not constitute the path as such, but is in a sense at one and the same time its condition and its effect. Humility is *vacare Deo* in all its aspects, and for this reason it is perfect simplicity and primordial purity of the soul before the divine influx. On the one hand it conditions incessant prayer, and on the other it is conditioned by it. He who is not humble, that is, simple and pure—we would willingly say "impersonal" and "objective"—cannot persevere in this prayer, and he who does persevere in it cannot remain in the imperfections that are contrary to simplicity, purity, humility.

* * *

Saint Bernard defines humility as "a virtue through which a man who has true knowledge of himself becomes contemptible in his own eyes".[8] And he adds that "the Lord, who is gentle and just, gives men the law of humility that by this means they may return to knowledge of the truth". This is to say that knowledge of oneself is indispensable for the knowledge of God. That is also the meaning of this teaching of the Prophet: "He who knows his soul knows his Lord."

Saint Bernard connects humility with truth; he understands it in a sense that has nothing exclusively moral about it, and this appears even more clearly when he speaks of the third degree of truth, which is "to purify the eye of the heart to contemplate things celestial and divine".

* * *

Meister Eckhart says that humility[9] consists in "being below", for otherwise it is impossible for God to give; thus lack of humility, ego-

---

[8] For Ibn Arabi likewise, humility is the sincere conviction of being a vile object in the eyes of God; perfect humility belongs only to the Sufi. The Prophet said: "Whoever has pride in his heart, be it only a rice grain, cannot enter Paradise." Shri Shankaracharya designates himself, at the beginning of one of his treatises, as "I, who am without worth"; likewise Shri Chaitanya desires the *bhakta* "always to look upon himself as inferior to a wisp of straw" and to be "humble like grass". It would be easy to multiply examples to show that humility is far from being peculiar to Christianity.

[9] Etymologically, the virtue of being like the soil (*humus*).

tism for example, does violence to the nature of God, which consists in giving.

*   *   *

Christ said to Saint Catherine of Siena in a vision: "I am He who is; thou art she who is not." This is the metaphysical foundation of all humility expressed in direct terms.[10]

For Thomism, humility is the measure of our nothingness before God.

*   *   *

"Humility", says Saint Teresa of Avila, "is to walk according to the Truth." For Saint Ignatius Loyola as well, humility is first of all the simplicity of soul that makes man submit himself quite naturally to the divine Law,[11] then indifference with regard to worldly things,[12] and finally the ascetic will to live in privations—material and moral—for the sake of God.[13]

---

[10] It will be noted that these terms are Vedantic, which means they are esoteric.

[11] Al-Qushayri: "It is to submit oneself to the direction of God." The same writer also gives this definition: "It is melting and contracting of the heart when subjugated by the Truth."

[12] According to al-Tirmidhi, "Man is humble when the blazing of the fire of desires has ceased" (*fanâ'*, "extinction").

[13] Al-Ghazzali has been reproached for bringing into his doctrine of humility the Aristotelian "measure" instead of understanding the quasi-infinite character of virtue; this "measure" shows, not that the Muslim conception stops halfway, but that al-Ghazzali's exposition gives only its purely social application (*adab*).

8

Microcosm and Symbol

Every truth can have incalculable consequences, and on the spiritual plane no truth can be inopportune in an absolute fashion. Spiritual truths are interdependent, and there are circumstances in which he who would tell the truth must either say nothing or tell the whole truth; now these circumstances are precisely those of the world today: the affirmation of the grossest errors calls for the affirmation of the subtlest truths—for cosmic reasons moreover, and independently of the practical aspect of things.

In order to state our thought clearly while being as brief as possible, we might also express ourselves in the following way: since it is our intention to affirm traditional wisdom as such, we are compelled to speak of things which, for the immense majority of men today, are not an effective possibility, but which nonetheless should be known theoretically, at least to some extent, if only for a fuller comprehension of traditional ideas and facts in general.

* * *

To define the difference between the metaphysical and the initiatic or mystical perspectives, it could be said that the first distinguishes between the Principle and manifestation in an objective mode, whereas the second considers these two terms in a subjective mode and hence distinguishes either *a priori* between the human "I" and the divine "He", or *a posteriori* between the human "he" and the divine "I", the "lived reality" being displaced as it were from the human to the Divine; the human ego has then become a kind of "he", and the divine "He" is henceforth known as unique, absolute, and infinite.[1] In cosmology, there is an analogous—though not

---

[1] The use of personal pronouns is entirely provisional here, at any rate as regards the divine Reality, which is obviously beyond objective and subjective points of view; in Sufic language this transcendence is expressed by the word *Huwa*, "He", while the points of view are respectively designated by the words *anta*, "Thou", and *anâ*, "I".

identical—relationship between the macrocosm, which serves as divine Model, and the microcosm: however, the latter is active and the former is passive, in the sense that the microcosm,[2] being so to speak the inner limit of the cosmos—the outer limit being the manifested divine Spirit—constitutes at the same time the way of exit from the cosmic illusion; and this exit is brought about through the Spirit, which is itself a direct manifestation of the Word.

Thus the divine Spirit is identical with the transcendent, universal, cosmic "I", which the relative being bears virtually within himself, so that the inner limit of the cosmos—the microcosm—must identify itself, in its process of deification, with the outer limit—the Empyrean—of this very cosmos. If we say that the microcosm is active and the macrocosm passive, this is true in only one respect, namely, insofar as the relative being intellectually determines the flux of forms, but not insofar as, being a form himself, he is in turn determined by the cosmic Intelligence, in which respect it is clearly the macrocosm that is active and the microcosm that is passive.[3]

Every diagram of spiritual realization starts in principle from the distinction between the body and the soul, then distinguishes within the soul between the sensorial soul (the psyche and the thinking mind) and the immortal soul (the true ego), and finally, within the immortal soul, between the individual soul and the Spirit (the Intellect), or in other words between the "brain" and the "heart"; strictly speaking, the heart does not come within the limits of the ego, but constitutes its transcendent center, vehicle of the uncreated Intellect. All these distinctions pertain as well to the realm of cosmology, a science that is to metaphysics what psychology—in the spiritual and "alchemical" sense that this word can bear—is to realization; but while cosmology considers the soul only *ad extra* and in prin-

---

[2] It is always the human microcosm that we have in view here; but what we say about it applies in the same way to any other total microcosm, that is, any microcosm constituted by the central state of a world. Now it is man who is this central state in relation to the terrestrial world; animals, plants, and minerals mark states which are more or less peripheral, and which are consequently partial, not total, microcosms.

[3] Let us recall in this respect that the cosmic Intelligence or divine Spirit is an aspect of the Word, of which it is said: "No man cometh unto the Father, but by me," or an aspect of the Prophet, of whom it is said: "No man shall meet Allah who hath not met the Prophet." In their highest meaning, these formulas signify that no one may reach the "Essence" who has not realized the "Attributes".

ciple goes no further than its threshold, realization considers it *ad intra*, to the very borders of the Ineffable.

In order to make this chain of ideas more easily accessible, we shall set forth the following table:

Principle

$$
\text{manifestation} \left\{ \begin{array}{l} \text{macrocosm} \\ \text{microcosm} \end{array} \right. \left\{ \begin{array}{l} \text{body} \\ \text{soul} \end{array} \right. \left\{ \begin{array}{l} \text{sensorial soul} \\ \text{immortal soul} \end{array} \right. \left\{ \begin{array}{l} \text{individual soul} \\ \text{Spirit, Intellect} \end{array} \right.
$$

The cosmology of the ancients, as well as that of the entire Middle Ages of the West and Near East, conceived of the earthly state as the center from which the planetary spheres ascend to the Empyrean, the symbolic throne of Divinity, who was thus conceived as the Infinite, "enveloping" or "containing" the finite. In an analogous fashion, Hindu doctrine takes the bodily or gross state (*sthûla-sharîra*) as the starting point of a series of increasingly universal degrees of existence, which culminate in a metacosmic, absolutely transcendent, infinite Reality that "envelops" not only the world, but Being itself. Initiatically, the point of departure is also the body—at least in a certain sense—since the body forms part of the microcosm and is as it were its "shell"; but the "direction" of the degrees of universality will appear the reverse, at least at the start, where the supreme Reality, rather than being conceived of as the most outward, farthest, or most incommensurable Void, appears on the contrary as the most inward, nearest Center—in short, as the unique, indivisible, absolute Subject. But finally, beyond the individuality there is neither subject nor object, neither inward nor outward; the Intellect, which realization conceives of *a priori* as inward, is none other, as we have said, than the universal Spirit, which envelops the worlds.

* * *

All that we have just said will enable one to understand that, from the initiatic point of view, there is strictly speaking no other field of action than the soul, the microcosm; as for the outer world, it is not taken into consideration except insofar as it influences the inner world or insofar as it is viewed as consubstantial with this inner world, hence as the cosmic aspect of the ego. According to this perspective, it is no longer a question of simply passing from "evil" to "good" on the basis of an individuality that is always maintained, but on the contrary of transcending the individuality itself, so that what was a passage from "evil" to "good" is replaced by a passage from the "I" to the Self;[4] it is precisely the analogy between these two passages that allows esoterism to use the symbols of exoterism as supports, aside from the fact that the first necessarily and *a fortiori* implies the realizations of the second. The microcosm, thus become the whole world, serves as the ground for the transmutation brought about thanks to the symbol; in other words, the soul is the fabric which will freely fashion itself in the image of the symbol and which will be determined, transmuted, regenerated, and absorbed by it.

We must now reply to the question of what exactly the symbol is or, more precisely, what the initiatic symbol is; we shall define it as a double manifestation of God, first as "form" and then as "Presence". The form, so as to act as a vehicle of the Presence, must in its own order directly reflect a divine Reality; now since the Presence is the cause and sufficient reason of the form, and not the reverse, the form can be derived only from a revelation sent by That which wills to be "present"; neither the form nor *a fortiori* the Presence can depend on human willing. This Presence manifests itself in the immediate materiality of the sacred symbol, and thereby in the man who is qualified, which is to say in conformity—by nature as well as by initiation and the disciplines it demands—with the nature of the symbol. This implies three conditions, two of which concern the symbol and one the man himself: first, the exactitude of the symbol; second, its consecration; and third, the consecration of the man—the microcosm—who is to assimilate the symbol. Thus the host must be made of a special bread—unleavened in the Latin Church—and not of ordinary bread; next it must be conse-

---

[4] According to a *hadîth*, "Thine existence is a sin (*dhanb*) with which no other sin can be compared." This is the most peremptory affirmation possible of an esoteric and supra-moral standpoint. We would hasten to add that what we schematically call a "passage from the 'I' to the Self" does not imply the destruction pure and simple of the first of the two terms, for the phenomenon of the "I" is in no way opposed to the realization of the Self, as is proven by the case of the *jîvan-mukta* and of the *Avatâra*.

crated, which presupposes precisely that it be made in such a way as to fulfill the conditions required for consecration; and finally, whoever desires to receive communion must be in a state of sanctifying grace,[5] which implies the complementary rites of baptism and confirmation. Or again, to cite an example of a very different but nonetheless analogous order: the sacred image—such as an icon of the Virgin or a representation of the Buddha—must be made according to the strict rules of the corresponding sacred art; next it must be blessed or consecrated; finally, whoever contemplates it ritually must have the "right" to do so, that is, he must have received the image from the very hands of the tradition, or in other words he must be a Christian in the first case and a Buddhist in the second. Or let us take the example of a symbol that is not fixed or static, but "enacted" or "actualized", such as an incantatory rite: the divine Name to be invoked must be correctly pronounced or else the condition of formal exactitude is not fulfilled; then it must be consecrated by the adequate intention of man, an intention expressed by concentration, fervor, perseverance—consecration, since it is a question of a dynamic symbol, being here necessarily subjective; finally, he who invokes must have a right to this method, that is, he must have received it from a master who likewise received it, which presupposes an initiation regularly transmitted throughout the centuries since the origin of the corresponding Revelation.

Before going further, we must forestall the following objection: is symbolism not inherent in the natural form of the symbolic thing, so that it cannot depend on a superadded value? Now what is in question here is spiritual symbolism and not symbolism pure and simple; every initiatic symbol, by its mere form, is necessarily a "natural" or "existential" symbol, but not every natural symbol is necessarily an initiatic symbol; otherwise, in the final analysis, every appearance would be such a symbol.[6]

The symbol "is" God and thereby is identified with the "Son", without whom no one may come to the "Father"; and this is so owing to the "vertical identity" in which only the essential nature

---

[5] There are certain ritual symbols that can be at once esoteric and exoteric in application, in accordance with certain modes of spiritual radiation.

[6] "If it is true that It [the Trinity] is present in all things, all things are not present in It" (Saint Dionysius the Areopagite, *The Divine Names*). Several categories of initiatic symbols may be distinguished: visual, auditory, enacted, and combinations

counts, and not the existential plane upon which that nature is manifested. It is not as man that Christ is God; on the other hand, the fact that he is man does not prevent his being really God; the levels of existence are therefore comparable to so many horizontal planes of divine reverberation, but the Light, which is vertical in relation to them, is everywhere identical by nature. The fact that this essential or vertical identity can be either indirect or natural, as is the case with everything insofar as it is necessarily—by its mere existence as well as by its positive qualities—a manifestation of "That which is", or direct and supernatural, as is the case with divine manifestations such as the God-Men and the saving symbols they have bequeathed to their posterity, does not enter into the essential definition of "vertical identity" and merely indicates its fundamental modes or degrees.

The relationship between the symbol and the microcosm corresponds analogically to the relationship between the male and female principles; this makes it easier to understand the meaning, in every spiritual path, of the activity and transcendence of the symbol, on the one hand, and the passivity, virginity, and fecundity of the microcosm, on the other, as well as to grasp in an altogether general manner the universal scope of the symbolism of Love.

thereof; the invocation of a divine Name, for instance, brings into play a faculty of sensation as well as a faculty of action, namely, the primordial faculties of hearing and speech; as for the visual symbol (the Hindu and Buddhist *yantra*), it may be either a sculpted or painted image, or a geometric form, or yet again an inscription, depending upon different schools and above all depending upon the religions, which do not make the same use of all the modes of symbolism. Regarding enacted symbols, we may mention the Hindu and Buddhist *mudrâs* and, in a very general way, sacred dances such as those of the dervishes. Apart from this, it is necessary to distinguish between fundamental or central symbols and complementary and secondary ones, not forgetting their different applications, either sensorial or purely mental. We may add to what we said previously about the invocation of a divine Name that the chanting of sacred texts also constitutes an incantatory mode: for instance, the long Buddhist *sûtras*, with their ceaseless repetitions interlacing in a series of monotonous and varied arabesques, allow of an imperceptible and all the more profound infiltration of the Spirit into the finer modalities of the contemplative, and thus they contribute to the liberating transmutation of the ignorant ego; the wisdom that should be transmitted imperceptibly emerges not only from the meaning of the formulas, but also and perhaps even primarily from their transcendent, divine quality—their "magic", one might say, in a transposed sense—a quality that is revealed in parallel fashion in the teachings of the literal meaning. These remarks apply *mutatis mutandis* to all symbols; and let us add that bodily beauty— hence outward beauty—is one of the ways in which the Buddhas save souls, which is true of every sacred form.

*   *   *

We said above that for the contemplative the world is reduced to his microcosm, ground of "theogenesis", and that the outer world is either held to be non-existent in practice, in a certain manner at least, or is regarded as inner, according to case and circumstance; on the other hand, the microcosm, since it is in practice "the world", is conceived of as outer, and only the symbol is considered the real ego. This does not in the least contradict the fact that the world, from this point of view, is reduced to the microcosm, for the outer world, to the extent that it has to be taken into consideration and hence is spiritually assimilated to the individual "I", is no more than a secondary and passive aspect of the interior and transcendent "I", represented by the symbol. It follows that for the spiritual man the ego consists on the one hand of the symbol, with which he must identify himself, and on the other hand of the macrocosm, which he must not regard as outer and therefore "other than myself"; the world, whose existence no one can humanly deny, is thus neutralized as to its illusorily outward character and at the same time becomes an expression of the doctrine, since it is the differentiated projection of the Intellect, which for its part is synthetically actualized by the symbol.[7]

If the world has become "I" for the contemplative, he will regard its imperfections as "his own" in a certain sense, the cosmic possibilities being the same everywhere; he is thus led to expect everything of himself and nothing of others, which is not unrelated to the symbolism of the "Lamb of God, which taketh away the sin of the world". This reversal is but one expression among others of the fundamental inversion brought about by the initiatic process, in accordance with the inverse analogy that exists between the Principle and manifestation, by virtue of which what seems great in the manifested is small in the Principle, and inversely; this inverse analogy must not be confused with direct analogy, which concerns

---

[7] From this it follows that spiritual liberation cannot be an act of "selfishness"; every spiritual path by definition is undertaken "for others" and is incomparably more profitable to them than those apparently most useful activities in which men engage at the expense of the "one thing needful". Upon contact with the symbol, the individual himself becomes symbolic in the sense that he represents God in the world and the world before God.

positive qualities or contents, not limiting containers or modes, and according to which every positive quality is the reflection of a divine Aspect or Attribute.

In an analogous fashion, the active becomes passive and the passive active, always insofar as they are limiting modes and not insofar as they reflect the respective principial aspects: the activity that reflects a divine Act cannot legitimately be transmuted into passivity; but specifically human activity necessarily becomes passivity before the divine Will, which henceforth determines it by giving it meaning and content. Or again: whatever affirms itself *a priori* as positive—the apparent reality of the objects of sense and the passions attached to them—becomes negative in the Truth, and whatever appears as negative from the point of view of sensorial experience—transcendent, and therefore invisible,[8] Reality, and all the consequences it entails for man—becomes positive to the degree that Knowledge transforms the mental and abstract concept into spiritual and concrete Life. Or again: whatever is dynamic in the ordinary man becomes static in the contemplative and inversely, in the sense that desires are absorbed into immutable Beatitude and doctrinal concepts blossom forth within Knowledge, which transforms them so to speak into tangible, lived realities, overflowing with inspiration. Or again, to give yet another example: what is subjective in the ordinary man—a sentiment or emotion—becomes objective or foreign to the sage,[9] and what appears to the ordinary man as objective—some object or other, a natural law, a truth—enters intimately into the life or will of the sage and as a result becomes similar to a psychic and therefore subjective disposition in the ordinary mortal; the profane man places his love *a priori* in facts, whereas the spiritual man places his in principles; this leads us to point out that a fact has a deep meaning only insofar as it manifests a universal law, whereas from the profane point of view principles seem to be just some facts among others.[10]

---

[8] This invisibility is of no concern to the "Eye of the Heart", which perceives the Principle in manifestation, the Cause in the effect, the Absolute in the relative, the Infinite in the finite.

[9] In another respect, this does not prevent an emotional element from being on the contrary "universalized" by serving as a support for participation in the divine Prototype to which it is related.

We said above that whatever appears small shall become great, and inversely: thus the symbol, at first small—since it appears *a priori* as a simple fact, a content of the human soul or human activity—becomes great in the sense that it reveals itself as the Principle, as Reality, which envelops and absorbs the individual, who in turn becomes small, a mere fact and content. In other words, the microcosm is *a priori* a sphere, whose symbol is then the center or heart; but for the being who has realized the Self, it is the symbol—or rather its "realized Reality"—that is comparable to a sphere, limitless in this case, whereas the microcosm is reduced to a purely symbolical content, henceforth possessing, by virtue of this very transmutation, a maximum of quality, an extrinsic attribute of theogenesis.[11] The entire initiatic process can therefore be defined as a reversal of the poles of attraction: the first pole of attraction, which is outward and multiple but finite, is neutralized by the action of the second pole, which is inward, unique, and infinite.

One question that should not be passed over is the following: what corresponds to the symbol in the macrocosmic order, that is, to the means of grace by which and through which a being comes to God? Let us first recall the definition itself of the symbol: it is the sufficient—and consecrated—vehicle of the real Presence; thus it represents an actualization of the Intellect and, in another aspect, a virtuality of the "divine State". Hence what corresponds to the symbol in the macrocosmic order is man, "made in the image of God"—not exclusively terrestrial man to be sure, but the state of existence that constitutes the center in every integral world, which is precisely the case with the human state in relation to our world; indeed man in this world of ours manifests the universal Intellect, the Holy Spirit insofar as it manifests itself. It is only through the

---

[10] This doctrine may be seen admirably formulated in the words of Saint Remy to Clovis: "Bow thy head, proud Sicamber, burn what thou hast worshiped and worship what thou hast burnt"—an inspired formula, which sums up in a masterful way the whole spiritual life: first, an indispensable "humbling" at the moment of "withdrawal" from the world, and then an inversion of values, which in a certain manner describes all that is essential in the initiatic process.

[11] All the relationships contained in the inversion brought about by the process of spiritual development appear in a very clear manner in the Far Eastern symbol of the *Yin-Yang*: the white dot is the "real Presence" in the night of ignorance, and the black dot is the individual mode in the clarity of Knowledge; for ignorance, the symbol is contained, whereas in reality it is the container.

human state—or through any other central state—that beings in "transmigration" can make their way out of the cosmos, just as in the human state itself it is only through the symbol that the soul can leave its state of indefinite tribulation in order to reintegrate its immutable and blissful Essence.

The Symbol

The Symbol thou shouldst carry in thy heart,
And in the Symbol thou shouldst always dwell;
It is a treasure and a shelter, and
A weapon and a saving boat as well.

It is a divine Grace which gives us life;
Within this saving Grace thou canst not fall.
And know: thou also art the Symbol and
The Sign of God, or thou art not at all.

Spiritual Perspectives

VIII

There is an inner dignity and an outer dignity, just as there is an inner humility and an outer humility.

Dignity is the ontological awareness an individual has of his supra-individual reality.

The criterion of true humility is its truth and its dignity.[1]

The criterion of true dignity is its truth and its humility.

*   *   *

There is no legitimate connection between humility and a leveling down, for such a leveling is a form of pride, since it denies the natural hierarchy of values and of men; by this negation it is also opposed to dignity. Humility—or simplicity—is never a synonym for egalitarian mediocrity, nor yet for weakness.

*   *   *

The spiritual content of dignity, unlike that of humility, is not accessible to all men, although in principle every man possesses the same dignity of being made in the image of God, of being the vicar of God on earth, and of having access to the Divine.

Dignity is opposed to vulgarity, frivolity, or curiosity as contemplation is opposed to agitation, or as "being" transcends "doing". It is the "motionless mover" that is incarnate in movement, the "being" that shows through "acting", the contemplation that is affirmed in

---

[1] Or its force, according to Saint Francis of Sales. It was said of the Curé d'Ars that in him humility had "a certain element of unction and dignity". The same saint said of humility that "it is to the virtues what the thread is to the rosary: take away the thread, and all the beads escape; take away humility, and all the virtues disappear".

action; it is the integration of the periphery in the center, as well as the revelation of the center in the periphery.[2]

Dignity is a universal possibility because it refers to Being, to the Cause, to the Principle. It is manifested in every realm of nature: an animal or plant, such as the swan or water-lily, expresses this folding back of the created upon its immutable Principle.

Sacerdotal functions imply in a certain sense a way of dignity. To act in the place of God, as does the officiating priest, is to act with dignity, to act divinely; it is to be central in the periphery or immoveable in movement.

* * *

Dignity is a way of remembering bodily the divine presence; it has need of effacement, as self-respect has need of humility. More precisely, effacement is already included in dignity and humility in self-respect. If there could be a humble pride, it would be self-respect.

Dignity is consciousness of a universal quality. Effacement is consciousness of our nothingness.

Sentimental humility individualizes this nothingness, and therein lies its contradiction. The same applies to affected dignity: it individualizes the theomorphism of Adam, which is just as contradictory, for it is not the individual who resembles God, but man as such, the human form, which includes all individuals.

Dignity is a repose, not an activity like affectation; it is not an individual affirmation, but on the contrary a retreat toward the impersonal center.

Dignity reflects the sacred aspect of man.

---

[2] The "non-action" (*wu-wei*) of the Far Eastern tradition will be recalled here; these two syllables were written above the throne of the Emperor, "Son of Heaven" and personification of this "non-action".

9

Meditation

Contrary to what is too often assumed, meditation cannot of itself provoke illumination; rather its purpose is negative in the sense that it has to remove the inner obstacles that stand in the way, not of a new, but of a pre-existent and "innate" knowledge of which one must become aware. Thus meditation may be compared not so much to a light kindled in a dark room as to an opening made in the wall of that room to allow the light to enter—a light that pre-exists outside and is in no way produced by the action of piercing the wall. Man is by definition a thinking being, and consequently he cannot regard thought as useless *a priori*, no matter what his deepest intentions may be; hence his starting point must necessarily be thought, not only for the needs of outer life, where this is self-evident, but even in his spiritual effort to go beyond the plane of mental limitations. Since he thinks, man must consecrate this faculty to the "one thing needful", just as he must consecrate all his other faculties, for everything has to be integrated into the spiritual; whoever gives thought to the world must also give thought to God, and this holds true for every fundamental activity of the human being, since we must go to God with all that we are.

Every spiritual path, regardless of its mode or level, comprises three great degrees: purification, which causes "the world to leave man"; expansion, which causes "the Divine to enter into man"; and union, which causes "man to enter into God". This might also be expressed somewhat differently; there is something in man that has to die, or has to be destroyed: this is soul-desire, whose existential limit is the sensorial body; there is something in man that has to be converted, or has to be transmuted: this is soul-love—soul-will—whose center of gravity is the ego; finally, there is something in man that has to become conscious of itself, that has to become itself, that has to be purified and freed of what is alien to itself, that has to awaken and expand and become all, because it is all—something that alone must be: this is soul-knowledge,[1] that is, the Spirit, whose subject is God and whose object is likewise God.

The role of meditation is thus to open the soul, first to the grace that draws it away from the world, second to what brings it nearer to God, and third to what reintegrates it into God, if one may speak in this way; according to circumstance, however, this reintegration may be only a fixation in a given "beatific vision", that is, a still indirect participation in divine Beauty.

* * *

The first thought that is capable of delivering man from earthly attachments is that of death, and more generally—and correlatively—that of the ephemeral nature of all things. This meditation, which also implies the idea of suffering and is intimately linked to the attitude of renunciation, throws light on a fundamental aspect of our existence; it can therefore serve as the basis and symbol for spiritual realization despite its apparently negative character, which is necessarily compensated for by a positive aspect. Indeed, to withdraw from the world is to open oneself to the divine Ray; it is to be disposed to know the Eternity of God. To flee from the impurity of the created is to take refuge in the Purity of the Uncreated; to leave suffering is to enter into Beatitude.[2]

Now whatever the intrinsic spiritual virtue of this meditation,[3] it is limited like every form and thus cannot constitute the only pos-

---

[1] In the final analysis, this knowledge must not be looked upon as an aspect opposed to love, but rather as the deepest reality of that which crystallizes into will, love, and intellection on the individual plane; thus conceived, knowledge is identified with the divine Light, from which all perfections are derived.

[2] If Buddhism makes use of this negative perspective and not some other, it is precisely because, by grafting itself onto the most immediately accessible experience, that of pain, it speaks to all beings. Every being can suffer, but not every being necessarily loves God; every being desires to escape suffering, which, owing to its quasi-absolute character in the experience of living beings, is like a springboard placed at the antipodes of the Infinite.

[3] We rather ought to speak of a category of meditation; but as we are here considering only fundamental contents and not all their possible modalities and combinations, we may dispense with taking into account the indefinitely diverse variations to which each formulation can give rise.

sible point of departure for the soul seeking the Infinite; it is therefore necessary to consider on the same ascetic plane an active and
positive attitude, and this attitude will be derived, not from the idea
of death or suffering, but from the certitude of meeting the Absolute, a certitude which, like that of death, takes precedence over
all the relative values of life. Every ascetic attitude, whether active
or passive—insofar as it is possible to see passivity in asceticism—is
equivalent to a stiffening or freezing, which may be likened to the
reflex of dread. But the attitude we wish to describe here overcomes
fear, not in a negative way by a withdrawn or fixed attitude, as is the
case in the meditation on death, but on the contrary by a combative
and therefore positive attitude: fear of Judgment—or, what amounts
to the same thing, the awareness that God sees us—will have the
effect of stimulating a voluntary affirmation capable of opening the
soul to Grace and eliminating what weakens it. What man has to
overcome by this meditation is no longer desire properly so called,
as was the case before, but the natural torpor of the soul, its sloth
with regard to the "one thing needful", passivity in the face of the
seductions of the world. In shaking off this somnolence, man opens
himself to the divine Influx and rouses himself through the spiritual
act, which reflects the pure Act of God; he overcomes the world,
not by fleeing from it, but by opposing it with an affirmation; he
does not withdraw from the created, but transforms it by an act, the
intimate and vigorous consent of the soul to God, and by perseverance, which fixes this act in duration. This attitude of vigilance and
combat—of "holy anger", if one will—has this in common with the
preceding attitude, that of purity: that it takes its stand as it were in
the present, which is pure and strong and which overcomes the past
and the future alike. It is, we repeat, the standpoint of fear, but a
fear that has become active and confident. In other words, there is
a passive and negative aspect of fear in the one case,[4] and an active
and positive aspect in the other; or again, there is on the one hand
the perfection of him who avoids evil and on the other hand the
perfection of him who accomplishes good.

* * *

---

[4] According to a Sufic teaching, when one fears a creature one flees away from it, but
when one fears God one flees toward Him.

After the perspective of fear, we shall consider that of love, its most direct expression being contemplation of the divine Perfections, which may be designated synthetically by the term "Beauty". The perspective of love is situated beyond fear and negation: instead of having painfully to reject the world on account of the ephemeral and deceptive nature of its always limited perfections, love on the contrary attaches itself to the divine Prototypes of these perfections, so that the world, henceforth emptied of its content—since this is to be infinitely rediscovered in God—will be merely a play of symbols and an accumulation of husks, and thus will have no further hold over man.[5] He who knows that all he loves here below is lovable only in virtue of the Essences[6]—and therefore infinitely pre-exists in Divinity—becomes detached from earthly shadows almost without wishing to; he knows that nothing is ever lost, the perfections of this world being no more than fleeting reflections of the eternal Perfections. In other words, the thing or the being that is loved is to be found infinitely more in God than in this world; God is, in infinite measure, every beloved thing and every beloved being. This meditation helps to overcome the world, not by renouncing it *a priori*, but by finding it again, beyond the created, in the Principle that is the Cause of all good; the soul thus consoled rests in God and there finds peace; the soul rests, recollected, satisfied, and freed from all dissipation, in awareness of infinite Beauty.

In creatures, beauty is above all an outward attribute, and it is really only by extension that one can speak, for example, of beauty of soul; but in this case again beauty is an appearance that envelops a deeper reality, a kind of inward truth. In a word, beauty is for us what is most easily graspable, and it is quite significant that it appears in the purest, most exclusive, and most perfect—though also the simplest and poorest—manner in the most peripheral kingdom, the mineral, where beauty is quasi-abstract and absolute. Now this outwardness of beauty is the inverse reflection of a principial relationship: if beauty appears outward in creatures, it is because it is inward in God; or again, if it is immediately graspable

---

[5] As an Arab dervish once said to us: "It is not I who have left the world; it is the world that has left me."

[6] "Verily, it is not for love of the husband that the husband is dear, but for love of *Âtmâ* in him. Verily, it is not for love of the wife that the wife is dear, but for love of *Âtmâ* in her. Verily, it is not for love of the sons that the sons are dear, but for love of *Âtmâ* in them" (*Brihadâranyaka Upanishad*).

in the created, it is in turn the most difficult aspect to grasp in the Uncreated. If God's Beauty were as easily accessible as that of creatures, the apparent contradictions of creation—the sufferings that we consider to be unjust or terrible—would be resolved of themselves, or rather they would vanish in total Beauty; it is thus that a woman's beauty can overwhelm and bring to naught all reasoning or that the beauty of a piece of music can drown mental distractions.[7] When we look at the sufferings of this world, we must never forget that God compensates them infinitely by His Beauty; but this is beyond rational demonstration.

Contemplative concentration on divine Beauty or Beatitude implies, in the attitude of the individual and in relation to the divine Prototype, a parallel analogy and an inverse analogy: the first is provided by the quietude, repose, and peace of the soul, for Beauty is balance and harmony; the second analogy is the individual's contentment with what he possesses in an immediate and ineluctable fashion, and consequently it is resignation toward all that he is according to the will of destiny;[8] this attitude is inversely analogous to divine Beauty in the sense that this Beauty represents an aspect of infinity, hence of extension, if one may express it thus, whereas contentment on the contrary, and by a kind of compensation, realizes a non-expansion or contraction in the individual.

Another attitude, complementary to the one of which we have just spoken, is that of fervor; this is likewise derived from the attitude of love, but whereas the preceding attitude rests in the Beauty or Beatitude of God, this new attitude soars toward His Goodness and Mercy: the soul clings with all its life and all its being to faith in the divine Mercy; it strives to "do violence" to that Mercy, to "force the Gates of Heaven".[9] This is the way of ardent trust, of intense hope, which dissolves every hardness of the soul and is affirmed outwardly by the love of one's neighbor, since it abolishes the indi-

---

[7] According to an Arab proverb, the beauty of man is in his intelligence, and the intelligence of woman is in her beauty.

[8] The Sufis call this virtue *ridhâ*, "resignation" or "contentment"; it is what the Hesychasts call "maintaining the spirit within the body". The reply of Diogenes to Alexander expresses very well the attitude in question.

[9] It will be recalled that "the kingdom of Heaven suffereth violence, and the violent take it by force".

vidual divisions born of an initial hardness of heart; it is the "faith which removes mountains".

Here again, in the attitude of the individual in relation to the divine aspect in view, there is a parallel analogy and an inverse one: Goodness or Mercy is warmth and center, and it is translated in the individual in a parallel mode as fervor and in an inverse mode as generosity, hence as a radiance or expansion; now the divine Goodness can be said to be "attractive", since it attracts from the periphery to the Center or from the current of forms to the blissful and liberating Essence.

*   *   *

On the plane of pure intellectuality, there is a negative attitude which corresponds to renunciation on the passional plane and which is as it were its core; but what is renunciation for the will becomes discernment for the intelligence: it is the distinction between the Real and the unreal and hence the negation of the world, including the "I". From this perspective, God alone "is"; the world—the microcosm as well as the macrocosm—is merely illusion or "nothingness"; there is no need for renunciation, since nothing is; it suffices to know, through the Intellect, that nothing is real.

The point of view that we have just set forth is discernment, hence separation between the Real and the unreal, and even annihilation of the unreal, and not directly union with the Real. Union is derived from a different point of view, which may be formulated thus: "outside God" nothing is except nothingness, and nothingness in no way is; now since I am not nothing, I am all; I am all That is, or in other words I am not other than He[10] in my supra-individual Essence, of which the ego is merely a refraction and hence a symbol. Thanks to this knowledge, God penetrates and sanctifies me,[11] while

---

[10] Let us recall the following formulas: *Aham Brahmâsmi* ("I am *Brahma*"), *Shivo'ham* ("I am Shiva"), and in Sufism the Hallajian expression *Anâ 'l-Haqq* ("I am God-Truth"), or again the expression *Subhânî* ("Glory be to me") of Bayazid.

[11] On condition that the knowledge is metaphysically exact; otherwise man will enter into a darkness much deeper than that of simple ignorance. Aside from the fact that spiritual dilettantism possesses neither greatness nor beauty, whoever appropriates to himself spiritual attitudes to which he has no right becomes the sport of powers of illusion and runs the risk of foundering in a darkness from which there is no return.

on the other hand He absorbs my existence; He makes me become That which I am in reality and from all eternity, namely, Himself. The mental act that corresponds to this reality is concentration on the Real, the Absolute, the Infinite; concentration in fact corresponds to a quasi-existential realization of God, which in any case presupposes the intellectual discernment we previously considered. According to this supreme point of view—which constitutes the esoteric complement of the affirmative attitude discussed above—it is only in God that I am really "I"; in the illusion of individuality I am as though separated from myself, and the created "I" is only a veil that hides me from "Myself", who am uncreated. It is no longer a question here of distinguishing That which is from that which is not, but of "being" That which is. We may also express this idea in the form of the following reasoning: it is certain that I am not nothing; not being nothing, I am all; being all, I am not other than He. This meditation is plenitude and not emptiness like the preceding one; it is totality and not unicity; it is like the sun filling space and flooding it with light; it is inaccessible and even mortal to the profane mind, whence the theological denials and prohibitions that always have in view the common interest, never that of a minority. And yet this restriction is not inherent to Christianity as such, for according to Saint Macarius of Egypt, "The crowns and diadems that the Christians receive are uncreated"; according to Saint Gregory Palamas, "The saints who participate in divine Grace become, in conformity with Grace, infinite and without origin"; and according to Meister Eckhart, "We are totally transformed in God and changed into Him; in the same way as in the Sacrament the bread is changed into the body of Christ, so am I changed into Him, so that He makes me one with His own Being and not simply like Him; by the living God, it is true that there is no longer any distinction."

* * *

This gradation of spiritual attitudes, far from being a merely arbitrary systematization, on the contrary corresponds rigorously to the nature of things, and every possible spiritual attitude can be reduced in the final analysis to one of the points of view we have just considered. We may designate these six fundamental attitudes respectively by the following terms: "negation", "affirmation"; "passivity", "activity"; "emptiness", "plenitude".[12] This amounts to saying that in "fear" there is an attitude which is negative and another which is positive; that in "love" there is an attitude which is passive and another which is active; that in "knowledge" there is an abstractive, distinctive, or objective attitude and another which is integrative, unitive, or subjective. The negative attitude of "fear" is renunciation, detachment; the affirmative attitude is effort, perseverance. The passive attitude of "love" is contentment and peace; the active attitude of "love" is faith and fervor.[13] The distinctive attitude of "knowledge" is discernment between the Real and the unreal, the extinction of the unreal within the Real; the unitive attitude is concentration on That which I am in reality, identity with That which I am.

---

[12] These six positions could also be respectively designated by the following terms: "cold", "dryness"; "humidity", "warmth"; "emptiness", "plenitude"; or again by these symbols: "crystal", "lightning" (or "sword"); "water", "fire"; "night", "sun".

[13] According to Hesychast doctrine, the two great graces which Christ bequeathed with his Name, and which as it were flow from it, are peace and love; they correspond respectively to the two attitudes which we have just mentioned and which we have dealt with previously, peace being the "static" aspect and love the "dynamic" aspect of the same mode of spirituality, *bhakti.*

Space

The North, the South; the East and then the West:
Their mysteries we carry in our breast.
Zenith, Nadir, Spirit and Earth, 'tis we:
Purity, Love, Strength, and Serenity.

Each value in the universal frame
Within our soul and spirit is the same.
Each quarter or each quality of Space
Shows a divine and cosmic Beauty's face.

So let us hear Eternal Wisdom's call:
Be thyself truly, and thou art the All.

Spiritual Perspectives

IX

The idea of sin presupposes the fact of the "fall", in other words—as Maimonides says—the passage from "necessary knowledge" to "probable opinions": before the fall Adam distinguished the true from the false; after the fall he distinguished good from evil. In the beginning will was inseparable from intelligence; the fall is a scission between the two. The distinction between what is "good" and what is "evil" is made by a will that has fallen into the void, and not by the Intellect, which is fixed in the immutable.

The good is a possibility of action; the true is not a possibility of knowing, but knowledge itself. Evil is a "willing"; but error is not a "knowing": it is an "ignorance". In other words evil is an act of the will, but error is not an act of the intelligence. Unlike the will, intelligence is not free through its possible action; it is free through its very substance, and thus through the necessity of its perfection.

*   *   *

Sin concerns every man insofar as individual liberty asserts itself outside the divine liberty; but this by no means signifies that every spiritual perspective must start from the act of sin; to identify man with sinful action is to create a danger of individualism.

Hindus believe in hell; consequently it cannot be denied that they possess the notion of sin; but since their disciplines have ignorance—and not sin—as their negative starting point, they suffer from no guilt complex. Sin appears to them as an imprudence or stupidity, and in any case as an ignorance; it is characterized less by its form than by its inner process.

*   *   *

There is a saying of Saint James that indicates how the contemplative ought to look upon sin and in what sense he is obliged to look on himself as a great sinner: "Therefore to him that knoweth to do good, and doeth it not, to him it is sin." This definition of sin goes far beyond the social level; it concerns the essential morality that is inseparable from spirituality, and its scope therefore embraces humanity in general, and not the specifically Judeo-Christian part of it.

The voice of conscience, far from being a mere sentimentality, is the inner criterion of our vocation—on condition, that is, that we dwell in the truth with regard to God, the world, and ourselves.

* * *

In the thought of a Saint Benedict or a Saint Bernard, the idea of "the greatest sinner" is equivalent to a definition of sin itself: the slightest inadvertence of our will is "sin" as such and without epithet, for in sin there is always something incommensurable because of what it denies, which is the primordial conformity of our will to God. If intellective knowledge has for its object the total Truth, free will has for its goal the supreme Good; knowledge liberates, whereas the will binds with a view to liberty. Will, like knowledge, is "perfectly itself" through its primordial object, since absolute liberty is only in God.

If, as Saint James says, every omission of a good—and so of a movement of our will toward God—is a sin, or "sin as such", this is because even the slightest inclination of the will not in accord with the meaning or the goal of our existence is either directly or indirectly, and in any case logically if not effectively, contrary to the highest Good. This way of looking at things in light of an individual alternative reveals a perspective which places the human problem on the plane of the will, and which consequently identifies man with will; the idea of redemption requires in fact the idea of the fall; if redemption is everything, the fall must also be everything.

* * *

"The worst of sinners": this is a subjective reality expressed in objective terms. I am necessarily "the worst", "the vilest", since I alone am "I".

Metaphysically, the obstacle which distances man from the Infinite is the ego, that is, the principle of individuation or the "passion" that is engendered by "ignorance", as the Hindus would say. For individualist mysticism the obstacle is not the ego as such, but a mode of it, namely, the extreme—and subversive—point of individuation: pride, which rears itself up against God and men, against Truth and destiny.

A doctrine, like that of Christianity, which must take account of all levels of understanding and all the human possibilities of spiritual realization will designate the higher term by the lower—the second being able to symbolize the former, and not the other way round; it is thus that the ego, in practice and method, becomes "pride".

* * *

The ordinary notion of "sin" is founded on action; other conceptions, in particular the idea of sin as "ignorance", place the accent on the root of evil and let action as such keep its inner indetermination. Action in fact can have divergent meanings; only the intention behind it can place it decisively in the hierarchy of values. Although action is everything from a social point of view, where the criterion lies in collective expediency, it may in itself be equivocal and enigmatic, whereas the root of evil, ignorance—and the passion resulting from it—do not give rise to any doubt or error of interpretation.

* * *

According to some Muslim theologians, there are in practice no small sins, for the transgression that is considered small by man will be considered great by God, whereas the small fault that man considers great will be counted as small; just as the Christian deems himself "the greatest of sinners", the Muslim, according to an expression of the Prophet, sees "the least sin rise up before him like a mountain". In Muslim esoterism sin is essentially to forget God, and this forgetting has about it something symbolically absolute by reason of the infinity of Him who is forgotten; from this point of view there can be no little sins. In the same way "the greatest of sinners" means, spiritually speaking, that there cannot be a greater sinner than he who commits "the greatest sin", which is nothing other than pride, the sin of Lucifer wanting to be like God.

*   *   *

Pride, like "idolatry" or polytheistic "association", or again like "ignorance" (*avidyâ*), is a cosmic tendency—in one sense "demi-urgic" and in another "satanic"—which insinuates itself into all manifestation; this explains why he who knows himself knows that he is "the greatest of sinners"—that is, "completely a sinner", since the negation of God contains something "relatively absolute"—and it also explains in what sense there is, according to a saying of the Prophet, "no greater fault than existence".

This perspective makes it possible to understand why in Islam humility is founded less on consciousness of sin than on conscious-ness of powerlessness before God. In this connection the following sentence from the Koran is very revealing: "Walk not on the earth in a proud manner, for in truth thou canst neither cleave the earth nor attain the mountains in height" (*Sûrah* "The Night Journey" [17]:37). Here the source of humility is the daily experience of our physical limitations, a meaning that also appears in the rite of ablution, the occasional cause of which is impurity of the body, and that is contained as well in the word *bashar*, "man": this term desig-nates man, not in his more or less theomorphic aspect—for he is then called *insân*—but in his aspect of mortality, powerlessness, and impurity.

Leaving aside the fact that humility has everywhere the same fundamental reasons, we can say in a relative sense that the Chris-tian is humble because he knows himself a sinner, and the Muslim because he can neither displace the moon nor abolish death.

*   *   *

If a spiritual man of an affective temperament can look upon him-self as the greatest of sinners, an intellective could—with the same logic and the same illogicality—look upon himself as the most ignorant of the ignorant. With the same logic: if our fall is a state of revolt, it is also, and with greater reason, a state of ignorance. With the same illogicality: if it is inconsistent to hold that the greatest of sinners is the man who takes himself to be such—sin *par excellence* being pride, which excludes the recognition of its own baseness, precisely—it is just as inconsistent to take oneself as the least wise of men, since the man who knows he is ignorant cannot be more ignorant than one who does not know this.

* * *

From the Judeo-Christian point of view, death proves the wrath of God; Edenic immortality proves that man was not yet under this wrath. For the Hindu there is here only a difference of degree; the fall was contained in the possibility of man, and this God "knew".

Man could not not fall, since God "could not not create".

God "created" by reason of His infinity: the Infinite requires its own affirmation, which is Being; Being requires creation; creation requires limitation and diversity; these in turn require negation and contradiction, and therefore evil. He who wants a world perfect in virtue and happiness also wants as a consequence an imperfect world full of sin and misfortune. The only choice is between the world and God; there is no choice between an imperfect world and a perfect world. In an analogous manner, there is no choice between a fallen Adam and an incorruptible Adam; there is only the choice between man and God. Hence the attitude of the saint who believes himself to be "the greatest sinner" and, at the spiritual antipodes of this perspective, the idea of non-duality, of identity in the absolute Subject.

* * *

Modern man always starts from the idea of his axiomatic innocence: he is not the cause of existence, he did not want the world, he did not create himself, and he is responsible neither for his predispositions nor for the circumstances that actualize them; he cannot be culpable, which amounts to saying that he has unlimited rights. The consequences of such an attitude are evident: it opens the door to all the vices of human nature and unleashes the downward force of its fall; this is enough to prove it false.

Every man who is injured in his elementary rights admits the existence of responsibility and culpability in others; he should therefore admit the possibility of culpability in himself; he should also recognize the existence of culpability as such, and so of guilt towards God. And such culpability incontestably exists, for every man freely does those things the responsibility for which he casts upon Heaven; every man, within the limits of his freedom, does what he reproaches God for having done in the universe. The opposite attitude is to ask pardon of God; the response, if one may put it thus, is that God asks pardon of man: this is salvation.

Spiritual contrition—the moral form of emptiness—has its full justification, not in the moral and relatively superficial idea of remorse, but in the essential nature of things, in our metaphysical knowledge of the universe and in the empirical consciousness of our destitution. God alone possesses Being; He alone is Plenitude; if man asks pardon of God, it is, in the final analysis, in order to conform to a normative reality, or simply to truth; it is because man exists without being able to move the sun or create one grain of dust, because he usurps the existence that belongs to Him who creates and who orders the stars, because he desires and accomplishes this usurpation within the limits of his freedom and on the plane of his life.

*   *   *

The fear of God is not in any way a matter of feeling, any more than is the love of God; like love, which is the tendency of our whole being toward transcendent Reality, fear is an attitude of the intelligence and the will: it consists in taking account at every moment of a Reality which infinitely surpasses us, against which we can do nothing, in opposition to which we could not live, and from the teeth of which we cannot escape.

10

The Servant and Union

The *Imâm* Abu al-Hasan al-Shadhili has said: "Nothing removes man further from God than the desire for union with Him." This statement may seem surprising at first, coming from someone who was one of the great proponents of esoterism in Islam; but everything becomes clear once it is understood that it refers to the ego and not the pure Intellect. Indeed, the "servant" (*'abd*) as such can never cease to be the servant; consequently he can never become the "Lord" (*Rabb*); the polarity "servant-Lord" is irreducible by its very nature, the nature of the servant or creature being in a certain sense the sufficient reason for divine intervention under the aspect of Lord.

Man cannot "become God";[1] the servant cannot change into the Lord; but there is something in the servant that is capable—though not without the Lord's grace—of surpassing the axis "servant-Lord" or "subject-object" and of realizing the absolute "Self". This Self is God insofar as He is independent of the "servant-Lord" axis and of every other polarity: while the Lord is in a certain manner the object of the servant's intelligence and will, and inversely, the Self has no complementary opposite; it is pure Subject, which is to say that it is its own Object, at once unique and infinite, and innumerable on the plane of a certain diversifying relativity. *Mâyâ*, which breaks up and diversifies both Subject and Object, is not opposed to the Self, of which it is simply the emanation or prolongation in illusory mode; and this mode proceeds from the very nature of the Self, which implies the possibility—through its Infinitude—of an "unreal

---

[1] If formulations of this sort are nevertheless encountered here and there, they are elliptical and not intended to be taken literally. When Saint Irenaeus and others speak of "becoming God", they understand thereby the Essence, or in other words they place themselves intellectually outside the polarity in question; no doubt they understand also, and perhaps even *a priori*, a union which is indirect or virtual, but which is already a kind of participation in Union in the advaitic sense.

reality", or conversely of an "existing nothingness". The Self radiates even into nothingness and lends it, if one may provisionally express oneself in a more or less paradoxical manner, its own Reality, which is made of Being, Consciousness, and Life or Beatitude.[2]

Thus the way of Union by no means signifies that the servant as such is united to the Lord as such or that man ends by identifying himself with God; it signifies that that something in man—beyond his individual outwardness—which is already potentially and even virtually divine, namely, the pure Intellect, withdraws from the "subject-object" complementarity and resides in its own transpersonal being, which, never entering into this complementarity, is none other than the Self. To the argument that the Self is an object of human intelligence and that in consequence it fits perfectly into the "subject-object" polarity, it must be answered that only the notion of the Self is such an object, and that the existence of this notion proves precisely that there is in the human mind something that already is "not other" than the Self; it is by virtue of this mysterious inward connection with the Self that we are able to conceive the Self objectively. If this something *increatum et increabile* were not within us,[3] it would never be possible for us to escape, at the center of our being, from the "servant-Lord" polarity.

Monotheistic theology, like the doctrine of the *bhaktas*, is in fact strictly bound up with this polarity; it therefore cannot surpass it, and for this reason the Intellect will always be reduced for it to an aspect of the servant; its general and as it were "collective" language cannot be that of sapiential esoterism, any more in the East than in the West. The Self is conceivable in a Christian climate only within the framework of a "theosophy", for it is the element of *sophia* that indicates an emergence from the domain of polarities and the surpassing of them; as for Muslims, they will not say that the Intellect (*'Aql*) is "uncreated" in its essence, but that the divine Intellect (*'Ilm*, "Science") takes possession of—or puts itself in place of—the human Intellect, which amounts to the same thing metaphysically;

---

[2] This is the Vedantic ternary *Sat, Chit, Ânanda*. By "Being" we mean here, not the sole ontological Principle—which is *Îshvara* and not *Sat*—but pre-ontological Reality, which is the complementary opposite of the pole "Knowing" (*Chit*). For *Chit* the Sufis would say *'Ilm* ("Science") or *Shuhûd* ("Perception"), the second term being the equivalent of the Vedantic *Sâkshin* ("Witness"); for *Sat* they would say *Wujûd* ("Reality") and for *Ânanda, Hayât* ("Life") or *Irâdah* ("Will", "Desire").

[3] *Et hoc est Intellectus* (Eckhart). "God formed man of the dust of the ground, and breathed into his nostrils the breath of life" (Gen. 2:7).

and this mode of expression is in conformity with the divine *hadîth* according to which "I (Allah) will be the ear by which he shall hear, the sight by which he shall see".[4]

* * *

It would be completely wrong to speak of the Lord "and" the Self, for God is One. If we speak of the Self, there is neither servant nor Lord: there is but the Self alone, possible modes of which are the Lord and the servant, or what are so called from a certain stand-point; and if we speak of the Lord, there is no Self in particular or different from the Lord; the Self is the essence of the Lord of the worlds. The "Attributes" (*Sifât*, in Arabic) of the Lord concern the servant as such, but the "Essence" (*Dhât*) does not.

From this it follows that man can speak to the Lord, but not realize Him and that he can realize the Essence or Self, but not speak to it; with regard to the Self, there is neither opposite nor interlocutor, for the Self or Essence, let it be repeated, is entirely outside the axis "Creator-creature" or "Principle-manifestation", although in this relationship it appears as hidden within the Creator; but it does not concern us as creatures or servants, and we are unable to attain it on the plane of this polarity, apart from the possibility of conceiving it, a possibility granted by the Lord by virtue of the universal nature of our intelligence and also by virtue of the universality of the Self. In other words, if we are able to attain the Self outside the said polarity, it is solely by the will of the Lord and with His help; the Self cannot be realized in defiance of the Lord or in defiance of the relationship "Lord-servant". Or again: although the object of unitive realization is the supra-ontological Essence and not the Lord, it cannot be effected without the Lord's blessing; and although the true subject of that union is the supra-personal Intellect and not the servant, it cannot be brought about without the servant's participation.[5]

---

[4] "In Eternity", declares the Sufi Abu al-Hasan Kharaqani, "man shall see God with divine eyes", and again: "I have neither body, nor tongue, nor heart, only God, and God is in me." And let us mention also the saying of Bayazid (Abu Yazid al-Bastami): "'I and Thee' signifies duality, and duality is an illusion, for Unity alone is Truth (*al-Haqq* = "God"). When the ego is gone, God is His own mirror in me."

[5] Bayazid: "The knowledge of God cannot be attained by seeking, but only those who seek it find it."

The ego, which is "accident", is extinguished—or becomes absolutely "itself"—in the Self, which is "Substance". The way is to withdraw the intelligence into its pure "Substance", which is pure Being, pure Consciousness, and pure Beatitude.

* * *

The subject of the realization of the Self is strictly speaking the Self as such: the essence of the servant "rejoins" the Essence of the Lord by a cosmic detour, through the operation of a sort of "divine respiration"; it is in this sense that it has been said that "the Sufi is not created", or again that the process of union (*tawhîd*) is "a message from Him by Him to Him".[6] Realization of the Essence or Self is effected not so much by the servant as through the servant; it comes about from God to God through man, and this is possible because, in the perspective pertaining to the Self—which has no opposite and of which *Mâyâ* is an emanation or "descent"—man himself is a manifestation of the Self, and not a sort of contrary situated on a separative axis. "There are paths going from God to men," states Abu Bakr al-Saydlani, "but there is no path from man to God"; this means not only that the servant is unable to attain the Lord, but also that the path of Union is not made by the servant as such;[7] on the other hand, when Abu Bakr al-Shibli affirms that "in the realization of God there is a beginning to be savored but not an end", he is referring on the one hand to the irruption of Grace such as it is experienced by the servant, and on the other hand to the Essence, which is itself infinite and consequently has no common measure with the initial and fragmentary experience of man.[8]

---

[6] Dhu al-Nun al-Misri: "True knowledge is knowledge of the Truth through the Truth, just as the sun is known through the sun itself." "The true knower (*'ârif*) exists not in himself, but by God and for God." "The end of knowledge is that man comes to the point where he was at the Origin." Bayazid: "He who knows God by God becomes immortal."

[7] Junayd: "The Sufi is someone who becomes without [personal] attributes and meets God."

[8] Bayazid: "The knower receives from God, as reward, God himself." "Whoever enters into God attains the truth of all things and becomes himself the Truth (*al-Haqq* = "God"); it is not a cause for surprise that he then sees in himself, and as if it were he, everything that exists outside God." Similarly Shankaracharya: "The *yogin*, whose intelligence is perfect, contemplates all things as dwelling in himself, and thus he perceives, by the eye of Knowledge, that everything is *Âtmâ*."

From the standpoint of the Self, as we have stated, there is no confrontation between a Principle and a manifestation; there is nothing but the Self alone, the pure and absolute Subject, which is its own Object. But, it will be asked, what then becomes of the world, which we cannot help still perceiving? This question has to some extent already been answered, but it will perhaps be useful to enlarge upon this crucial point: the world is *Âtmâ*—the Self—in the guise of *Mâyâ*; more especially it is *Mâyâ* insofar as the latter is distinct from *Âtmâ*, which goes without saying, for otherwise the verbal distinction would not exist; but while being *Mâyâ*, it is implicitly, and necessarily, *Âtmâ*, in rather the same way that ice is water or is "not other" than water. In the Self in the direct or absolute sense, there is no trace of *Mâyâ*—save the dimension of infinitude which has been referred to and from which *Mâyâ* indirectly proceeds—but *Mâyâ* is "not other" than the Self at the degree of *Mâyâ*;[9] it is not the servant, since the polarities are surpassed. *Mâyâ* is the reverberation of the Self in the direction of nothingness,[10] or the totality of the reverberations of the Self; the innumerable relative subjects "are" the Self under the aspect of "Consciousness" (*Chit*), and the innumerable relative objects are once again the Self, but this time under the aspect of "Being" (*Sat*); their reciprocal relationships—or their "common life", if one wishes—constitute "Beatitude" (*Ânanda*), but in manifested mode, of course; this Beatitude is made up of everything in the world that is expansion, play, or movement.

According to the perspective "servant-Lord", as has been stated above, the Essence is implicitly "contained" in the ontological Principle—whence the infinite Majesty of that Principle[11]—but this is the mystery of all mysteries and in no way concerns us; in order to illustrate more clearly the diverse angles of vision included in the science of the supernatural, the perspective of discontinuity or separativity may be represented by a system of concentric circles—or polygons, if preferred[12]—which are so many isolated images of the

---

[9] It is in this sense that it is said in the *Mahâyâna* that *samsâra* "is" *Nirvâna*.

[10] Nothingness cannot exist, but the "direction toward" nothingness exists, and indeed this observation is fundamental in metaphysics.

[11] The "Personal God" is in fact none other than the personification of the Essence.

[12] In this case the dimensions or constitutive structures of the worlds and microcosms would be taken into account, not just their existence.

center. We have seen that according to the perspective of the Self, everything "is" the Essence, and that if we nonetheless establish a distinction on this plane—as our existence obliges us to do—it is between the Essence as such and the Essence as "I" or "world";[13] this is the perspective of continuity, of universal homogeneity or immanence, represented by such figures as the cross, the star, the spiral; in these figures the periphery is attached to the center, or rather the whole figure is simply an extension or development of the center; the entire figure is center, if one may put it this way, whereas in the figures with discontinuous elements the center is to all intents nowhere, since it is without extent.

What, then, is the practical consequence of these affirmations as far as our spiritual finality is concerned? Just this: if we consider the total Universe in connection with separativity, according to the axis "Creator-creature", no union is possible, unless it be a union of "grace" that safeguards or maintains the duality; but if we consider the Universe in relation to the Unity of the Essence or Reality, that is, in relation to the homogeneity and indivisibility of the Self, union is possible since it "pre-exists", and separation is only an illusory "fissure"; it is this "fissure" that is the mystery, not the union.[14] But it is a negative and transitory mystery, an enigma that is an enigma only from its own point of view and within the limits of its subjectivity; it can be resolved intellectually and, with all the more reason, ontologically.[15]

*   *   *

Since Paradise affords perfect beatitude, it may be asked how and why anyone would desire something else and something more, namely, a realization that transcends the created and reintegrates the individual accident in the universal Substance. To this objection, which is justifiable in certain psychological cases, the reply is that it is not a question of choosing this and scorning that, but of

---

[13] Pantheism is the error of introducing the nature of *Âtmâ-Mâyâ* into the polarity "Lord-servant" or of denying that polarity on the very plane where it is real.

[14] For the Vedantists, *Mâyâ* is in a sense more mysterious, or less obvious, than *Âtmâ*.

[15] The intellectual solution being the notion of contradictory or privative possibility, a possibility necessarily included in All-Possibility or in the very nature of Infinitude. It would be absurd to object that this notion is insufficient, since anything more adequate is of the order of "being", not "thinking".

following our spiritual nature such as God has willed it, or in other words of following grace in the manner in which it concerns us; the true metaphysician—the *pneumatikos*—cannot but accept the consequences implied by the scope of his intelligence: man follows his "supernatural nature" insofar as it is imprescriptible and with the help of God, but man as servant will take what the Lord grants him. It is true that the Sufis, in order to underline the absolute transcendence of supreme Union, have not hesitated to describe Paradise as a "prison" and to make use of other metaphors of the kind,[16] but they have also called that Union the "Paradise of the Essence",[17] an expression which has the advantage of conforming to scriptural symbolism; the word "Paradise" or "Garden" then becomes synonymous with "supernatural beatitude", and if on the one hand it specifies no degree of reality, it also implies no limitation.

The objection mentioned above might be countered equally well by the assertion that it is impossible to assign limits to the love of God; it is therefore unreasonable to ask why a given soul, possessing an intuition of the Essence, tends toward the Reality it senses through the existential darkness; such a question is devoid of meaning, not only in relation to the "naturally supernatural" aspirations of the gnostic, but also on the plane of the affective mystic, where the soul aspires to everything it can conceive above itself and not to anything less. It is obviously absurd to wish to impose limits upon knowledge: the retina of the eye catches the rays of infinitely distant stars; it does so without passion or pretension, and no one has the right or the power to hinder it.

---

[16] For Bayazid, "The true knowers are the ornaments of Paradise, but for them Paradise is a place of torment." Or again: "Paradise loses its value and brightness for one who knows and loves God", a statement possessing an impeccable metaphysical logic, since from the standpoint of happiness, as in every other respect, there is no common measure between the created and Uncreated. The verbal audacities encountered in Bayazid and others are explained by a constant concern to escape from all inconsistency and "hypocrisy" (*nifâq*), and all told they do no more than follow the line of the great Testimony of Islam: "There is no God if it is not the only God"; the "Garden", despite its positive aspect of "nearness" (*qurb*), is not God; there is therefore in Paradise a negative element of "remoteness" (*bu'd*). Bayazid moreover provides the key to his language when he specifies that "the love of God is what causes thee to forget this world and the beyond", and similarly Ibrahim ibn Adham counsels renunciation of the one as of the other; in the same spirit, Abu Bakr al-Wasiti expresses the view that "a devout person who seeks Paradise thinks to accomplish the work of God, whereas he accomplishes only his own", and again, Abu al-Hasan Kharaqani enjoins us to "seek the Grace of God, for it surpasses alike the terrors of hell and the delights of Heaven".

[17] Or "Garden of Quiddity" (*Jannat al-Dhât*).

The Path

There are the servants of the Sovereign Good;
There are the seekers of the Inner Sun.
There are two manners of approaching God
The Most High; yet the twofold Path is one.

Spiritual Perspectives

X

No "egoism" is possible in the attitude of the pure contemplative, for his "I" is the world, the "neighbor". What is realized in the microcosm radiates in the macrocosm by reason of the analogy between all the cosmic orders; spiritual realization is a kind of "magic", which necessarily communicates itself to the surroundings. The equilibrium of the world has need of contemplatives.[1]

To lose oneself for God is always to give oneself to men. To reduce all spirituality to social charity means, not only putting the human above the Divine, but also deeming oneself indispensable and attributing an absolute value to what one is capable of giving.

Why is social benevolence not in itself a virtue, and why does it not bring with it knowledge of God? It is because it can perfectly well go hand in hand with complacency, which annuls its spiritual quality. Without the inner virtues, such as humility and generosity, good works have no connection with sanctity; they may even indirectly take man further away from God.

According to circumstances virtue is possible without good works, but from the point of view of the love of God good works are nothing without intrinsic virtue, just as—in another order of ideas—detachment is possible without renunciation, whereas renunciation is meaningless except with a view to detachment.

* * *

Certain Hindus of old blessed our epoch, not because it is good, but because, being bad, it includes by way of compensation spiritual graces that make easy what is in itself difficult, provided that man

---

[1] It is a question of a relative equilibrium consonant with particular cyclic conditions. Saint John of the Cross said that "a spark of pure love is more precious to God, more useful for the soul, and more rich in blessings for the Church than all other works taken together, even if to all appearances one does nothing".

177

is sincere, pure, humble, and persevering. In former ages the spirit was more or less everywhere, but was more difficult to reach and to realize just because it was everywhere present: its very overflowing excluded facility. It was there, but had a tendency to disappear; today it is hidden, but has a tendency to give itself.

There is an economy of mercy, although mercy in its essence goes beyond any economy, for principially it comes before justice. Mercy is not measured except in its outward aspect; justice, which is neither the first nor the last word of God, limits it only accidentally and with respect to a particular plane of existence.

Apart from compensatory graces, which are in themselves independent of the evil of our times, there are advantages in this evil itself: the world has become so emptied of substance that it is hard for a spiritual man to be too attached to it; the man of today, if he is contemplative, is already half-broken owing to this very fact. Formerly, worldliness was all the more seductive for having aspects of intelligence, nobility, and plenitude; it was far from being wholly contemptible as it is in our day; no doubt it made possible, in the souls of the elite—who alone concern us here—a sort of guileless and total attachment, which required a corresponding renunciation; the evil of the world did not yet make itself felt in the actual appearance of the world.

* * *

Why is man unable to enter into contemplation as long as his heart is full of anger against his neighbor? It is because man cannot go beyond his "I"—his individuality—except on condition that he sees it as individuality as such, without any distinction of person.

Before sacrificing, says the Gospel, man must be reconciled with his brother; a saint—we do not remember who—said that it is just as absurd to want to contemplate God with one's heart full of bitterness against one's neighbor as it is to pluck out one's eye in order to see better.

Moral imperfection is here simply the human expression of an incompatibility of perspectives. Hatred of a particular person—or of a collectivity, which amounts qualitatively to the same thing—is inconsistent with love of the totality; and it is the totality that one must love in order to be able to love God. Perfection requires one to love man, not a particular man.

* * *

Spiritual realization is theoretically the easiest thing and in practice the most difficult thing there is. It is the easiest because it is enough to think of God; it is the most difficult because human nature is forgetfulness of God.

Sanctity is a tree that grows between impossibility and a miracle.

* * *

Love is in the depths of man even as water is in the depths of the earth, and man suffers from not being able to enjoy this infinity which he bears in himself and for which he is made.

It is necessary to dig deep into the soil of the soul through layers of aridity and bitterness in order to find love and to live on it.

The depths of love are inaccessible to man in his state of hardness, but reveal themselves externally through the language of art and also through that of nature. In sacred art and in virgin nature the soul can taste, by analogical anticipation, something of the love which lies dormant in it and for which it has only nostalgia without the experience.

* * *

In this low world in which we live, there is the immense problem of separation; how can one make men understand that in God they are separated from nothing?

To the angels our formal—or separative—world presents itself as a pile of debris: what is in reality united is separated in form and by form. The formal world is made up of congealed essences.

Man escapes from form—and from separateness—in his own supernatural center, on the shore of eternal and blissful essences.

* * *

The soul is a tree whose roots are deeply embedded in the "world"—in things, both in ourselves and around us, which are capable of being felt, tasted, lived; the "world" is diversity, as well as the passional movements that respond to it, whether in the flesh, in sentiment, or in thought.

The "one thing needful" is the transferring of our roots into what appears to be nothingness, emptiness, unity. Since the soul cannot plant its roots in the void, the void is "incarnated" in the symbol; it is in everything that brings us nearer to God.

* * *

There is one great certainty in life, and this is death; he who really understands this certainty is already dead in this life. Man is hardly at all preoccupied with his past sufferings if his present state is happy; what is past in life, whatever its importance, no longer exists. Now everything will one day be past; that is what a man understands at the moment of death; thus the future is already part of the past. To know that is to be dead; it is to rest in peace.

But there is yet another certainty in life—whether we can have this certainty depends only on ourselves—and it is the certainty of living in the divine will; this certainty compensates for that of death and conquers it. To put it another way: when we have the certainty of being in conformity with the divine will, the certainty of death is full of sweetness. Thus the meaning of our life on earth can be reduced to two certainties: that of the ineluctability of our destiny and that of the meaning or value of our will. We cannot avoid the meaning of life any more than we can avoid death; that great departure, which cannot have a shadow of doubt for us, proves to us that we are not free to act no matter how, that from this present moment we ought to conform to a will stronger than our own.

* * *

In his empirical existence man finds himself in contact with God, the world, the soul, and the neighbor. On each of these levels it might be said that God speaks a different language: in the world He touches us through destiny, which is in time, and through the symbols that surround us, which are in space; in the soul He is truth, which is objective, and the voice of conscience, which is subjective; in our neighbor He appears as the need we must satisfy and also as the teaching we must accept: the divine function of the neighbor is at once passive and active.

One cannot serve God without also seeing Him in destiny, in truth, in the neighbor.

*   *   *

What are the great misfortunes of the soul? A false life, a false death, a false activity, a false rest.

A false life: passion, which engenders suffering; a false death: egoism, which hardens the heart and separates it from God and His mercy; a false activity: dissipation, which casts the soul into an insatiable vortex and makes it forget God, who is Peace; a false rest or a false passivity: weakness and laziness, which deliver up the soul without resistance to the countless solicitations of the world.

*   *   *

To this false life is opposed a true death: the death of passion; this is spiritual death, the cold and crystalline purity of the soul conscious of its immortality. To false death is opposed a true life: the life of the heart turned toward God and open to the warmth of His love. To false activity is opposed a true rest, a true peace: the repose of the soul that is simple and generous and content with God, the soul that turns aside from agitations and curiosity and ambition, to repose in divine beauty. To false rest is opposed a true activity: the battle of the spirit against the multiple weaknesses that squander the soul—and this precious life—as in a game or a dream.

To false knowledge, to vain thought, is opposed a manner of being: that of the spirit united to its divine Source, beyond discursive thought, which is scission, indefinite dispersion, movement without issue. To false existence, to crude and blind fact, is opposed true knowledge, true discernment: to know that God alone is absolute Reality, that the world is only through Him and in Him, and that outside Him I am not.

*   *   *

To think of God. In the mind the divine presence is like snow; in the heart—as existential essence—it is like fire. Freshness, purity, peace; warmth, love, bliss. The lily and the rose.

The divine presence penetrates the soul—the existential ego, not thought in itself—like a gentle heat; or it pierces the heart—as intellective center—like an arrow of light.

*   *   *

Prayer—in the widest sense—triumphs over the four accidents of our existence: the world, life, the body, the soul; we might also say: space, time, matter, desire. It is situated in existence like a shelter, like an islet. In it alone are we perfectly ourselves, because it puts us into the presence of God. It is like a diamond, which nothing can tarnish and nothing can resist.

*   *   *

Man prays, and prayer fashions man. The saint has himself become prayer, the meeting-place of Earth and Heaven; he thereby contains the universe, and the universe prays with him. He is everywhere where nature prays, and he prays with her and in her: in the peaks, which touch the void and eternity; in a flower, which scatters its scent; in the carefree song of a bird.

He who lives in prayer has not lived in vain.

APPENDIX

A Sampling of Letters and
Other Previously Unpublished Materials

1

The first thing necessary is a sense of the essential, or a sense of truth; and likewise a sense of the sacred; then a sense of nobility; then a sense of beauty; and finally a sense of greatness.

These are the tendencies that constitute qualification for the spiritual life and the supreme Path.

Do not get lost then in the insignificant, and do not forget the essential truths; do not feel at ease in profaneness or worldliness or in what is lacking in nobility; tolerate no ugliness, either in your ambience or in your soul; and avoid all pettiness.

Then you may knock, and it shall be opened unto you.

2

I am glad to learn you have finally found a life setting that suits your aspirations, that is, a setting arranged in view of the "one thing needful". "Easy solutions"—since you bring up this moral problem and this typically modern way of looking at things—are always legitimate if God is the aim, for "my yoke is easy, and my burden is light"; worldly people make a cult out of difficulty, which is merely a form—and a fairly hypocritical form at that—of individualism; it is to forget that greatness comes from God and not from man. The greatness of the divine qualities reveals itself in the one who opens himself to them, if one may express oneself thus.

In the spiritual life, difficulties often reside in apparently simple things; victory belongs to him who, in secret, knows how to persevere in little things. To think of God, to empty oneself for Him, to escape from that habitual dream in which the ego mirrors and repeats itself—this seems easy *a priori*; what could be simpler than to repeat an ejaculatory prayer? But to do this always, to renounce anew our dream, to acquire the habit of keeping ourselves in God's presence, thus to go against the congenital tendencies of our soul—tendencies toward dissipation as well as laziness—this is a great thing, the "dimensions" of which cannot be measured from outside. If you read the lives of saints, you will see that they were great above all through simple but consequential attitudes; the more visible glories were somehow superimposed upon these.

Worldly people like to appease their conscience by musing about sublime realities, as if by thinking about them they participated in them; it is of course good to think about them, and one cannot help doing so; however, it is important not to let this habit take the place of real virtues. One must dedicate oneself to a discipline that is not above our strength—that may even appear to be beneath it—but one must dedicate oneself to it totally. And one will then see, over time, that it is above our strength, but that everything is possible with God's help; nothing is possible without it. There are things which are little in themselves but which, when practiced with perseverance, lead to great things; this is what is forgotten by those who constantly bring up the reproach of "easiness".

People often speak to me of concentration and complain they are lacking in it; this is above all a lack of imagination, for he who knows that God is infinitely lovable and that there is nothing to fear outside of Him has little difficulty in maintaining himself in a certain state of recollectedness. A man sentenced to death has no trouble remembering death, and likewise a man parched with thirst effortlessly remembers water; it is not difficult for a young man to think about his betrothed. So should every man think of God; if he does not do so, it is because he lacks "imagination". And this is the great surprise of death: the soul, once it is wrested out of the body and this earthly world, is confronted with God, and it sees the fulgurating and infinite Essence of all that it loved—or could have loved—on earth. In a word, to "concentrate" on God is to know right now that all we love, and all we could love, is to be found infinitely in God, and that all we love here below we love, though without being aware of it, only because of God. We attach ourselves to the fleeting reverberations on water as if the water were luminous; but at death we see the sun with immense regret—unless we became aware of the sun in time.

I claim no merit in being able to speak in this way, for God "forced matters", if I may say so, by placing me in a destiny that made me appreciate very early my helplessness and the marvels of His grace.

3

Many questions arise simply because man lets himself be enticed into the domain where questions lie instead of keeping firmly to the domain of certainty. If a man is confused by something, he should first of all come back to the certainty that it is not this world as such which is important, but the next world, and above all that *lâ ilâha illâ 'Llâh*; and he should say to himself: in the face of this truth, which in principle is the solution to all questions, this or that question just does not arise; it is enough if he has the Answer of answers. And then God will give him a light also for what is earthly and particular.

4

What God asks of us in the first place—for this concerns all men— is to save our souls; whether this salvation is tied to metaphysical knowledge and esoteric practices is quite another question. And here man has three possibilities: either he has no inner relation with ultimate truth, understands nothing of the wisdom of God, and does not wish to know anything about it; or he understands and loves this wisdom to some degree, but for some reason cannot follow a corresponding Path; or—and this is the third possibility— he understands and loves wisdom and can seek to realize it methodically.

Now what you say in your letter about your psychological difficulties moves me to suppose that yours is the second possibility. You have read about initiatic qualifications: a disposition to neurosis is not compatible with stringently and methodically practiced spiritual exercises. What I say here opens up to you the following perspectives: since God asks only one thing of you with certainty, because He asks it of every man—namely, to save your soul, and consequently to incorporate yourself into a tradition that offers you the means to do this—the criterion of the Way for you is not in esoterism in the first instance, but in orthodoxy. Thus from a purely principial point of view, your Way could be found in either Latin or Greek Christianity, or also in Islam; none of these forms would exclude your need for a metaphysical deepening.

What you should do above all is to practice free prayer, in which you must tell God, as you would tell a human person, all your troubles. Someone once said to me: "But I cannot pray," and I answered, "Then say to God, 'I cannot pray.' But express it! Then the spell will soon be broken."

5

There are people who torment themselves for even slight faults, committed even in the distant past, and yet in the present they do what pleases God. Now it is a fault to reproach ourselves with something God does not reproach us with.

God does not reproach us with a sin of which we are fully aware and which we have the sincere intention to commit no longer if at the same time we practice what He requires and what brings us closer to Him. For whoever invokes God with this attitude is a new man.

Moreover, God does not ask us abstractly to be perfect, but asks us concretely not to have a particular fault and not to commit a particular sin or stupidity. Abstention from evil is something precise, practically speaking, whereas perfection is an indefinite ideal, at least on the moral plane.

Furthermore, we must not ask ourselves whether God asks this or that of us; if we accomplish what God certainly asks of us— namely, prayer, invocation, the elementary virtues, and reasonable attitudes—we shall learn *ipso facto* what He may ask additionally.

God does not ask us for something of which we are unaware, any more than He reproaches us with what no longer exists. God considers realities, not dreams. Objectivity is the key to every spiritual and moral value.

6

In order to vanquish a negative heredity—or any blemish, for there are also faults that have been acquired and traumas that have been endured—man must avail himself not only of that sacramental grace which is Invocation, but also of his intelligence, of his will, and of prayer. With the intelligence he must seek the causes, accidental or substantial, of the affliction, for consciousness of the affliction reveals the remedy; one must never ask, "What should I do?" when one realizes one's fault—this consciousness is virtually the cure. "To recognize one's malady is no longer to have it," and "There is no lustral water like unto knowledge." A man who absolutely does not know how to vanquish a fault does not sincerely wish to vanquish it.

With the will man must resist evil and accomplish the good; to know is to will, and to will is to realize. To rely on the help of Heaven without abstaining from evil and without striving toward the good is hypocrisy; to be sincere is to will, and to will is to be able. But here man might object that he cannot do all he wills; we reply that he can always strive, and if he cannot do everything, he can do at least something.

It is here that prayer intervenes; if a man feels himself weak and imperfect, he has a right and even a duty to ask Heaven for help. He has this right to the degree he is sincere, and he has this duty to the degree he is weak. And he alone is weak who is unaware that underlying weakness there is strength, and that every quality belongs to God.

7

The quintessence of all tradition and all spirituality is discernment between the Real and the illusory and concentration on the Real. Everything is contained in this twofold definition. This is doctrine and method in a more outward sense; now there are many doctrines and many methods, but there is only one discernment between the Real and the illusory, the Absolute and the contingent, the Infinite and the finite, just as there is only one concentration on the Real, only one Union, only one Deliverance.

The most diverse traditions agree that the best support for concentration and the best means to obtain Deliverance at the end of the *Kali-Yuga* is the invocation of a revealed divine Name, one that is destined by the Revelation itself for *japa*. Consequently, when I speak of "concentration on the Real", I am thinking of *japa*.

One must enclose oneself in the divine Name as in a shelter during a tempest. One must also invoke it as if the Name were a miraculous sword during a battle, and thus vanquish the enemies we carry within ourselves. At other moments, it is necessary to rest in the divine Name and be perfectly content with it and to give oneself up to it with profound recollectedness, as if in a marvelously beautiful sanctuary full of blessings. And at still other times, one must cling to the divine Name as if it were a rope thrown to a drowning man; it is necessary to call upon God so that He hears us and may save us; we must be aware of our distress and of God's infinite Mercy. Another manner in which *japa* can be practiced is to concentrate on the idea that *Âtmâ* alone is real, that neither the world nor ourselves are real; then it is as if we no longer existed, and the divine Name alone shines in us as if in a great void. Finally, it is necessary to unite to the divine Name as if we were but one substance with it; we then have no more ego, and it is the Name that takes the place of our heart; it is neither our body nor our soul, but rather the Name, that is "us"; and we are "ourselves" not in this or that thought, nor in this or that act, but uniquely in the divine Name, which is mysteriously identical to the Named, or in the sacred invocation, which unites us mysteriously to the Invoked.

8

Your mistake is to be haunted by the idea that everything depends on your efforts; you forget the virtue of *dhikr*, the grace resulting from the Name—or from the *Shahâdah*—independently of your merits. Japanese Buddhism has developed this aspect of the question rather well. What matters in our spiritual life is first of all metaphysics, which distinguishes the Real from the unreal—while affirming that "each thing is *Âtmâ*"—and then the invocation, which brings the Real into us, or rather draws us into the Real. One must invoke with faith. The Name is He. One who remains in the Name can never be lost. The passional nature may protest at first—out of either bitterness or boredom—but it cannot indefinitely resist the all-powerful Name; sooner or later it will submit. Bitterness, sadness, boredom, doubt—all this is ourselves, or rather it is that something in ourselves we must overcome. We must put the Name in place of ourselves. We are incapable of being perfect, but the Name is all perfection; it suffices that it is perfect in us. Failing virtue and efforts, one must have faith while abstaining from evil. The basis of faith for us is metaphysical truth. I have explained the basis of the way of the divine Name in a book that will be sent to you as soon as it is published; but it would also be worth your while to read oriental texts, such as Ramakrishna, Ramdas, Ma Ananda Moyi, Shivananda.

9

Victory over our faults must at the same time be total victory over our past. True regret for past errors is constructive, not self-destructive; it is a return to God and not to the misery of the soul; and return to God brings about joy and not sorrow. When after years of struggle we have overcome a fault, or after years of blindness we have been delivered from it by grace, we should not spend the rest of our life lamenting and asking ourselves why we were not cured sooner. For the past is an aspect of our personality—hence of our *karma*—and there is no reason to ask ourselves why we are what we are; above all there is no reason to regret being ourselves, to regret having been in our place at the moment when grace came and where we have every reason to be content and grateful.

A fault necessarily appears absurd and unforgivable when it has been overcome; a difficulty appears easy when it has been resolved; in spiritual realization what appeared at first like a mountain reveals itself retrospectively as a fog—whence the temptation, when the event is over, to want to decipher the enigma of our absurdity and lament our difficulties with regard to what is easy. Now victory over this self-destructive tendency is part of our victory over our faults. A sage even went so far as to say that, if we are now in a good state, we ought not to regret our past sins; he meant by this that it is vain, when we have arrived at the goal, to ask ourselves why we reached it by such a detour or why we did not reach it earlier; for that would amount to asking why blindness is blind and why one person is not another. On the one hand, the absurd is unintelligible by definition; on the other hand, the human person is what he is; and it is only the result that counts!

10

Your arguments move in psychological and other categories that are situated wholly outside what I am able to imagine. That one cannot bear a few weeks of rest in a wonderful garden—in which I myself have taken walks—and thus to be in contact with a nature that brings us back to ourselves, whose peacefulness and beauty help us recall what we are before God and through Him, and outside of external activities—not to be able to bear this setting or this situation is something beyond my personal experience, to say the least. Certainly, I do not have the duty to change you; yet I still have the right to tell you—although this was not *a priori* my intention—that you identify yourself with an activity that is wholly extrinsic and that you are fleeing your intrinsic, and hence real, being; this is so basic that one does not need to be a spiritual master to observe it. One can in principle tend toward God in any milieu and in any activity, but one must do it!

11

It is quite natural that the more perfect should sometimes suffer at the hands of the less perfect, but not that he should reproach the world for the existence of imperfection; for what is must be. We must give a folly its true name, but we cannot reasonably wonder at the existence of fools; and if there are fools, then there must also be follies. It can moreover happen that through some inward folly we provoke our neighbor to some outward folly; how foolish he is will depend on how foolish we are.

All evil ultimately comes from men having forgotten their being; they no longer repose in pure being, they are no longer conscious of it, but are completely yoked to their doing and let things pull them and push them this way and that. Men do not even know any longer what existence is, nor do they know that they carry a skeleton about with them and that they are locked up in the prison of their five senses; still less do they know what lies in the center of their souls, namely, the kingdom of Heaven and the Glory of God, and that they only have to go through a door to escape from the noise of the ego and the world and to be in a golden quietness.

12

Do not let yourself become discouraged by a situation which is easy to understand and which therefore does not present any intellectual problem; the problem is purely practical, that of moral and spiritual adaptation to an absurd ambiance. You must first of all tell yourself that this human ambiance, though so full of assurance and arrogance, is monstrously abnormal, and this from the point of view of both its convictions and tendencies. These people may well be unanimous in their errors and vices, but it is you who are normal; remain then imperturbable in the face of this collective hypnosis and remain completely true to yourself. In a world that is proud, glacial, and stupidly passional, remain peacefully in your little garden; this is a temporary trial. In metaphysical terms, the appearance of such a horrible world is an unavoidable necessity that accords with cosmic laws, which require that error manifest itself; evil must come, said Christ. In Morocco, you were more or less in a little paradise; but one grows through experience, so one must not be surprised at the trials destiny sends.

When faced with a problem, one must first of all look for the objective and subjective causes; to be able to see clearly the outward and inward aspects of a difficulty is already much; this allows us not to be excessively troubled and to draw the conclusions that matter, conclusions that are both practical and spiritual: on the one hand, to do one's work and render oneself as inconspicuous as possible, while remaining indifferent to scorn and hostility; on the other hand, to withdraw into prayer, to establish oneself so to speak in prayer, to practice individual prayer as well as the ejaculatory orison—to live with hope and to expect nothing from the world, but nonetheless to ask God to come to our aid, inwardly and outwardly. It is difficult to be alone, but it is something that must be learned; this is what Heaven asks of you in this moment. "Verily, after hardship comes ease", it is said in Arabic.

13

When the petty, the futile, assails you do not be petty and futile yourself, but be great through thanking God for this experience, which shows you once again that worldly things are petty and futile; and submit your case to God, without tormenting yourself with questions. Do not try to puzzle things out on their own meaningless level, do not seek to compel what is meaningless to have a meaning, and do not be meaningless yourself; but take things by their root, which lies in your own self. Do not contend with the petty, but understand why it is the petty and why it is there and must be there; remember what greatness is, and give your neighbor greatness where you can; for every being is bound up with God and so has greatness in Him; pettiness is only a darkening cloud and an outward din.

In the all-holy Truth and in pure Prayer there is no narrowness and no bitterness, but only breadth and soft, cooling peace.

14

The facts you relate in your second letter are indeed miraculous. They highlight the spiritual and providential meaning of the trials that followed them. Such trials have a twofold cause: the exhausting of our past errors—which may come from a former existence—and the cosmic reaction against our current ignorance; there are also sufferings whose meaning is that of a martyrdom, which a saintly man can assume for others. In your case, there is no need to worry about your incapacity to concentrate or meditate; it would have sufficed to offer your sufferings to God and to invoke His Name without concentration. In a great suffering as in a great joy, it is the experience that serves as meditation, and it is the acceptance of a suffering—in view of God—that serves as concentration. I know this myself, for I have suffered horribly in my life.

In the lives of saints, for example Saint Teresa of the Child Jesus, suffering due to an almost total lack of physical well-being, and above all due to cold and illness, plays an important role. Assuming that Saint Teresa had followed a way requiring intellectual concentration, her attitude toward suffering would have been the same. Suffering is—by direct "vision"—a meditation on death. To understand and accept the cosmic and spiritual meaning of pain is the temporary equivalent of concentration. It could be said in such a case, solely on condition of the attitude I have just defined, that the Angels concentrate for us—just as it is said that the Angels pray in place of the person whom illness prevents from praying, on condition that he have the intention to do so.

15

There is something vengeful and self-destructive in man which, once it is awakened, refuses to draw back and seeks to submerge and utterly consume everything; there is something Luciferian in the vengefulness that would shatter a life for the sake of a "yes" or a "no", as if there were no greater pleasure than the feeling that one has been wronged. But in a certain sense only God can be wholly right, and it is to Him, not to men, that we must bow; in other words, if we sometimes have to bow to men and magnanimously meet them half-way—not by renouncing justice and truth, but by surmounting the offence as such and acting on the basis of love of our neighbor—this is above all because we owe it to God, because we are not nearly good enough to lay a total claim to our rights; we cannot make a divinity out of revenge because of some unrecognized right or some unrecognized truth and take vengeance on the world and ourselves, indeed on existence in general and thus, in a fashion, on God. Only God is good, and in a certain sense one can do absolute and total wrong only to God. Before God man always has enough sin to enable him to retain his consciousness of guilt, even when he has suffered an injustice. A man may be right, but there is already a wrong as it were in the ego. The key to all this is the quite simple but immeasurable and inexhaustible Truth of truths: namely, there is no divinity except the One God.

Men have greed and hardness in them, and against this Prayer takes its stand like a cooling, extinguishing, and at the same time unshakeable strength. Whereas greed is hot and aggressive, hardness is cold and shuts itself off; it is selfishness toward one's neighbor and indifference towards God; it is the lukewarmness and grayness of the worldly man, whose soul fritters itself away in petty, noisy, everyday trivialities, being without unifying warmth and liberating beauty and love; such a soul is not music, but chatter or clatter; and this is the complement to greed, which like a beast of prey is ever insatiably on the prowl for new victims for its lusts.

16

Clearly it is never too late to start a life dedicated to the "one thing needful". But to start such a life, it is necessary to affirm the intention of doing so in a prayer addressed to the Blessed Virgin, to ask for her help and her blessing by promising her to remain faithful to this commitment, that is, the commitment to practice the invocation of a specific sacred formula. Since a life of prayer must have a fundamental rhythm that we never desist from, one should practice the invocation three times a day no matter what the length of each session is; when one has the time and strength to do so, however, one can also recite the Formula or the Name at each moment. If one cannot practice the invocation while seated, one can recite the Formula while walking in a street, and even mentally; but one must never neglect one of the three daily moments, even if it as short as only a few minutes when time is lacking. Apart from the prayer addressed initially to the Blessed Virgin, one should start with a little retreat of at least two hours in order to pronounce without interruption the Formula, for it is necessary to have a beginning in everything; and this retreat can be repeated from time to time. One must never ask whether one is "worthy" of such a way, nor whether one is sufficiently gifted for it, for one has no choice; we have an immortal soul, and we do what we can.

I am not telling you what you must do; I am telling you what my Christian friends are doing and what I advise them to do; moreover, what I advise is self-evident if one has a deep understanding of the issues.

17

The empirical ego is the web of our tendencies and experiences; it is the "I" that aspires to happiness and whose form is modified upon contact with the phenomena it undergoes or produces. It is for this I—"servant", "sinner", and "believer"—that exoteric, anthropomorphic, voluntaristic, and lawgiving Religion is intended.

Beside the empirical I, there is in principle the intellectual I; we say "in principle", for in fact this higher ego does not assert itself in every human being; with the ordinary man, it is limited to belief and to spiritually indifferent—and indeed ineffectual—reasoning. With the born intellectual, on the contrary, metaphysical intelligence determines his whole personality and consequently his attitude in the face of the Absolute. It is for this intellectual ego, to express it thus, that Wisdom is intended and possesses a saving virtue, because this ego aspires *a priori* to the True.

Wisdom requires a certain support from Religion, since every human being has an empirical I, but this does not mean that the sage has need of a dogmatic and voluntaristic exoterism; what he needs is a sacred discipline that satisfies the nature of the ordinary ego—in other words, a formal and ritual framework and with it a peace-giving and protective *barakah*.

Unquestionably, average Sufism tends to reduce Wisdom to Religion, while elevating Religion to the rank of Wisdom; but Sufism in itself necessarily possesses a dimension that escapes these limitations, which after all are natural and even inevitable in a religious society.

The sage is not without form, but he is without prejudice; he is *hanîf*, and his Religion is the *Fitrah*.

Every human being aspires legitimately to happiness; Felicity—*Ânanda*—is a divine dimension. The man predestined to Wisdom—the "intellectual ego"—cannot find ultimate happiness elsewhere or otherwise than in and through the Truth. It is the Truth that attracts him; happiness lies therein; beatitude is hidden in the Intellect itself—the Intellect that is Serenity and Certitude. And he who says Truth implies all that it demands, which is to say, essentially, Virtue and Invocation: conformity to the True and the Way to the True.

An observation is called for here, and it is the following: Virtue, far from being merely an embellishment or a matter of "sentimentality", is on the contrary strictly necessary, for without it the Truth and the Way are in danger of turning to poison, of giving rise either to the "sin against the Holy Spirit" or to mental derangement; the injunction not to "cast pearls before swine" has not merely an outward and social meaning, but an inward and spiritual import as well. The qualifications of intelligence and will are proportionate to the Truth and the Way only when conjoined with humility, generosity, and a sense of the sacred; in this last quality, fear and love are combined. The soul exists, and hence it must conform to the True, according to its means.

18

The Prophet said: "Guard yourself against suspicion, for the devil seeks to arouse discord among you," or something of the kind. One ought never to brood, if only because the unintelligible or the absurd belongs to the stuff of which the world is made. One should say to oneself in the face of some apparently insoluble difficulty: first of all, everything, every occurrence, has a cause, whether we know it or not; our ignorance takes nothing from it and adds nothing to it. Second, this cause makes no difference to the truth that *lâ ilâha illâ 'Llâh*; what is, is, and what is not, is not. A man sometimes lets himself be overcome by bitterness, because he has allowed the corresponding spiritual possibility—that of sobriety—to be altogether crowded out by his dreams and pleasures; but whoever meets his fellow men with magnanimity and at the same time maintains a certain coolness toward the world—a kind of anticipation of all disillusionment, a foreknowledge of the nothingness of all that is earthly, a refusal to dream—will not be taken unawares by some unexpected bitterness breaking in upon him and will not be despoiled of the irreplaceable good of love. Know man, and know thyself; only God is good.

19

You want me to speak to you a little about the manner of invoking God "like the birds". There is a holy gravity and a holy carefreeness in the invocation. Holy gravity is based on the sense of the sacred and devotional fear; it is to invoke God solemnly, deeply, contemplatively, worshipfully, and to be aware of His Majesty, as if one found oneself in the most venerable and the most marvelous of sanctuaries. Holy carefreeness on the contrary is based upon trust, a sense of Mercy, spiritual childlikeness: it is to invoke God like a child playing in a garden, or like a bird, precisely, which sings for the sake of singing, or because God makes it sing, or because God is God—in short, without worrying about why things are the way they are. These are the two poles or the two complementary modes of invocation, or simply of prayer.

"I love because I love", as Saint Bernard would say. And this applies to the serious mode as well as the light. Love immobilizes him who contemplates Majesty, as it makes him who offers himself up to Mercy sing and dance with joy.

20

Canonical prayer is traditional because it is good; it is not good because it is traditional. Gold is costly because it is precious; it is not precious because it is costly. Within the framework of the Islamic Revelation, the *Fâtihah* is important by reason of its content, and not because it belongs to this framework; the same content may occur elsewhere in an appropriate form. We do not pray in order to perform a traditional and orthodox rite; we pray in order to say something to God.

Canonical prayer is not only a human discourse; it is also divine, which means that besides its literal value it has a sacramental import. It is on our level, yet at the same time beyond us.

21

To consider the supreme Name as a "means" is legitimate only on condition that one specify that the goal is the Named and not some experimental contingency; one can practice the *dhikr* "to be saved" only on condition that this personal motivation fits into the notion of God as the infinite Source of all good. God does not allow us to desire "a state of inviolable inner bliss, calm, and strength" outside the Source of this state; now to conceive of the divine Source is to subordinate the state to that Source and draw all the conclusions this entails; the great Traditions of humanity offer the Source, before which one must place in parenthesis all secondary motivations. If God wills that a man committed to a spiritual path should be deprived of all bliss until death, the man cannot alter this; there is no other choice, since one can choose only the Real, whatever the terrestrial effects of this choice may be depending on individual cases.

22

Outward man is man subjected to the attraction of phenomena and engaged in the contingencies of life—man acting in the world. Inward man on the contrary is man alone before God and attracted by the divine Center. The inward man is the witness of the outward man; the Intellect is the witness of the inward man. One could speak also of the outward "I", the inward "I", and the Self, each being the witness of the one whom it dominates.

One of the requirements of the human condition is to realize an equilibrium between the inward man and the outward man: the first must establish itself over the second, just as the Intellect—or Grace—establishes itself over the inward man, or in other words just as the Universal establishes itself over the individual, determining it and transforming it. Just as the Intellect imposes truths on the inward man—or just as Grace communicates beauties to him—so the inward man will impose virtues, protective limits, and salutary habits on the outward man. The inward ego must not let itself be invaded and submerged by the outward ego; it must not yield in its life, and still less must it yield in its substance, to the dissipation and hubbub of the world.

The inward man realizes the contemplative attitudes, and the outward man realizes the virtues and good habits; the first, by his knowledge and fervor, must neutralize and transmute the contingent perceptions and activities of the second.

23

It often surprises me how deeply most men are sunk in phenomena, how much they identify themselves with their own everyday world of appearances, and how little strength of imagination they have; this surprised me even as a child insofar as I was capable of noticing it; I did notice it without any doubt, for otherwise I should not so often have felt myself to be as one standing outside, disinterested, as it were an onlooker. For the contemplative man the experience of vastly different worlds—the West, Islam, the Red Indians—can and must have a particular spiritual significance; the forms become transparent; they act as supports, yes, but they are no longer confining. What is distraction for one can for another be soaring flight.

24

Clearly it is necessary to address oneself to God with faith; and faith entails the right intention. One must not invoke God with an intention beneath the invocation: that is, one must not invoke in view of some earthly goal or other, nor to be able to tell oneself that one is a saint; but one can invoke either because one feels miserable and helpless, or because one loves the fragrance of His Presence and Peace, or again because God is That which is. It is also important to know that, when we pronounce the divine Name with sincerity, God sees everything we are in need of; the invocation contains all possible prayers we might have, including our gratitude.

One must not wait for the divine Name to afford serenity; we must on the contrary offer serenity to it, for to have serenity is to have faith, and to have faith is to have serenity. Before the Name can give us happiness—if it wills to give this to us—we must know that it itself is happiness and that as a result the invocation is happiness; this is part of faith.

Moreover, happiness consists not only in receiving; it consists also, and essentially, in giving.

25

If only it were easier for a man to do what most people are incapable of doing, namely, to step outside himself and see himself from outside—an outside that is in reality the inside! Then he would be standing in a vast, silver silence, and he would see his ego as something quite small, as something strangled, seething, and noisy.

What makes spiritual realization so difficult is that the ego is inverted, as if turned inside out, a stranger to Reality. Within this inversion it is not so difficult to chase after mirror-reflections of Reality, if the corresponding gifts are there; but to step out of this invertedness into the open—that is difficult, humanly speaking.

26

The terms *oratio* and *jejunium* imply that invocation of the Name—or of the Names—must always be accompanied by perfect sobriety, which is to say that one must not expect any results during the invocation; all our satisfaction should come solely from the fact that we are practicing the invocation or that we are in the presence of the Name. One must not hope for any sensible grace; it is necessary to behave as if grace will come only at the moment of death. For what saves us is not the awareness of some grace or answer; it is uniquely the fact that we pray. For this we have our whole life; we must therefore be mindful of the equilibrium of the soul in order to avoid alternations between the phases of enthusiasm and aridity. If we are indifferent to aridity, it will surely dissipate; we must firmly fix in ourselves the idea that it is not our states that count; it is uniquely our faithfulness to prayer. Our soul must not complicate matters; when complications arise, it is necessary on the one hand to eliminate them through intelligence by seeking out their causes, and on the other hand to combat them through personal prayer by asking for help from Heaven.

If you have temptations of weariness, this proves you are putting too much psychic effort into the spiritual practice, and this tires the soul; one must invoke in a more impersonal and more detached manner, and not engage oneself overly in the individualism that is typical of voluntarist mysticism; one needs to have the sense of quietude. Our sentiments are nothing; perseverance is everything. From yet another side, ups and downs are natural for the soul; everything situated in duration undergoes phases; every continuous motion contains rhythms. Likewise, temptations and reactions are natural for the soul, and this should not surprise us; we need simply entrust ourselves to Heaven and beseech its help.

27

In the spiritual life one must jump over one's own shadow; from the human point of view, this is the liberating miracle. And scarcely anyone can do it.

28

You make allusion to this "critical age"—between forty-five and sixty years old—of which I have sometimes spoken. It is a time when a veil seems to come between the world and ourselves, as if everything were put into question and as if we would have to start from the very beginning again. One must then find a new *modus vivendi* with regard to what is relative as well as with regard to the Absolute; it is necessary to arrive through meditation at a definitive position with regard to life and its contents; this is evident. It is especially necessary not to sacrifice concentration to our uncertainties, for certitude comes precisely from concentration. If you want to know what you must change in your existence, how you ought to simplify it, which things it is appropriate to renounce—because they become too invasive—you must start by reposing in the *mantra* as if you had no worries; this is what the Hindus call *prapatti* and the Muslims *tawakkul*; then clarity will certainly come; problems resolve themselves to the extent we detach ourselves inwardly.

There is also the question of one's will towards the *mantra*, how to strengthen it or determine it. The answer is simple: by the imagination, for the will obeys the imagination, the "subconscious" if you prefer; it is our spiritualized imagination, our deep conviction, which makes concrete for us what we must want in an absolute manner. When we base ourselves uniquely on the will as such, we are incapable of wanting what surpasses us; but imagine a man in the face of a danger or seduction: in both cases, it is easy for him to act, that is, to obey the determination that comes from the object; it is easy to love beauty and to flee death. So if we have the impression that our will is weak—our will for concentration on the *mantra*—it is because we do not see sufficiently, not "concretely" enough, the necessity of the *mantra*, or its infinite beauty, or our misery; and this also proves that we concern ourselves with things we should not concern ourselves with, things outside our *dharma*. At the time of death, one may regret many things, but what one will never regret is to have omitted something in order to "think of the Buddha".

What we do in the morning is very important for the whole day; it is good not to leave the morning's invocation before having the certitude that it has determined our whole being and therefore our whole day. The brain is a sponge that absorbs the river of appearances; it is not enough to empty it of the images from which it lives;

one must also satisfy its need for absorption and its habitual movements; this is what psalmodies do, the reading of sacred texts, meditations, invocations. One must infuse into the mind, to the extent it can bear, the consciousness of the Real and of the unreal; this consciousness will be the framework for everything else. The world is a multiplicity that disperses and divides, at least *a priori*; the celestial Word—true "manifestation of the Void" (*shûnyamûrti*)—is on the contrary a multiplicity that brings together and leads to Unity, whence the importance of ritual recitations. The celestial Word absorbs the soul, and transposes it imperceptibly, through a kind of "divine ruse"—in the sense of the word *upâya*—into the serene and immutable climate of the Absolute; the fish of the soul enter into the divine net without distrust. In this sense, psalmodies of sacred texts are very efficacious; they show us in a way what we should think and what we should be.

To fight sadness, we have no other means than to fix the gaze of the intelligence and the soul on the Infinite, which contains everything that is perfect and lovable. This point of view is easily realizable, it seems to me, in a perspective like that of the Amidists, but in principle it is present everywhere; it is up to us to discover it. To overcome the temptation of sadness, one should use the appropriate meditations and practice the invocation with the desired intention, for one or two hours, in a sanctuary or in virgin nature. One must cut off sadness at its root and not allow it to accumulate; if it arises one day, it should disappear the same day; one must make an effort, with all the means, to overcome it—that is, by ritual recitations, by the *mantra*, by meditation.

29

In order to practice ejaculatory prayer, there is no need to be in a state of moral perfection; one must open oneself to the divine Perfection transmitted by the Names. Certainly our intention must be pure: we must abstain from what takes us away from God whether in principle or in fact and fulfill what brings us close to God either in principle or in fact; on the basis of this intention, even if it is not put into practice perfectly, we have the right, and even the duty, to address ourselves to God.

You can of course sometimes invoke the Name of Jesus alone, and sometimes this Name together with the Name of Mary; but as you say—you even speak of a sign—it is doubtless better to invoke both Names. Jesus and Mary are like the Taoist *Yin-Yang*: each contains its complement, so that when invoking Jesus one is implicitly invoking Mary, and conversely; yet the explicit actualization of each of these Names is fully justified, for objective as well as subjective reasons. In the last analysis—and metaphysically speaking—the Name of Jesus refers to the Absolute, and the Name of Mary to the Infinite.

30

We do not believe that in the hereafter the delivered man—in the sense of the Sanskrit word *jîvan-mukta*—has quite simply disappeared after his union with the Self; it seems to us rather that he leaves in Paradise a form-symbol endowed with distinctive consciousness, which disappears only with the apocatastatic disappearance of Paradise itself—the *mahâpralaya*—when the whole Universe is reabsorbed or integrated into the divine Substance. In this we rejoin the doctrine of the three bodies of the Buddha: earthly, celestial, and divine; this is illustrated also by the example of Christ, whose earthly appearance did not for an instant abolish the divine Reality. The Prophet, during his "night journey" (*Laylat al-mi'râj*), met various Prophet predecessors in Heaven, who were nevertheless "delivered ones" by definition.

Sleep is to death—and death to the Last Judgment—what *pralaya* is to *mahâpralaya*, what the Last Judgment is to the *apocatastasis*.

31

To conquer avidity (exteriorizing, passional expansion) we must realize its opposite, Abstention (crystallizing, ascetic contraction), and its positive analogue, Life (interiorizing, fervent expansion).

To conquer indifference (petrifying, prideful contraction) we must realize its opposite, Life, and its positive analogue, Abstention.

To conquer sloth (corrupting solution) we must realize its opposite, the Act (victorious fixation that unites), and its positive analogue, Repose (stabilizing, peace-giving solution).

To conquer dissipation (agitated fixation that separates) we must realize its opposite, Repose, and its positive analogue, the Act.

To conquer outwardness (scattering separation that deprives) we must realize its opposite, Immanence (liberating union), and its positive analogue, Transcendence (discerning, illuminative separation).

To conquer egoism (compressive union) we must realize its opposite, Transcendence, and its positive analogue, Immanence.

32

You say in your letter that a *jîvan-mukta* is so to speak "absolute", so there could be no "gradations between a *jîvan-mukta* of the *Krita-Yuga* and another of the *Kali-Yuga*"; and you add that you cannot conceive of a being "superior", for example, to Shri Ramana Maharshi. My answer is that this is easily conceivable when one knows all the aspects of the issue; the question is to know how to situate the gradations. For it is necessary to distinguish *a priori* between outward man and inward man, as Meister Eckhart might say; outward man—on pain of not existing—belongs to the realm of cosmic phenomena, whereas inward man pertains to the supernatural immanence of the Self in the soul. In concrete terms, I would say, to take one example, that Rama and Krishna are incomparably greater—as human phenomena or as major *Avatâras*—than any *jîvan-mukta* of our times; Shankaracharya too—as a minor *Avatâra*—is incomparably greater than any of his disciples who has realized *moksha*; and no one is going to make me believe that any *jîvan-mukta* is as great as Christ.

This applies to the outward man, the man who is simply human, the cosmic phenomenon. But even from the point of view of the inward man, there is inequality, and this in parallel to equality: the Self is always the Self, certainly, but the human modality always remains the human modality and determines an indefinite number of variations with regard to the particular modality of the meeting between the human and the Divine. Hindu dialectic, which is always elliptical concerning the human aspect of things, hardly accounts for this diversity; it mentions only "identity", which indeed is the only decisive element. Sufism is more explicit in this connection; it emphasizes that "identity" is the "overriding" divine Presence in our center, but that the meeting between the Divine and the human takes place through an indefinite number of modes or combinations; otherwise identity would mean that man as such could be the Divine as such, which is impossible. I have dealt with these issues in *Logic and Transcendence* in the chapter "The Servant and Union".

There is no need for the *jîvan-mukta* to be a perfect man in his constitution; certainly he is perfect as to his behavior, but not necessarily as to his physical form or his animic scope or gifts, whereas primordial man possessed constitutional perfection in all respects, which is also and *a fortiori* the case for the *Avatâras* and hence for all the founders of religions, as well as for the Virgin Mary. Christ expressed the incommensurability between the "me" and the Self by saying: "Why callest thou me good? There is none good but one, that is, God." When it is said that "the *yogin* is *Brahma*", one ought to specify "in a certain respect"; if this is not done, it is because one wishes to offer a principial definition, not a description. The question of the *jîvan-mukta* pertains largely to what is inexpressible, for the simple reason that it is not possible to grasp mentally the nature of the Self.

33

When the soul has become a blessed star, it still carries in it something of its earthly life, something like a distinguishing mark or heraldic shield, which may be compared to the symbolic summing-up of its life or life's work; for this reason indeed the saints are portrayed with their signs. All these signs point to this or that Name of God and are like diverse symbols of this or that Name. For everything is prefigured in the divine Qualities.

The elect are already connected to God in the here-below: a luminous ray binds them to God, but they are still as if covered with earth or as if blind; they do not see it, or they see it only indistinctly. They feel they are still on earth, but for God they are already with Him, in luminous immortality.

34

I and world: the one needs the other. Not only does the ego need the world as content and means of nourishment, but also the world is incapable of doing without its complement, for it wants to be experienced and is insatiable in its craving to be experienced; it is in its nature to do everything it can to keep alight the fire of the ego or, differently considered, to maintain the ice of the ego in its coldness and hardness—in short, to prevent our escaping from its play. And that is why we should be surprised at nothing that the cosmos dazzles us with.

At the same time the dream-stuff "world" is already in a sense undone from within, for all its images that attach us to itself testify to That which it is not and which is infinitely more than it, That which it would like to hide and yet must reveal, on pain of having no existence.

There is only one Being; there is only one Witness, one Beholder; and there is only one Joy, which reposes in itself and at the same time, in a profusion of Self-giving, showers down in a thousand forms and movements.

In the supreme Name God has become world or form; wake has become dream so that the dream might become wake. The supreme Name is the miraculous barque that carries us from the seemingly insuperable dream-stuff of the world to the liberating shore of divine Wakefulness.

35

A hundred years ago some poet racked his brains over some worthless play; somewhere in the world someone is dreaming of success; a statesman is greedily absorbed in some petty project; yesterday a Zen monk swept the floor-boards in Kyoto; and today, quite near, a cricket chirps in the grass. The world is mad.

One might object that every being, every man, is thus completely locked into a narrow world of experience, in a picture book, in a dream. Yes and no, and in a certain sense absolutely not! I have seen venerable men in whom one could perceive no trace of being locked into a dream world nor any trace of aridity; they looked as if they had experienced everything that can be experienced and as if they were conscious of all possible limits and of the Unlimited.

36

You ask me in your letter what you should do to be saved. I am very old, and I cannot write long letters any more. So I must be brief.

The answer is: Pray. For if you practice prayer all your life you cannot be lost.

Of course you must abstain from sin and also from the manifold perversions of the modern world.

You may be a member of the ancient, traditional, Tridentine Catholic Church, or of an Orthodox Church, or of a traditional, non-sectarian Protestant Church. But the main thing is prayer; to understand this it is good to read the Psalms.

The most important practice is ejaculatory prayer—for instance, the Prayer of Jesus: *Domine Jesu Christe miserere nobis.* Or the beginning of the Lord's Prayer: *Pater noster qui es in Caelis.* Or just *Jesu-Maria.*

This is all I can say in a few words.

37

Life: even if it is short, it is long; and even if it is long, it is short.

It is long because one day follows another, seemingly without end; it is short because it is only the dream of a night.

Yet this dream is all; it is all because it contains the seed of our Eternity.

EDITOR'S NOTES

Numbers in bold indicate page numbers in the text for which the following definitions, descriptions, citations, and explanations are provided.

Chapter 1: Dimensions of Prayer

1: "Thou shalt love the Lord thy God with all thy heart, and with all thy soul, and with all thy mind, and *with all* thy *strength*: this is the first commandment" (Mark 12:30; *cf.* Luke 10:27).

3: "Brahma *is Reality; the world is appearance; the soul is not other than* Brahma": this summation of *Advaita Vedânta* is traditionally ascribed to Shankara (788-820), whom the author regarded as the greatest of Hindu metaphysicians (see editor's note for Ch. 3, p. 29, Note 1).

Spiritual Perspectives I

5: *Joan of Arc* (1412-31), the Maid of Orléans, experienced a number of supernatural visitations, which took the form of blazing lights and voices, including those of Saint Michael, Saint Catherine, and Saint Margaret, who revealed her mission to save France.

In the author's original French, the term rendered "evidence" in the phrase *ontological evidence* is *évidence*, which includes the idea of obviousness or self-evidence, while at the same time suggesting corroboration or proof.

Christ's words to the Apostle Thomas: "Jesus saith unto him, Thomas, because thou hast seen me, thou hast believed: blessed are they that have not seen, and yet have believed" (John 20:29).

The Sermon on the Mount (Matt. 5-7) includes the following Beatitude: "Blessed are they that *mourn*: for they shall be *comforted*" (Matt. 5:4).

6: *The faith "that moves mountains"*: "If ye have faith as a grain of mustard seed, ye shall say unto this mountain, Remove hence to yonder place; and it shall remove; and nothing shall be impossible unto you" (Matt. 17:20).

Note 1: *Evagrius Ponticus* (346-99), who spent much of his life among the Desert Fathers of Egypt, stressed the importance of *apatheia*, or "*apathy*"— that is, imperturbable detachment and calm.

Hesychasts—monks of the Eastern Christian tradition whose aim is to attain to a state of *hesychia* or inner stillness through the practice of the Jesus Prayer or other "prayer of the heart" (see editor's note for "Spiritual Perspectives III", p. 41, Note 4)—include the sixth century Palestinian hermits *Barsanuphius* and *John.*

Note 2: *Anselm* (*c.* 1033-1109), Archbishop of Canterbury and one of the most important of the medieval scholastics, prefaced his ontological argument for the existence of God with the words: "I do not seek to understand so that I may believe; but I believe so that I may understand", the second phrase being *credo ut intelligam* in Latin.

Note 3: *Simeon the New Theologian* (949-1022), widely regarded as the greatest of Eastern Christian mystical writers, says in his *Discourses* that tears are both an effect and a deepening of the initiatic mystery of Baptism.

"*He that believeth on me,* as the scripture hath said, *out of his belly shall flow rivers of living water*" (John 7:38).

John Climacus (*c.* 570-649), a monk and later abbot of Sinai, is best known for his *Ladder of Paradise,* a treatise on the spiritual life in which the thirty steps (chapters) of the "ladder" (*klimax* in Greek) correspond to the age of Christ at his Baptism.

Vladimir Lossky (1903-58) published *The Mystical Theology of the Eastern Church* in 1944.

9: *Meister Eckhart* (*c.* 1260-1327), a German Dominican writer, was regarded by the author as the greatest of Christian metaphysicians and esoterists (see editor's notes for Ch. 4, p. 62, Note 12; "Spiritual Perspectives IV", p. 79, Note 2; and "Spiritual Perspectives IV", p. 82).

"And he that taketh not his cross, and followeth after me, is not worthy of me" (Matt. 10:38).

Note 9: *The story of Majnun and Layla,* one of the best known in the Islamic world, tells of a young man nicknamed *majnun,* literally "madman", because of his love for a beautiful woman with hair as black as the "night" (*layla*); because their love remained unfulfilled in this world, the story is often interpreted as an allegory for the soul's longing for God.

Dante Alighieri (1265-1321) celebrated his love for the young woman *Beatrice* in his *La Vita Nuova,* "The New Life", promising her a poem (*The Divine Comedy*) "such as has been written for no lady before" and making her his spiritual guide in *Paradise* (see editor's note for Ch. 2, p. 15 and "Spiritual Perspectives VII", p. 129, Note 3).

Chapter 2: Fundamental Keys

14: *"Our Father who art in Heaven,* Hallowed be thy Name" (Matt. 6:9; Luke 11:2).

Made in the image of God: "And God said, Let us make man in our image, after our likeness" (Gen. 1:26).

15: *Amore e'l cor gentil sono una cosa*—"Love and the noble heart are one thing"—is the first line of a poem in Dante's *La Vita Nuova,* "The New Life" (see editor's notes for "Spiritual Perspectives I", p. 9, Note 9 and "Spiritual Perspectives VII", p. 129, Note 3).

Spiritual Perspectives II

19: Note 1: For Meister *Eckhart,* see editor's notes for "Spiritual Perspectives I", p. 9; Ch. 4, p. 62, Note 12; "Spiritual Perspectives IV", p. 79, Note 2; and "Spiritual Perspectives IV", p. 82.

20: Note 2: *Chaitanya* (1486-1533), a Vaishnavite Hindu spiritual teacher and ecstatic devotee of Krishna, was regarded by his followers as an *Avatâra* of both Krishna and Radha (see editor's note for Ch. 4, p. 73).

Ramakrishna (1834-86), a devotee of the Hindu Goddess Kali, was one of the greatest Hindu saints of modern times (see editor's note for "Appendix", p. 189, Selection 8).

Omar ibn al-Farid (*c.* 1182-1235), author of the "Wine Ode of the Sufi", and *Jalal al-Din Rumi* (1207-73), founder of the Mevlevi Sufi order, were Muslim poets and mystical writers.

22: *Voltaire* (1694-1778)—pseudonym of François-Marie Arouet—a deist and the best known of the French "Philosophes", was violently opposed to the Roman Catholic Church and sharply critical of its monastic institutions for their alleged indifference to social problems.

The *Carthusian* Order is a strictly contemplative monastic order known for its austerity and requiring of its members a vow of silence and complete renunciation of the world.

23: *God alone is good*: "Why callest thou me good? There is none good but one, that is, God" (Matt. 19:17; Mark 10:18).

25: *He calls this totality of contemplation "love"*: cf. 1 Corinthians 13.

Chapter 3: Prayer and the Integration of the Psychic Elements

29: Note 1: *Shri Shankaracharya* (788-820) was the pre-eminent spokesman for *Advaita Vedânta*, the Hindu perspective of "non-dualism" (see editor's note for Ch. 1, p. 3).

The *Pater*, or *Pater Noster*—"Our Father" in Latin—is the Lord's Prayer, the most common of Christian canonical prayers (*cf.* Matt. 6:9-13; Luke 11:2-4); the *Fâtihah*—"The Opening" in Arabic—is the first *sûrah*, or chapter, of the Koran, consisting of seven short verses used in all Muslim prayers.

30: Note 2: According to traditional Christian teaching, *two natures*, one divine and one human, are united in the single Person of *Christ*, who is the *Logos* or Son of God.

32: Note 4: *Christ's saying concerning holy childlikeness:* "Whosoever shall not receive the kingdom of God as a little child, he shall not enter therein" (Mark 10:15; *cf.* Luke 18:17).

Spiritual Perspectives III

37: *Gregory of Nyssa* (*c.* 330-*c.* 395), a bishop of the early church and an influential mystical and ascetical writer, taught that the *nous* or intellect is the fundamental reason for man's intrinsic dignity as the "image of God".

Note 1: *Maximus the Confessor* (580-662), a prolific writer on doctrinal, ascetical, exegetical, and liturgical subjects, is the most authoritative of the "neptic" Fathers, spiritual writers of the Christian East for whom intellection, or "intuition", provides direct knowledge of spiritual realities.

For *Meister Eckhart,* see editor's notes for "Spiritual Perspectives I", p. 9; Ch. 4, p. 62, Note 12; "Spiritual Perspectives IV", p. 79, Note 2; and "Spiritual Perspectives IV", p. 82.

Kali, worshiped by *Ramakrishna* (see editor's note for "Spiritual Perspectives II", p. 20, Note 2 and "Appendix", p. 189, Selection 8) as the supreme deity, is the destructive and transformative manifestation of the Hindu goddess Parvati, consort of Shiva.

38: Note 2: *Ramanuja* (1017-*c.* 1157) is widely regarded as the classic exponent of *Vishishta Advaita,* that is, the Hindu *darshana* or perspective of "qualified non-dualism", in which emphasis is placed on the personal nature of God.

For *Shankara,* see editor's notes for Ch. 1, p. 3 and Ch. 3, p. 29, Note 1.

40: Note 3: *Macarius of Egypt* (*c.* 300-*c.* 390), or Macarius the Great, a Desert Father renowned for his sanctity and miracles, founded a community of ascetics that became one of the chief centers of early Egyptian monasticism.

Dorotheus (sixth century), founder and archimandrite of a Palestinian monastery near Gaza, wrote a series of "Instructions" on the ascetical life.

For *Evagrius Ponticus*, see editor's note for "Spiritual Perspectives I", p. 6, Note 1.

For the book by *Vladimir Lossky*, see editor's note for "Spiritual Perspectives I", p. 6, Note 3.

41: Note 4: The *Jesus Prayer* is the most common orison of the *Hesychasts* (see editor's note for "Spiritual Perspectives I", p. 6, Note 1) and consists of the words, or some variation, "Lord Jesus Christ, Son of God, have mercy upon us."

44: *Thomas* Aquinas (*c.* 1225-74), a giant among the medieval scholastics and author of the monumental *Summa Theologica*, is considered by the Roman Catholic Church to be the greatest Christian theologian in history.

"*Blessed are they that have not seen, and yet have believed*" (John 20:29).

45: *In God Love is Light*: "God is light, and in Him is no darkness at all" (1 John 1:5); "*God is love*" (1 John 4:8).

46: Muhyi al-Din *Ibn Arabi* (1165-1240), author of numerous works including *Meccan Revelations* and *Bezels of Wisdom*, was a prolific and profoundly influential Sufi mystic, known in tradition as the *Shaykh al-Akbar*, that is, the "great master".

47: *The "peace" that Christ gave the Apostles*: "Peace I leave with you, my peace I give unto you: not as the world giveth, give I unto you. Let not your heart be troubled, neither let it be afraid" (John 14:27).

Callistus of Xanthopoulos, later Patriarch of Constantinople, and *Ignatius* of Xanthopoulos (*fl.* late fourteenth century) were fellow monks on the Holy Mountain of Athos, who together compiled a *Century*—that is, one hundred chapters—of "Directions to Hesychasts".

Note 9: *Nikitas Stithatos*, an eleventh-century monk, three of whose "centuries" are preserved in the *Philokalia*, entered the monastery of Studios at Constantinople *c.* 1020 and may have become abbot in his old age, sometime between 1076-92.

Note 10: The *Alexandrians* included Clement (*c.* 150-*c.* 215) and Origen (*c.* 185-*c.* 254), whose Catechetical School in Alexandria was marked by strong Platonic tendencies and a preference for mystical and allegorical interpretations of Scripture (see editor's note for "Spiritual Perspectives III", p. 54, Note 21).

"Holy silence" is one of several possible translations of the Greek *hesychia*, whence the term Hesychasm.

48: *Palamite teaching* is the doctrine of Gregory Palamas (*c.* 1296-1359), an Athonite monk and later Archbishop of Thessalonica, best known for his defense of the psychosomatic contemplative techniques used by the Hesychast Fathers.

Note 11: *Angelus Silesius*, that is, the "Silesian Angel", was the pen name of Johannes Scheffler (1624-77), a Roman Catholic priest and mystical poet greatly influenced by the teachings of Meister Eckhart.

The *Curé d'Ars* was Jean-Baptiste Marie Vianney (1786-1859), a parish priest and much sought-after confessor from the French village of Ars, who was widely known for his gift of reading souls.

The tears of Saint Mary Magdalene at the Savior's feet: "A woman in the city, which was a sinner, when she knew that Jesus sat at meat in the Pharisee's house, brought an alabaster box of ointment, and stood at his feet behind him weeping, and began to wash his feet with tears, and did wipe them with the hairs of her head, and kissed his feet, and anointed them with the ointment" (Luke 7:37-38).

49: *The ante-Nicene Fathers* were spiritual authorities of the early Church who lived and wrote prior to the Council of Nicaea, the first of the Ecumenical Councils, which was convened in 325.

50: Note 16: *The hymn of praise to charity in the First Epistle to the Corinthians*: 1 Corinthians 13.

L'oeil du coeur (Paris: Dervy-Livres, 1974), pp. 105-6; English edition: *The Eye of the Heart: Metaphysics, Cosmology, Spiritual Life* (Bloomington, Indiana: World Wisdom Books, 1997), p. 127.

52: Note 19: Mansur *al-Hallaj* (858-922), the first Sufi martyr, was dismembered and crucified for his mystical pronouncement, "I am the Truth" (see editor's note for "Spiritual Perspectives IV", p. 83, Note 6).

53: Note 20: "*The kingdom of God is within you*" (Luke 17:21).

54: *Saint Louis* IX (1214-70) was King of France from 1226 and one of the leading Crusaders.

Note 21: *Origen* was the most prolific and influential of the early Church Fathers, writing many hundreds of books, including *De Oratione*, "On Prayer", and *Contra Celsum*, "Against Celsus", a defense of Christianity against the pagan philosopher Celsus (see editor's note for "Spiritual Perspectives III", p 47, Note 10).

Prays without ceasing: "Pray without ceasing" (1 Thess. 5:17).

55: Regarding *love of the neighbor* and the implications of that love for the *individual* and the *collectivity*, whether *qualitative* or *quantitative*, the author writes elsewhere: "Love of God is higher than love for man; in a distantly analogous way, love for the collectivity takes precedence over love for the individual. The collective interest comes before individual interest if both interests are of the same order, or if the parties concerned are qualitatively equivalent; this means that the collectivity must be of the same quality as the individual either by the fact of its totality or by reason of a specific quality, a caste for example; in no case does the purely quantitative collectivity come before the qualitative individual. . . . Society comes before the individual, if need be, as the norm comes before the exception, not as quantity crushes quality—which implies, precisely, that society should be organized with a view to man's spiritual welfare" (*Stations of Wisdom* [Bloomington, Indiana: World Wisdom Books, 1995], pp. 105-8).

Note 22: *Augustine* (354-430), Bishop of the North African city of Hippo, was the greatest of the Western Church Fathers.

With all our heart: "Thou shalt love the Lord thy God with all thy heart" (Matt. 22:37; Mark 12:30; Luke 10:27).

Richard of Saint Victor (d. 1173) was prior of the Abbey of Saint Victor in Paris.

Chapter 4: Modes of Prayer

58: *The example of Saint Peter.* "Peter answered and said unto him, Though all men shall be offended because of thee, yet will I never be offended. Jesus said unto him, Verily I say unto thee, That this night, before the cock crow, thou shalt deny me thrice" (Matt. 26:33-34; *cf.* Mark 14:29-30; Luke 22:33-34).

60: For *Ramakrishna,* see editor's notes for "Spiritual Perspectives II", p. 20, Note 2 and "Appendix", p. 189, Selection 8.

Note 4: *John of the Cross* (1542-91) was a Spanish priest and mystic and co-founder, with Teresa of Avila (see editor's note for "Spiritual Perspectives VII", p. 137), of the reformed or Discalced Carmelites.

Note 7: "And God said unto Moses, *I am that I am*" (Ex. 3:14).

"*I am God*" (Koran 20:14; 27:9; 28:30).

62: "*I sleep, but my heart waketh*" (Song of Sol. 5:2).

Note 12: *Meister Eckhart* (see editor's notes for "Spiritual Perspectives I", p. 9; "Spiritual Perspectives IV", p. 79, Note 2; and "Spiritual Perspectives IV", p. 82) wrote a number of Biblical commentaries, including a lengthy study of the Prologue to the Fourth Gospel (John 1:1-14), in which many of his distinctively esoteric teachings are found.

64: Note 15: "*In the resurrection they neither marry, nor are given in marriage,* but are as the angels of God in heaven" (Matt. 22:30; *cf.* Luke 20:35).

The *houris* are celestial maidens, "fair ones with wide, lovely eyes" (*Sûrah* "The Smoke" [44]:54 *passim*), who are promised as a reward to the faithful in the Muslim Paradise.

Bernard of Clairvaux (1090-1153) was a Cistercian monk and author of numerous homilies on the Song of Songs.

65: Note 16: *Bernardino of Siena* (1380-1444) is known as "the apostle of the Holy Name" because of his devotion to the Name of Jesus; Ciro Cannarozzi edited Bernardino's *Vernacular Sermons* in seven volumes from 1934 to 1958.

The letters *I H S*—that is, *iota, êta,* and *sigma*—which are an abbreviation for   , or *IÉSOUS*, the Name of Jesus in Greek, are traditionally regarded as an acronym for the Latin phrases *in hoc signo,* "by this sign [one may conquer]", or *Jesus [Iesus] Hominum Salvator,* "Jesus [is] the Savior of men".

Note 17: *Nicholas Cabasilas* (*c.* 1320-*c.* 1390) was a late Byzantine mystical writer whose principal work, a set of seven discourses on *Life in Christ,* explains how spiritual union with Christ may be achieved through the three sacraments of Baptism, Chrismation (or Confirmation), and Eucharist.

66: Note 20: *Irenaeus* (*c.* 130-*c.* 200) taught that "the Son of God became the Son of man so that man, by entering into communion with the Word and thus receiving divine sonship, might become a son of God" (*Against Heresies,* 3:19).

67: For *Thomas* Aquinas, see editor's note for "Spiritual Perspectives III", p. 44.

"For *God* so *loved the world,* that He gave His only begotten Son, that whosoever believeth in him should not perish, but have everlasting life" (John 3:16).

"For whosoever will save his life shall lose it: and whosoever will *lose his life* for my sake shall find it" (Matt. 16:25; *cf.* Mark 8:35, Luke 9:24, and John 12:25).

68: Note 23: The author writes, "In Islam spiritual possibilities appear as superimposed levels, but in Christianity there is all told only one spiritual level—if we leave out the question of its modes—in which man participates in a more or less direct or indirect way. A Muslim may be either an exoterist or an esoterist, and in the latter case he may be a saint; a Christian can only be either a child of his times or a saint, whatever may be covered by the word 'saint', according to the case. In Islam there is, so to speak, no sanctity apart from esoterism; in Christianity there is no esoterism apart from sanctity" ("Contours of the Spirit", Part Three of *Spiritual Perspectives* *and Human Facts,* trans. P. N. Townsend [Bedfont, Middlesex: Perennial Books, 1987], p. 87).

Note 25: "*My kingdom is not of this world*" (John 18:36).

"And the *light shineth in darkness*; and the darkness comprehended it not" (John 1:5).

68-9: Note 25: The quoted passage is taken from the author's chapter "The Particular Nature and Universality of the Christian Tradition", which appears in *The Transcendent Unity of Religions* (Wheaton, Illinois: The Theosophical Publishing House, 1984, 1993), p. 135; see also *The Fullness of God: Frithjof Schuon on Christianity,* ed. James S. Cutsinger (Bloomington, Indiana: World Wisdom, 2004), pp. 14-15.

69: "Go ye therefore, and *teach all nations,* baptizing them in the Name of the Father, and of the Son, and of the Holy Ghost" (Matt. 28:19).

The "Peace" of Christ: "Peace I leave with you, my peace I give unto you: not as the world giveth, give I unto you. Let not your heart be troubled, neither let it be afraid" (John 14:27).

Note 25: *The offence which must needs come:* "It must needs be that offences come; but woe to that man by whom the offence cometh" (Matt. 18:7).

Note 26: The *Cabala,* or Jewish mystical and esoteric tradition, reveals what *Moysi doctrina velat,* that is, what "the teaching of Moses concealed".

Note 28: "Knowledge and Love" appears as Part Six of *Spiritual Perspectives and Human Facts* and in the present volume as "Spiritual Perspectives" I-IV.

69-70: In the author's original French, the term rendered "obviousness" in the phrase *overwhelming obviousness or absoluteness* is *évidence,* which includes the idea of self-evidence as well as referring to corroboration or proof.

70: The *Shahâdah,* or Testimony of Faith in Islam, begins with the Arabic words *lâ ilâha illâ 'Llâh,* "There is no god but God".

For "*The world is false,* Brahma *is real*", or "is Reality", see editor's note for Ch. 1, p. 3.

For the word "evidence" in the phrase *the Evidence that delivers,* see editor's note above, pp. 69-70.

71: For the word "evidence" in the phrase *aspect of Truth or Evidence,* see editor's note above, pp. 69-70.

The Muslim *formula of consecration,* with which all but one of the *sûrah*s or chapters of the Koran begin, consists of the Arabic words *bismi 'Llâhi 'r-Rahmâni 'r-Rahîm,* often translated "In the Name of God, the Beneficent, the Merciful".

72: *Repose of hearts*: "He it is who sent down peace of reassurance into the hearts of believers that they may add faith unto their faith" (*Sûrah* "The Victory" [48]:4).

Note 37: *Mahmud Shabistari* (*c.* 1250-1320) was the author of *The Rose Garden of Mystery,* one of the greatest works of Persian Sufism.

73: *Rama* is the seventh *Avatâra* or incarnation of the Hindu God Vishnu and the hero of the *Râmâyana,* the oldest of the Hindu epics; according to the story, Rama's wife, *Sita,* an incarnation of the Goddess *Lakshmi,* was abducted by the demon king *Ravana* and taken from India to the island of *Lanka,* where she was eventually rescued by Rama.

In Hindu tradition, *Radha* was one of the *gopîs,* or cowherd girls, who loved *Krishna,* the eighth of the incarnations of Vishnu, and she was the one whom he especially loved in return; although not an *Avatâra,* she is understood to be the *shakti,* or radiant power, of Krishna and an embodiment of *Ânanda.*

The *Mahâbhârata,* an ancient Indian poem of epic proportions, includes the *Bhagavad Gîtâ,* regarded by many Hindus as the most sublime and profound of all sacred texts.

Amitabha (Sanskrit) or *Amida* (Japanese) is the name of the Buddha of "infinite light", who, as a Bodhisattva named Dharmakara, vowed not to enter *Nirvâna* until he had brought all who invoked his Name into the paradise of his Pure Land, also known as *Sukhâvatî* ("place of bliss") or the Western Paradise.

Shakyamuni, meaning "sage of the Shakyas", is one of the traditional epithets of Siddhartha Gautama, the historical Buddha, who was a member of the Shakya clan.

Note 38: After rescuing *Sita*, *Rama* began to doubt her fidelity and ordered her banished to the forest and killed; spared by her executioner, she was finally able to convince Rama of her devotion, though her own heart was now broken, and she fell to the *Earth*, which opened to receive her into the depths from which she had first been born.

74: According to Buddhist tradition, *tathâgata* (Sanskrit, Pali), signifying the one "thus gone"—and interpreted to mean the traceless pathfinder of the way to Truth—is the title which the historical Buddha chose for himself.

The Sanskrit words *gâte, pâragâte, pârasamgâte*—"gone, gone for the other shore, attained the other shore"—are part of the "Great Wisdom" *mantra* with which the *Mahâyâna* Buddhist "Heart Sutra" concludes.

Note 41: In Tibetan Buddhism, *Amitayus* is the aspect of Amitabha concerned with limitless life.

When *Vairochana* is understood symbolically to occupy the center, *Amitabha* is regarded as the *Dhyâni Buddha* of the West, *Akshobhya* of the East, *Amoghasiddhi* of the North, and *Ratnasambhava* of the South.

In Hindu tradition, *Sarasvati* is the consort of *Brahmâ* and the patroness of learning and the arts.

Spiritual Perspectives IV

77: "*God does what He wills*" (*Sûrah* "The Family of Imran" [3]:40 *passim*).

78: *Made in His image*: "God created man in His own image, in the image of God created He him; male and female created He them" (Gen. 1:27).

"And the *Word* was *made flesh*" (John 1:14).

79: *God alone is good*: "Why callest thou me good? There is none good but one, that is, God" (Matt. 19:17, Mark 10:18; *cf.* Luke 18:19).

Note 2: *Basil* the Great (*c.* 330-79), one of the Cappadocian Fathers, and *Cyril of Alexandria* (d. 444), Patriarch of that city, were key figures in promoting the classical Patristic teaching that the purpose of the Incarnation is the deification of man.

According to *Meister Eckhart,* all food is Holy Communion for those who are pure in heart (see editor's notes for "Spiritual Perspectives I", p. 9; Ch. 4, p. 62, Note 12; and "Spiritual Perspectives IV", p. 82).

80: For *Macarius of Egypt,* see editor's note for "Spiritual Perspectives III", p. 40, Note 3.

Note 2: For *Angelus Silesius,* see editor's note for "Spiritual Perspectives III", p. 48, Note 11.

Note 3: *The Sufi Hasan al-Shadhili* (1196-1258) was the founder of the Shad-hiliyya Sufi *tarîqah,* an initiatic lineage from which are derived a number of other Sufi orders, including the Alawiyya and the Darqawiyya (see editor's note for Ch. 10, p. 169).

81: *Vishnuites,* or Vaishnavites, are members of a Hindu theistic sect who worship the God Vishnu as the Supreme Deity.

Note 4: *The Shaykh Ahmad al-Alawi* (1869-1934), a famous Algerian Sufi, was the author's spiritual master.

82: For *Shankara,* see editor's notes for Ch. 1, p. 3 and Ch. 3, p. 29, Note 1.

For *Ibn Arabi,* see editor's note for "Spiritual Perspectives III", p. 46.

The teaching of Meister *Eckhart* (see editor's notes for "Spiritual Perspectives I", p. 9; Ch. 4, p. 62, Note 12; and "Spiritual Perspectives IV", p. 79, Note 2) that *aliquid est in anima quod est increatum et increabile . . . et hoc est Intellectus*—"there is something in the soul that is uncreated and uncreatable . . . and this is the Intellect"—was among the articles for which he was charged with heresy, and which he himself subsequently retracted "insofar as they could generate in the minds of the faithful a heretical opinion" (The Bull *In agro dominico* [1329]).

83: Note 6: Abu Hamid Muhammad *al-Ghazzali* (1058-1111), an Islamic jurist and theologian, entered upon the Sufi path in search of a direct confirmation of God, which he described in his *Mishkât al-Anwâr*, "Niche of Lights", among other works.

Hallajian refers to Mansur al-Hallaj, who in a moment of mystical ecstasy declared, *Anâ'l-Haqq*, "I am the Truth", Truth being one of the Names of God (see editor's note for "Spiritual Perspectives III", p. 52, Note 19).

Chapter 5: Trials and Happiness

92: "*The kingdom of God is within you*" (Luke 17:21).

Faith demands works: "Faith without works is dead" (James 2:20).

Note 1: A biography of the Persian king *Artaxerxes*, who reigned from 464-425 B.C. (*cf.* Ezra 7), is included in the *Lives of the Noble Greeks and Romans* by the Greek historian *Plutarch* (*c.* 46-*c.* 120).

93: For *Bernard* of Clairvaux, see editor's note for Ch. 4, p. 64, Note 15.

Note 2: *The "logic" of the Burning Bush*: "The Lord appeared unto [Moses] in a flame of fire out of the midst of a bush" (Ex. 3:2), and "God said unto Moses, I AM THAT I AM; and He said, Thus shalt thou say unto the children of Israel, I AM hath sent me unto you" (Ex. 3:14).

Spiritual Perspectives V

96: "But when thou doest alms, *let not thy left hand know what thy right hand doeth*" (Matt. 6:3).

100: "Though I speak with the tongues of men and of angels, and have not charity, I am become as *sounding brass*, or a tinkling cymbal" (1 Cor. 13:1).

103: "*Beauty is the splendor of the true*" is an axiom that the author attributes to Plato (*c.* 427-*c.* 347 B.C.).

104: *Wisdom after the flesh*: "In simplicity and godly sincerity, not with fleshly wisdom, but by the grace of God, we have had our conversation in the world" (2 Cor. 1:12).

Hardened heart: "He hath blinded their eyes, and hardened their heart; that they should not see with their eyes, nor understand with their heart, and be converted, and I should heal them" (John 12:40; *cf.* Exod. 7:13, Deut. 2:30, 2 Chron. 36:13, Isa. 63:17, *passim*).

105: "Behold, I send you forth as sheep in the midst of wolves: *be ye therefore wise as serpents*, and harmless as doves" (Matt. 10:16).

106: Umar al-Khayyam—*Omar Khayyam* (1048-1125)—was a Persian astronomer, mathematician, and poet, whose *Rubaiyat* ("quatrains") conceal a mystical apprehension of God under a veil of seeming skepticism and hedonism.

Chapter 6: What Sincerity Is and Is Not

108: *Boethius* (*c.* 480-*c.* 524), canonized—as Saint Severinus—for his martyrdom, was a Christian philosopher, statesman, and master of the seven liberal arts.

For *Augustine*, see editor's note for "Spiritual Perspectives III", p. 55, Note 22 (for the same citations see also "Spiritual Perspectives VII", p. 133).

Thomas Aquinas—see editor's note for "Spiritual Perspectives III", p. 44—quotes both of these passages in his *Summa Theologica*, Q. 162, Art. 6, Pt. II-II, in discussing the question "whether pride is the most grievous of sins".

109: Note 1: "*Unto the pure all things are pure*: but unto them that are defiled and unbelieving is nothing pure; but even their mind and conscience is defiled" (Tit. 1:15).

111: Note 2: *Hate thy soul*: "If any man come to me, and hate not his father, and mother, and wife, and children, and brethren, and sisters, yea, and his own life also, he cannot be my disciple" (Luke 14:26).

Editor's Notes

Spiritual Perspectives VI

115: For the axiom *"Beauty is the splendor of the true"*, see editor's note for "Spiritual Perspectives V", p. 103.

Ibn al-Arif (1088-1141), an Andalusian Sufi master, was best known for his writings on the science of the virtues.

God alone is good: "Why callest thou me good? There is none good but one, that is, God" (Matt. 19:17, Mark 10:18; *cf.* Luke 18:19).

116: Note 1: The *Philokalia* is a collection of ascetical and mystical writings by spiritual masters of the Christian East, compiled by Saint Nikodimos of the Holy Mountain (1748-1809) and Saint Makarios of Corinth (1731-1805).

117: *The soul is all that it knows* is the doctrine of Aristotle (384-322 B.C.), for whom "the thinking part of the soul, while impassible, must be capable of receiving the form of an object; that is, it must be potentially identical in character with its object without being the object" (*On the Soul*, 3.4).

Chapter 7: Dimensions of the Human Vocation

121: *Dominion over all other earthly creatures*: "And God blessed them, and God said unto them, Be fruitful, and multiply, and replenish the earth, and subdue it: and have dominion over the fish of the sea, and over the fowl of the air, and over every living thing that moveth upon the earth" (Gen. 1:28).

122: The Latin phrase *credo quia absurdum est*, "I believe because it is absurd", comes from an apologetic work, *On the Flesh of Christ*, by Quintus Septimius Florens *Tertullian* (*c.* 160-*c.* 225)—see author's Note 3—an early Church Father and ascetical writer.

Note 3: For the Latin phrase *credo ut intelligam* and its use by *Anselm*, see editor's note for "Spiritual Perspectives I", p. 6, Note 2.

Spiritual Perspectives VII

125: *Made in the image of God*: "And God said, Let us make man in our image, after our likeness" (Gen. 1:26).

126: For *Ramakrishna*, see editor's note for "Spiritual Perspectives II", p. 20, Note 2 and "Appendix", p. 189, Selection 8.

Note 1: *Bernadette* of Lourdes (1844-79), to whom the Blessed Virgin miraculously appeared several times, suffered much from persistent ecclesiastical questioning and publicity.

Teresa of the Child Jesus (1873-97)—also known as Thérèse of Lisieux— gained admission to the Carmelite convent at Lisieux when she was fifteen years old in spite of the opposition of its superior, who objected to a religious profession at so young an age.

127: Note 2: *Russian heretics* such as the Khlysti or Khlysts (from the word *khlestat*, meaning "to lash or whip"), a sect which emerged in the seventeenth century and with which Rasputin (*c.* 1871-1916) was reputedly associated, combined self-flagellation and sexual license in their efforts to cultivate humility.

129: Note 3: *Dante* Alighieri (1265-1321) places himself among the greatest poets of history, including Homer, Horace, Ovid, Lucan, and his master *Virgil* (70-19 B.C.), as he journeys through Limbo in the *Inferno*, Canto IV:88-102 (see editor's notes for "Spiritual Perspectives I", p. 9, Note 9 and Ch. 2, p. 15).

131: "For whosoever exalteth himself shall be abased; and *he that humbleth himself shall be exalted*" (Luke 14:11; *cf.* Luke 18:14).

"But when thou doest alms, *let not thy left hand know what thy right hand doeth*" (Matt. 6:3).

Note 4: For *Ibn Arabi*, see editor's note for "Spiritual Perspectives III", p. 46.

131-32: *The "talents" of the parable*: "The kingdom of heaven is as a man travelling into a far country, who called his own servants, and delivered unto them his goods. And unto one he gave five *talents*, to another two, and to another one; to every man according to his several ability; and straightway took his journey" (Matt. 25:14-15).

132: *God alone is good*: "Why callest thou me good? There is none good but one, that is, God" (Mark 10:18).

Note 5: For *Joan of Arc*, see editor's note for "Spiritual Perspectives I", p. 5.

133: For *Augustine*, see editor's note for "Spiritual Perspectives III", p. 55, Note 22.

For *Boethius*, see editor's note for Ch. 6, p. 108.

Note 6: *Cabalists* are Jewish mystics and esoterists; the *Baal Shem* (Hebrew for "master of the Name") is the title given to one who possesses a secret knowledge of the Name of God, notably to the founder of the eighteenth-century Hasidic current of cabalism, Israel ben Eliezer (1700-60).

135: *Basilian spirituality* is based upon the monastic *Rule* of Basil the Great (*c*. 330-79), one of the Cappadocian Fathers.

Note 7: *Diadochos of Photike* (*c*. 400-*c*. 486), whose works include a century of texts *On Spiritual Knowledge and Discrimination*, is one of the most important of the Orthodox Fathers anthologized in the *Philokalia* (see editor's note for "Spiritual Perspectives VI", p. 116, Note 1).

136: For *Bernard* of Clairvaux, see editor's note for Ch. 4, p. 64, Note 15.

For *Meister Eckhart*, see editor's notes for "Spiritual Perspectives I", p. 9; Ch. 4, p. 62, Note 12; "Spiritual Perspectives IV", p. 79, Note 2; and "Spiritual Perspectives IV", p. 82.

Note 8: For *Ibn Arabi*, see editor's note for "Spiritual Perspectives III", p. 46.

For *Shankaracharya*, see editor's notes for Ch. 1, p. 3 and Ch. 3, p. 29, Note 1.

For *Chaitanya*, see editor's note for "Spiritual Perspectives II", p. 20, Note 2.

137: *Catherine of Siena* (1347-80), a Roman Catholic visionary, ascetic, and mystical spouse of Christ, was the author of a *Dialogue*, or *Treatise on Divine Providence*, which consists of a series of conversations between God and the human soul.

Note 6: *Teresa of Avila* (1515-82), a Spanish Carmelite nun and mystic, wrote extensively on the stages of the spiritual life and the levels of prayer, as in her most important work, the *Interior Castle*, in which the soul's journey to God is envisioned as a progression from the outer courtyard of a crystal castle to the innermost of its seven mansions or rooms (see editor's note for Ch. 4, p. 60, Note 4).

Ignatius Loyola (1491-1556), founder and first general of the Society of Jesus, composed a series of *Spiritual Exercises*, which combine meditation on the events of Christ's life with a prescribed pattern of prayerful reflection that guides one through the three principal stages of the spiritual life: purification, illumination, and union.

Note 11: Abu al-Qasim *al-Qushayri* (d. 1074), author of a commentary on the Koran, is best known for an *Epistle to the Sufis*, a manual on the mystical path.

Note 12: Muhammad ibn Ali *al-Tirmidhi* (d. *c.* 932), surnamed *al-Hakim*, "the philosopher", was the first Sufi authority to connect the degrees of spiritual knowledge with a hierarchy of sanctity, headed by the *qutb*, the spiritual "pole" or "pivot" for a given age.

Note 13: For Abu Hamid Muhammad *al-Ghazzali*, see editor's note for "Spiritual Perspectives IV", p. 83, Note 6.

Chapter 8: Microcosm and Symbol

140: Note 3: "*No man cometh unto the Father, but by me*" (John 14:6).

"*No man shall meet Allah who hath not met the Prophet*" (*hadîth*).

143: Note 6: *Dionysius the Areopagite* (dated *c.* 500 by many scholars) was a disciple of Saint Paul (Acts 17:34) and perhaps the greatest of all Christian masters of apophatic theology.

145: "The next day John seeth Jesus coming unto him, and saith, Behold the *Lamb of God, which taketh away the sin of the world*" (John 1:29).

Note 7: "*One thing* is *needful*" (Luke 10:42).

147: *Made in the image of God*: "And God said, Let us make man in our image, after our likeness" (Gen. 1:26).

Note 10: *Remy*, or Remigius (*c.* 438-*c.* 533), known as the "Apostle of the Franks", was Metropolitan of Reims when he baptized King *Clovis* I (*c.* 466-511), founder of the Frankish monarchy, together with three thousand of his subjects.

Spiritual Perspectives VIII

151: The *motionless mover*, or Unmoved Mover, is the classic expression of Aristotle for the divine Principle, as in the *Metaphysics*, 1072b.

Note 1: *Francis of Sales* (1567-1622), a leading figure in the Counter-Reformation, was a noted preacher and the founder of the Visitation Order, whose most important spiritual writings include an *Introduction to the Devout Life* and a *Treatise on the Love of God*.

For the *Curé d'Ars*, see editor's note for "Spiritual Perspectives III", p. 48, Note 11.

Chapter 9: Meditation

153: "*One thing* is *needful*" (Luke 10:42).

157: Note 8: For *Hesychasts*, see editor's notes for "Spiritual Perspectives I", p. 6, Note 1 and "Spiritual Perspectives III", p. 41, Note 4.

The reply of Diogenes to Alexander. According to Plutarch (see editor's note for Ch. 5, p. 92, Note 1), the Greek Cynic philosopher *Diogenes* of Sinope (*c.* 412-323 B.C.), having refused to join other notable statesmen and philosophers in an audience with *Alexander* the Great (356-323 B.C.), was sought out by the emperor, who found him lounging in the sun and asked him whether there was any boon he wished granted; Diogenes replied, "Yes, I would have you stand so that you do not block the sun."

Note 9: "And from the days of John the Baptist until now *the kingdom of Heaven suffereth violence, and the violent take it by force*" (Matt. 11:12).

158: *Faith which removes mountains*: "If ye have faith as a grain of mustard seed, ye shall say unto this mountain, Remove hence to yonder place; and it shall remove: and nothing shall be impossible unto you" (Matt. 17:20).

Note 10: The Sanskrit phrase *Aham Brahmâsmi*, "I am *Brahma*", is found in the *Brihadâranyaka Upanishad* (1.4.10).

Shivo'ham, "I am Shiva", is the refrain of a devotional hymn by Shankara (see editor's notes for Ch. 1, p. 3 and Ch. 3, p. 29, Note 1), "Nirvana Satakam".

For *Hallajian*, see editor's note for "Spiritual Perspectives IV", p. 9, Note 6.

Bayazid (Abu Yazid) al-Bastami (d. 874), known as the "sultan of the gnostics", is said to have been the first of the great Sufi masters to teach the doctrine of *fanâ'* or spiritual extinction in God.

159: For *Macarius of Egypt*, see editor's note for "Spiritual Perspectives III", p. 40, Note 3.

For *Gregory Palamas*, see editor's note for "Spiritual Perspectives III", p. 48.

For this teaching of *Meister Eckhart*, see editor's note for "Spiritual Perspectives IV", p. 79, Note 2.

Spiritual Perspectives IX

163: Moses *Maimonides* (1135-1204) was the greatest of medieval Jewish philosophers, his most important work being a *Guide for the Perplexed.*

164: *"Therefore to him that knoweth to do good, and doeth it not, to him it is sin"* (James 4:17).

Benedict of Nursia (*c.* 480-*c.* 550), known as the "patriarch of Western monasticism", composed a short *Rule* for his monks, in which he laid special emphasis on the virtues of humility and self-abnegation.

For *Bernard* of Clairvaux, see editor's note for Ch. 4, p. 64, Note 15.

Chapter 10: The Servant and Union

169: The Sufi master *Abu al-Hasan al-Shadhili* left no written works, but many of his sayings and litanies, whose repetition is said to have effected numerous miracles, have been preserved (see editor's note for "Spiritual Perspectives IV", p, 80, Note 3).

Note 1: For *Irenaeus*, see editor's note for Ch. 4, p. 66, Note 20.

170: For the Latin phrases *increatum et increabile* and *et hoc est Intellectus* (see author's note 3) in the teaching of Meister *Eckhart*, see editor's note for "Spiritual Perspectives IV", p. 82.

171: Note 4: *Abu al-Hasan Kharaqani* (*c.* 962-1034), a Sufi with a reputation for great ascetical rigor, was an illiterate peasant, initiated not by a living master but by the spirit of *Abu Yazid al-Bastami* (see editor's note for Ch. 9, p. 158, Note 10).

172: *Abu Bakr al-Saydlani* was an early eleventh century Sufi about whom very little is known; al-Qushayri (see editor's note for "Spiritual Perspectives VII", p. 137, Note 11), describing him simply as a "righteous man", says that he tended a cemetery where other Sufis were buried and that he was obliged to give special attention to one particular gravestone, repeatedly engraving the name of the person who was buried there, only to have the stone disappear every time; perplexed about this al-Saydlani consulted a fellow Sufi and was told, "That *shaykh* preferred anonymity in the world." This anecdote may help to explain al-Saydlani's own obscurity, and it bears closely upon the author's theme in this chapter.

Abu Bakr al-Shibli (*c.* 861-945), an important Sufi of Baghdad and the author of a number of paradoxical aphorisms, was a high government official before entering the spiritual path.

Note 6: *Dhu al-Nun al-Misri* (*c.* 796-859), regarded as the *qutb*, or spiritual "pole", among the Sufis of his time, was a gifted poet and a leading authority on *ma'rifah*, that is, *gnosis* or metaphysical knowledge.

Note 7: Abu al-Qasim al-*Junayd* (d. 910), known for his insistence that Sufism should be firmly based on exoteric Muslim law and practice, taught that the ultimate return of all things into God is anticipated in the experience of *fanâ'*.

Note 8: For *Shankaracharya*, see editor's notes for Ch. 1, p. 3 and Ch. 3, p. 29, Note 1.

175: Note 16: *Ibrahim ibn Adham* (d. *c.* 790), born into a royal family at Balkh in Central Asia, renounced his life of worldly wealth and power and is credited with having made the first Sufi classification of the stages of the ascetical life.

Abu Bakr Muhammad *al-Wasiti* (d. after 932), praised by later Sufis as a "leader of *tawhîd*" and "the master of the East in the science of subtle allusions", was well known for his pungent aphorisms.

Spiritual Perspectives X

177: Note 1: For *John of the Cross*, see editor's note for Ch. 4, p. 60, Note 4.

178: *Before sacrificing, says the Gospel, man must be reconciled with his brother.* "If thou bring thy gift to the altar, and there rememberest that thy brother hath aught against thee; leave there thy gift before the altar, and go thy way; first be reconciled to thy brother, and then come and offer thy gift" (Matt. 5:23-24).

180: "*One thing* is *needful*" (Luke 10:42).

Appendix: A Sampling of Letters and Other Previously Unpublished Materials

183: Selection 2: "*One thing* is *needful*" (Luke 10:42).

"*My yoke is easy, and my burden is light*" (Matt. 11:30).

187: Selection 6: "*To recognize one's malady is no longer to have it*" (*cf. Tao Te Ching*, Ch. 71).

"*There is no lustral water like unto knowledge*" is a traditional Hindu teaching often quoted by the author, based upon the *Bhagavad Gîtâ*, 4:38.

189: Selection 8: Many of the most important teachings of *Ramakrishna*—see editor's note for "Spiritual Perspectives II", p. 20, Note 2—are collected in *The Gospel of Sri Ramakrishna* (1942), translated by Swami Nikhilananda.

Swami *Ramdas* (1884-1963), a devotee of the Hindu *Avatâra* Rama and a personal friend of the author, described the practice and fruits of invocatory prayer in his spiritual autobiography *In Quest of God* (1925).

Ma Ananda Moyi (1896-1982)—or Anandamayi Ma—was a highly venerated Hindu saint, whose life and teachings first became known in the West in 1943 through a collection of her sayings titled *Aux Sources de la joie* ("At the Fountainhead of Joy").

Swami *Shivananda* Sarasvati (1887-1963), who worked as a physician before undertaking the life of a renunciate, wrote several works on meditation and the spiritual path, including *Self-Realization* (1954) and *Japa Yoga* (1952).

191: Selection 11: *What lies in the center of their souls, namely, the kingdom of Heaven*: "The kingdom of God is within you" (Luke 17:21).

Selection 12: *Evil must come*: "It must needs be that offences come; but woe to that man by whom the offence cometh!" (Matt. 18:7).

"*Verily, after hardship comes ease*" (*Sûrah* "Expansion" [94]:5).

192: Selection 14: *Teresa of the Child Jesus* suffered from tuberculosis, dying at the age of twenty-four (see editor's note for "Spiritual Perspectives VII", p. 126, Note 1).

193: Selection 15: *Only God is good*: "Why callest thou me good? There is none good but one, that is, God" (Mark 10:18).

There is no divinity except the One God is a translation of the first part of the Muslim *shahâdah*.

194: Selection 16: "*One thing* is *needful*" (Luke 10:42).

195: Selection 17: *Sin against the Holy Spirit*: "All manner of sin and blasphemy shall be forgiven unto men: but the blasphemy against the Holy Ghost shall not be forgiven unto men" (Matt. 12:31; *cf.* Mark 3:29, Luke 12:10).

"Give not that which is holy unto the dogs, neither *cast* ye your *pearls before swine*, lest they trample them under their feet, and turn again and rend you" (Matt. 7:6).

196: Selection 18: "*Guard yourself against suspicion, for the devil seeks to arouse discord among you*" (*hadîth*).

197: Selection 19: For *Bernard* of Clairvaux, see editor's note for Ch. 4, p. 64, Note 15.

202: Selection 28: *Amidists* are Buddhists of the *Jôdo* or Pure Land sect, whose central spiritual practice is the invocation of Amida, the Buddha of "infinite light" (see editor's note for Ch. 4, p. 73).

203: Selection 30: The "*night journey*", or *Laylat al-mi'râj*, was the miraculous ascension of the Prophet Muhammad from Jerusalem through the various Heavens to the Throne of Allah.

204: Selection 32: *Ramana Maharshi* (1879-1950), widely regarded as the greatest Hindu sage of the twentieth century, experienced the identity of *Âtmâ* and *Brahma* while still in his teens, and the fruit of this experience remained with him as a permanent spiritual station throughout his life.

For *Meister Eckhart*, see editor's notes for "Spiritual Perspectives I", p. 9; Ch. 4, p. 62, Note 12; "Spiritual Perspectives IV", p. 79, Note 2; and "Spiritual Perspectives IV", p. 82.

For *Rama and Krishna*, see editor's notes for Ch. 4, p. 73.

For *Shankaracharya*, see editor's notes for Ch. 1, p. 3 and Ch. 3, p. 29, Note 1.

205: Selection 32: "*The Servant and Union*" is Chapter 10 of the present volume.

"*Why callest thou me good? There is none good but one, that is, God*" (Mark 10: 18).

207: Selection 36: The author gives the Latin form of these prayers: *Domine Jesu Christe miserere nobis* is the Prayer of Jesus, or Jesus Prayer, "Lord Jesus Christ, have mercy upon us"; *Pater noster qui es in Caelis* is the first phrase of the Lord's Prayer, "Our Father, who art in Heaven"; *Jesu-Maria* is the two-fold invocation of "Jesus-Mary".

SOURCES

The chapter selections in this anthology have been translated from the following French editions of Schuon's work. Bibliographical information is also provided for previous English translations.

1. "Dimensions of Prayer": published as "Dimensions de la prière" in *La transfiguration de l'homme* (Paris: Éditions Maisonneuve Larose, 1995), pp. 96-99; English edition: "Dimensions of Prayer", *The Transfiguration of Man* (Bloomington, Indiana: World Wisdom Books, 1995), Part Two: "Man, Truth, and the Path", pp. 97-100.

2. "Fundamental Keys": published as "Clefs fondamentales" in *Avoir un centre* (Paris: Éditions Maison-Neuve, 1988), pp. 127-30; English edition: "Fundamental Keys", *To Have a Center* (Bloomington, Indiana: World Wisdom Books, 1990), Part Three: "Spiritual Perspectives", pp. 141-45.

3. "Prayer and the Integration of the Psychic Elements": published as "De l'oraison et de l'intégration des éléments psychiques" in *L'oeil du coeur* (Paris: Dervy-Livres, 1974), pp. 120-25; English edition: "Prayer and Integration of the Psychic Elements", *The Eye of the Heart: Metaphysics, Cosmology, Spiritual Life* (Bloomington, Indiana: World Wisdom Books, 1997), Part Three: "Spiritual Life", pp. 159-65.

4. "Modes of Prayer": published as "Des modes de l'oraison" in *Les stations de la sagesse* (Paris: Buchet/Chastel, 1958), pp. 161-89; English editions: "Modes of Prayer", *Stations of Wisdom*, trans. G. E. H. Palmer (London: John Murray, 1961; London: Perennial Books, 1980), Chapter 6, pp. 125-47; revised translation (Bloomington, Indiana: World Wisdom Books, 1995), pp. 121-45.

5. "Trials and Happiness": published as "Epreuves et bonheur" in *Résumé de métaphysique intégrale* (Paris: Le Courrier du Livre, 1985), pp. 117-23; English edition: "Trials and Happiness", *Survey of Metaphysics and Esoterism*, trans. Gustavo Polit (Bloomington, Indiana: World Wisdom Books, 1986. 2000), Part Three: "The World of the Soul", pp. 215-20.

6. "What Sincerity Is and Is Not": published as "Ce qu'est la sincérité et ce qu'elle n'est pas" in *L'ésotérisme comme principe et comme voie* (Paris: Dervy-Livres, 1978), pp. 119-24; English edition: "Sincerity: What It is and What It is Not", *Esoterism as Principle and as Way*, trans. William Stoddart (Bedfont, Middlesex: Perennial Books, 1981), pp. 123-27.

7. "Dimensions of the Human Vocation": published as "Dimensions de la vocation humaine" in *L'ésotérisme comme principe et comme voie* (Paris: Dervy-Livres, 1978), pp. 141-44; English edition: "Dimensions of the Human Vocation", *Esoterism as Principle and as Way*, trans. William Stoddart (Bedfont, Middlesex: Perennial Books, 1981), pp. 147-50.

8. "Microcosm and Symbol": published as "Microcosme et symbole" in *L'oeil du coeur* (Paris: Dervy-Livres, 1974), pp. 111-19; English edition: "Microcosm and Symbol", *The Eye of the Heart: Metaphysics, Cosmology, Spiritual Life* (Bloomington, Indiana: World Wisdom Books, 1997), Part Three: "Spiritual Life", pp. 147-58.

9. "Meditation": published as "De la meditation" in *L'oeil du coeur* (Paris: Dervy-Livres, 1974), pp. 148-54; English edition: "On Meditation", *The Eye of the Heart: Metaphysics, Cosmology, Spiritual Life* (Bloomington, Indiana: World Wisdom Books, 1997), Part Three: "Spiritual Life", pp. 167-76.

10. "The Servant and Union": published as "Le serviteur et l'union" in *Logique et transcendance* (Paris: Les Éditions Traditionnelles, 1972), pp. 231-39; English edition: "The Servant and Union", *Logic and Transcendence*, trans. Peter N. Townsend (New York: Harper and Row, 1975; London: Perennial Books, 1984), Chapter 14, pp. 209-16.

*   *   *

Spiritual Perspectives I-IV: published as "Connaissance et amour" in *Perspectives spirituelles et faits humains* (Paris: Éditions Maisonneuve and Larose, 1989), V, pp. 169-228; English editions: "Love and Knowledge", *Spiritual Perspectives and Human Facts*, trans. Macleod Matheson (London: Faber and Faber, 1954), Part Five, pp. 126-70;

trans. Peter N. Townsend (Bedfont, Middlesex: Perennial Books, 1987), Part Five, pp. 133-77.

Spiritual Perspectives V-X: published as "Des vertus spirituelles" in *Perspectives spirituelles et faits humains* (Paris: Éditions Maisonneuve and Larose, 1989), VI, pp. 231-87; English editions: "The Spiritual Virtues", *Spiritual Perspectives and Human Facts*, trans. Macleod Matheson (London: Faber and Faber, 1954), Part Six, pp. 171-213; trans. Peter N. Townsend (Bedfont, Middlesex: Perennial Books, 1987), Part Six, pp. 181-223.

* * *

The poems facing pages 5, 19, 37, 77, 95, 113, 125, 151, 163, and 177 are taken from Schuon's *Road to the Heart* (Bloomington, Indiana: World Wisdom Books, 1995), a collection of poetry originally written in English. Titles and pages from that volume are as follows:

"Synthesis", p. 88; "One Word", p. 28; "Prayer", p. 65; "The Name", p. 18; "Remembrance", p. 102; "War", p. 90; "Tell Me", p. 59; "The Symbol", p. 19; "Space", p. 58; "The Path", p. 83.

* * *

The selections appearing in the Appendix have been translated from a variety of previously unpublished sources, including "The Book of Keys", a collection of private spiritual texts written by Schuon for his spiritual community, and "Memories and Meditations", Schuon's autobiographical memoirs. Most of the spiritual texts were written in French, though some are in German; the memoirs, drawn from journal entries spanning many years, were composed in German.

1. "The Book of Keys", No. 1087, "Qualifications".
2. Letter of 2 February 1956.
3. "Memories and Meditations", p. 246.
4. Letter of 7 November 1949.
5. "The Book of Keys", No. 957, "Moral Realism".
6. "The Book of Keys", No. 718, "The Invincibility of the Absolute".
7. Letter of 24 April 1961.
8. Letter of 31 January 1956.

9. "The Book of Keys", No. 643, "The True *Tawbah*".
10. Letter of 17 October 1993.
11. "Memories and Meditations", p. 254.
12. Letter of 4 September 1978.
13. "Memories and Meditations", pp. 258-59.
14. Letter of 13 May 1949.
15. "Memories and Meditations", pp. 251-52.
16. Letter of 27 February 1978.
17. "The Book of Keys", No. 1126, "Empirical Ego and Intellectual Ego: Religion and Wisdom".
18. "Memories and Meditations", p. 246.
19. Letter of 17 July 1978.
20. "The Book of Keys", No. 1102, "Canonical Prayer".
21. "Reflections on the Subject of a Letter" (undated manuscript).
22. "The Book of Keys", No. 82, "Man, Outward and Inward".
23. "Memories and Meditations", p. 247.
24. Letter of 16 December 1984.
25. "Memories and Meditations", p. 251.
26. Letter of 1973 (no other date).
27. "Memories and Meditations", p. 248.
28. Letter of April 1959.
29. Letter of 19 November 1979.
30. Notebook entry (no title, entry number, or date).
31. "The Book of Keys", No. 399, "*Al-Tawbah*".
32. Letter of 17 February 1978.
33. Notebook entry (no title, entry number, or date).
34. "Memories and Meditations", pp. 260-61.
35. "Memories and Meditations", p. 256.
36. Letter of 22 July 1986.
37. "The Book of Keys", No. 1144, "Life".

GLOSSARY
OF FOREIGN TERMS AND PHRASES

Ab extra (Latin): "from outside"; proceeding from something extrinsic or external.

Ad extra (Latin): "at the extremity"; from the point of view of a boundary or limit.

Ad intra: (Latin): "at the interior"; considered from within.

Âdi-Buddha (Sanskrit): in Buddhist cosmology, the universal or primordial Buddha, in whom is personified supreme suchness or emptiness, and from whom come both the *Dhyâni-Buddha*s and the historical Buddhas, including Siddhartha Gautama.

Advaita (Sanskrit): "non-dualist" interpretation of the *Vedânta*; Hindu doctrine according to which the seeming multiplicity of things is regarded as the product of ignorance, the only true reality being *Brahma*, the One, the Absolute, the Infinite, which is the unchanging ground of appearance.

Ânanda (Sanskrit): "bliss, beatitude, joy"; one of the three essential aspects of *Apara-Brahma*, together with *sat*, "being", and *chit*, "consciousness".

Apara-Brahma (Sanskrit): the "non-supreme" or penultimate *Brahma*, also called *Brahma saguna*; in Schuon's teaching, the "relative Absolute".

Apocatastasis (Greek): "restitution, restoration"; among certain Christian theologians, including Clement of Alexandria, Origen, and Gregory of Nyssa, the doctrine that all creatures will finally be saved.

241

Âtmâ or *Âtman* (Sanskrit): the real or true "Self", underlying the ego and its manifestations; in the perspective of *Advaita Vedânta*, identical with *Brahma*.

Aum or *Om* (Sanskrit): the most sacred syllable in Hinduism, containing all origination and dissolution; regarded as the "seed" of all *mantras*, its three *mâtrâs* or letters are taken to be symbolical of the *Trimûrti*, while the silence at its conclusion is seen as expressing the attainment of *Brahma*.

Avatâra (Sanskrit): the earthly "descent", incarnation, or manifestation of God, especially of Vishnu in the Hindu tradition.

Avidyâ (Sanskrit): "ignorance" of the truth; spiritual delusion, unawareness of *Brahma*.

Âyah (Arabic, plural *âyât*): in Islam, a "sign" or "mark" of Allah's existence or power, especially a miracle; also a verse of the Koran.

Barakah (Arabic): "blessing", grace; in Islam, a spiritual influence or energy emanating originally from God, but often attached to sacred objects and spiritual persons.

Barzakh (Arabic): as used in the Koran, a "barrier" or "separation" between paradise and hell, or this life and the next, or the two seas (fresh and salt); in the interpretation of Sufism, an "isthmus" connecting different planes of reality.

Basmalah (Arabic): traditional Muslim formula of blessing, found at the beginning of all but one of the *sûrahs* of the Koran, the full form being *Bismi 'Llâhi 'r-Rahmâni 'r-Rahîm*, "In the Name of Allah, the Beneficent, the Merciful".

Bhakta (Sanskrit): a follower of the spiritual path of *bhakti*; a person whose relationship with God is based primarily on adoration and love.

Bhakti or *bhakti-mârga* (Sanskrit): the spiritual "path" (*mârga*) of "love" (*bhakti*) and devotion; see *jnâna* and *karma*.

Brahmâ (Sanskrit): God in the aspect of Creator, the first divine "person" of the *Trimûrti;* to be distinguished from *Brahma,* the Supreme Reality.

Brahma or *Brahman* (Sanskrit): the Supreme Reality, the Absolute.

Buddhi (Sanskrit): "Intellect"; the highest faculty of knowledge, to be contrasted with *manas,* that is, mind or reason.

Chit (Sanskrit): "consciousness"; one of the three essential aspects of *Apara-Brahma,* together with *sat,* "being", and *ânanda,* "bliss, beatitude, joy".

Dharma (Sanskrit): in Hinduism, the underlying "law" or "order" of the cosmos as expressed in sacred rites and in actions appropriate to various social relationships and human vocations; in Buddhism, the practice and realization of Truth.

Dharmakâya (Sanskrit): literally, *"dharma* body"; in *Mahâyâna* Buddhism, the supreme and non-manifest form of the Buddhas, personified as the *Âdi-Buddha.*

Dhikr (Arabic): "remembrance" of God, based upon the repeated invocation of His Name; central to Sufi practice, where the remembrance is often supported by the single word *Allâh.*

Dhyâni-Buddha (Sanskrit): Buddha "of meditation"; a Buddha, such as Amitabha (Amida in Japanese), who appears to the eye of contemplative vision, but is not accessible in a historical form.

Distinguo (Latin): literally, "I mark or set off, differentiate", often used in the dialectic of the medieval scholastics; any philosophical distinction.

Fanâ' (Arabic): "extinction, annihilation, evanescence"; in Sufism, the spiritual station or degree of realization in which all individual attributes and limitations are extinguished in union with God.

Fâtihah (Arabic): the "opening" *sûrah,* or chapter, of the Koran, recited in the daily prayers of all Muslims and consisting of the words: "In the Name of Allah, the Beneficent, the Merciful. Praise to Allah, Lord of the Worlds, the Beneficent, the Merciful. Owner of the Day of Judgment, Thee (alone) we worship; Thee (alone) we ask for help. Show us the straight path, the path of those whom Thou hast favored, not (the path) of those who earn Thine anger nor of those who go astray."

Fiat lux (Latin): "Let there be light" (*cf.* Gen. 1:3).

Fitrah (Arabic): in Islam, the natural predisposition of man, as created by God, to act in accordance with the will of Heaven; the original uprightness of humanity (*cf. Sûrah* "The Romans" [30]:30); in Schuon's usage, the primordial norm or "nature of things".

Gnosis (Greek): "knowledge"; spiritual insight, principial comprehension, divine wisdom.

Guru (Sanskrit): literally, "weighty", grave, venerable; in Hinduism, a spiritual master; one who gives initiation and instruction in the spiritual path and in whom is embodied the supreme goal of realization or perfection.

Hadîth (Arabic, plural *ahâdîth*): "saying, narrative"; an account of the words or deeds of the Prophet Muhammad, transmitted through a traditional chain of known intermediaries.

Hanîf (Arabic): in Islam, one who remains true to the *fitrah*.

Haqîqah (Arabic): "truth, reality"; in Sufism, the inward essence of a thing, corresponding to an archetypal Truth in God.

Haqq (Arabic): "the True, the Real"; in Islam, one of the Names of Allah, who alone is truly real.

Imâm (Arabic): in Islam in general, the "leader" of congregational prayer; in Sufism, a spiritual guide or master.

Increatum et increabile (Latin): "uncreated and uncreatable"; transcending the domain of time and relativity, as the Absolute or its prolongations.

In divinis (Latin): literally, "in or among divine things"; within the divine Principle; the plural form is used insofar as the Principle comprises both *Para-Brahma*, Beyond-Being or the Absolute, and *Apara-Brahma*, Being or the relative Absolute.

Îshvara (Sanskrit): one who "possesses power"; God understood as a personal being, as Creator and Lord; manifest in the *Trimûrti* as *Brahmâ*, *Vishnu*, and *Shiva*.

Japa-Yoga (Sanskrit): method of "union" or "unification" (*yoga*) based upon the "repetition" (*japa*) of a *mantra* or sacred formula, often containing one of the Names of God.

Jejunium (Latin): "fasting, abstinence from food".

Jiriki (Japanese): "power of the self"; a Buddhist term for spiritual methods that emphasize one's own efforts in reaching the goal of liberation or salvation, as for example in Zen; in contrast to *tariki*.

Jîvan-mukta (Sanskrit): one who is "liberated" while still in this "life"; a person who has attained a state of spiritual perfection or self-realization before death; in contrast to *videha-mukta*, one who is liberated at the moment of death.

Jnâna or *jnâna-mârga* (Sanskrit): the spiritual "path" (*mârga*) of "knowledge" (*jnâna*) and intellection; see *bhakti* and *karma*.

Jnânin (Sanskrit): a follower of the path of *jnâna*; a person whose relationship with God is based primarily on sapiential knowledge or *gnosis*.

Jôdo (Japanese): "pure land"; the untainted, transcendent realm created by the Buddha Amida (Amitabha in Sanskrit), into which his devotees aspire to be born in their next life.

Jôdo-Shinshû (Japanese): "true pure land school"; a sect of Japanese Pure Land Buddhism founded by Shinran, based on faith in the power of the Buddha Amida and characterized by use of the *nembutsu*.

Kali-Yuga (Sanskrit): in Hinduism, the fourth and final *yuga* in a given cycle of time, corresponding to the Iron Age of Western tradition and culminating in a *pralaya* or the *mahâpralaya*; the present age of mankind, distinguished by its increasing disorder, violence, and forgetfulness of God.

Karma (Sanskrit): "action, work"; one of the principal *mârga*s or spiritual "paths", characterized by its stress on righteous deeds (see *bhakti* and *jnâna*); in Hinduism and Buddhism, the law of consequence, in which the present is explained by reference to the nature and quality of one's past actions.

Krita-Yuga (Sanskrit): in Hinduism, the first *yuga* in a given cycle of time; the Golden Age or Eden of Western tradition, distinguished by *rita*, that is, "order, justice".

Lâ ilâha illâ 'Llâh (Arabic): "There is no god but God"; see *Shahâdah*.

Mahâpralaya (Sanskrit): in Hinduism, the "great" or final "dissolving" of the universe at the end of a *kalpa*, or "day in the life of *Brahmâ*", understood as lasting one thousand *yuga*s.

Mahâyâna (Sanskrit): "great vehicle"; the form of Buddhism, including such traditions as Zen and *Jôdo-Shinshû*, which regards itself as the fullest or most adequate expression of the Buddha's teaching; distinguished by the idea that *nirvâna* is not other than *samsâra* truly seen as it is.

Mantra (Sanskrit): "instrument of thought"; a word or phrase of divine origin, often including a Name of God, repeated by those initiated into its proper use as a means of salvation or liberation; see *japa-yoga*.

Materia prima (Latin): "first or prime matter"; in Platonic cosmology, the undifferentiated and primordial substance serving as a "receptacle" for the shaping force of divine forms or ideas; universal potentiality.

Mâyâ (Sanskrit): "artifice, illusion"; in *Advaita Vedânta*, the beguiling concealment of *Brahma* in the form or under the appearance of a lower reality.

Moksha (Sanskrit): "release" or "liberation" from *samsâra*; according to Hindu teaching, the most important of the aims of life, attained by following one of the principal *mârgas* or spiritual paths (see *bhakti, jnâna,* and *karma*).

Mudrâ (Sanskrit): "seal, sign"; in Hinduism and Buddhism, a stylized and symbolic gesture, especially one involving the hands and the fingers, often seen in iconography and sacred dance and employed in meditation as a vehicle for inducing a particular state of consciousness.

Mukta (Sanskrit): one who has attained *moksha* or "liberation"; see *jîvan-mukta.*

Nembutsu (Japanese): "remembrance or mindfulness of the Buddha", based upon the repeated invocation of his Name; same as *buddhânusmriti* in Sanskrit and *nien-fo* in Chinese.

Nirvâna (Sanskrit): "blowing out, extinction"; in Indian traditions, especially Buddhism, the extinction of the fires of passion and the resulting, supremely blissful state of liberation from egoism and attachment; compare with the Sufi idea of *fanâ'.*

Niyama (Sanskrit): "discipline", whether on the bodily or psychic level; in Hinduism, the second step in the eightfold path of the *yogin,* consisting in the practice of cleanliness, contentment, austerity, recitation of sacred scriptures, and devotion to God; see *yama.*

Oratio (Latin): literally, "language, speech"; in Christian usage, words addressed to God; prayer.

Paramâtmâ or *Paramâtman* (Sanskrit): the "supreme Self".

Pater noster (Latin): "Our Father"; used in Christianity to refer to the Lord's Prayer, consisting of the words: "Our Father who art in

Heaven, Hallowed be thy Name. Thy kingdom come. Thy will be done on earth as it is in Heaven. Give us this day our daily bread. And forgive us our debts, as we forgive our debtors. And lead us not into temptation, but deliver us from evil. For thine is the kingdom, and the power, and the glory, for ever. Amen" (Matt. 6:9-13).

Pneumatikos (Greek): a "spiritual man"; one in whom the element of spirit predominates over the soul and the body (*cf.* 1 Thess. 5:23; 1 Cor. 2:14-15).

Pontifex (Latin): "bridge-maker"; man as the link between Heaven and earth.

Prakriti (Sanskrit): literally, "making first" (see *Materia prima*); the fundamental, "feminine" substance or material cause of all things; see *Purusha*.

Pralaya (Sanskrit): "dissolution"; Hindu teaching that all appearance is subject to a periodic process of destruction and recreation; see *mahâpralaya*.

Prapatti (Sanskrit): "seeking refuge"; pious resignation and devotion to God.

Purusha (Sanskrit): "man"; the informing or shaping principle of creation; the "masculine" demiurge or fashioner of the universe; see *Prakriti*.

Samsâra (Sanskrit): literally, "wandering"; in Hinduism and Buddhism, transmigration or the cycle of birth, death, and rebirth; also the world of apparent flux and change.

Sannyâsin (Sanskrit): "renunciate"; in Hindu tradition, one who has renounced all formal ties to social life.

Sat (Sanskrit): "being"; one of the three essential aspects of *Apara-Brahma*, together with *chit*, "consciousness", and *ânanda*, "bliss, beatitude, joy".

Sattva (Sanskrit): in Hinduism, one of the three *guna*s, or qualities, of *Prakriti*, of which all things are woven; the quality of luminosity, manifest in the material world as buoyancy or lightness and in the soul as intelligence and virtue.

Shahâdah (Arabic): the fundamental "profession" or "testimony" of faith in Islam, consisting of the words *lâ ilâha illâ 'Llâh, Muhammadan rasûlu 'Llâh*: "There is no god but God; Muhammad is the messenger of God."

Shakti (Sanskrit): creative "power", expressed in Hinduism in the form of divine femininity.

Sharî'ah (Arabic): "path"; in Islam, the proper mode and norm of life, the path or way willed and marked out by God for man's return to Him; Muslim law or exoterism.

Shaykh (Arabic): literally, "old man, elder"; in Sufism, one who has attained spiritual mastery through submission to the discipline and instruction of another *shaykh* and who can thus trace his lineage to the foundation of a given *tarîqah*.

Shûnyamûrti (Sanskrit): "the form or manifestation of the void"; traditional epithet of the Buddha, in whom is "incarnate" *shûnyatâ*, ultimate "emptiness", that is, the final absence of all definite being or selfhood.

Sophia (Greek): "wisdom"; in Jewish and Christian tradition, the Wisdom of God, often conceived as feminine (*cf.* Prov. 8).

Sûrah (Arabic): one of the one hundred fourteen divisions, or chapters, of the Koran.

Sûtra (Sanskrit): literally, "thread"; a Hindu or Buddhist sacred text; in Hinduism, any short, aphoristic verse or collection of verses, often elliptical in style; in Buddhism, a collection of the discourses of the Buddha.

Talmud (Hebrew): "learning, study"; in Judaism, a body of writings and traditional commentaries based on the oral law given to Moses on Sinai; the foundation of Jewish civil and religious law, second in authority only to the *Torah.*

Tariki (Japanese): "power of the other"; a Buddhist term for forms of spirituality that emphasize the importance of grace or celestial assistance, especially that of the Buddha Amida, as in the Pure Land schools; in contrast to *jiriki.*

Tarîqah (Arabic): "path"; in exoteric Islam, a virtual synonym for *sharî'ah,* equivalent to the "straight path" mentioned in the *Fâtihah*; in Sufism, the mystical path leading from observance of the *Sharî'ah* to self-realization in God; also a Sufi brotherhood.

Tawakkul (Arabic): complete "reliance" on God and "trust" that He alone is sufficient for all one's needs.

Tawbah (Arabic): in Islam, "repentance" from sin; the title of *Sûrah* 9, taken from verse 104: "Know they not that Allah is He who accepteth repentance from His bondsmen and taketh the alms, and that Allah is He who is relenting, the merciful."

Tawhîd (Arabic): "unification, union"; in Islam, the affirmation of divine unity as expressed in the first phrase of the *Shahâdah,* "There is no god but God" (*lâ ilâha illâ 'Llâh*); in Sufism, the doctrine of mystical union; see *fanâ'.*

Torah (Hebrew): "instruction, teaching"; in Judaism, the written law of God, as revealed to Moses on Sinai and embodied in the Pentateuch (Genesis, Exodus, Leviticus, Numbers, Deuteronomy).

Trimûrti (Sanskrit): literally, "having three forms"; in Hindu tradition, a triadic expression of the Divine, especially in the form of *Brahmâ,* the creator, *Vishnu,* the preserver, and *Shiva,* the transformer.

Upâya (Sanskrit): "means, expedient, method"; in Buddhist tradition, the adaptation of spiritual teaching to a form suited to the level of one's audience.

Vacare Deo (Latin): literally, "to be empty for God"; to be at leisure for or available to God; in the Christian monastic and contemplative tradition, to set aside time from work for meditation and prayer.

Vedânta (Sanskrit): "end or culmination of the Vedas"; one of the major schools of traditional Hindu philosophy, based in part on the Upanishads, esoteric treatises found at the conclusion of the Vedic scriptures; see *advaita.*

Virtus (Latin): "manliness, virility"; strength of character, moral excellence.

Yama (Sanskrit): "restraint", whether on the bodily or psychic level; in Hinduism, the first step in the eightfold path of the *yogin*, which consists in resisting all inclinations toward violence, lying, stealing, sexual activity, and greed; see *niyama.*

Yantra (Sanskrit): literally, "instrument of support"; a geometrical design, often representing the cosmos, used in Tantric Hinduism and Tibetan Buddhism as a visual support or focus for meditation.

Yin-Yang (Chinese): in Chinese tradition, two opposite but complementary forces or qualities, from whose interpenetration the universe and all its diverse forms emerge; *yin* corresponds to the feminine, the yielding, the moon, and liquidity; *yang* corresponds to the masculine, the resisting, the sun, and solidity.

Yogin (Sanskrit): one who is "yoked or joined"; a practitioner of *yoga*, especially a form of *yoga* involving meditative and ascetic techniques designed to bring the soul and body into a state of concentration.

Yuga (Sanskrit): an "age" in Hinduism, one of the four periods into which a cycle of time is divided.

For a glossary of all key foreign words used in books published by World Wisdom, including metaphysical terms in English, consult: www.DictionaryofSpiritualTerms.com.
This on-line Dictionary of Spiritual Terms provides extensive definitions, examples and related terms in other languages.

INDEX

'abd, 169
ablution, 166
Absolute, 7, 31, 59, 66n, 69-
70, 92, 121, 155, 195, 201;
consciousness of, 62; God as,
78; relative, 13; truth of, *xix*;
and Name of Jesus, 203; and
necessity, 85; and relativity,
contingency, 13, 67, 95, 146n,
187; and Word, 60
Abu al-Hasan Kharaqani, 171n,
175n, 231
adab, 137n
Adam, 152, 163, 167
Âdi-Buddha, 74n
Advaita Vedânta. See *Vedânta*
Akshobhya, 74n, 221
al-Alawi, Ahmad, 81n, 222
alchemy, spiritual, 15, 92, 93,
116
Alexander the Great, 157n, 230
Alexandrian perspective, 52
Alexandrians, 47n, 215
Allah, 70, 116, 140n, 171, 234;
Name of, 60n, 65n, 71, 72,
72n
All-Possibility, 61n, 174n
Amida (Amitabha), *xxii* (n), 73,
74n, 220, 221, 234
Amidism, Amidists, 61n, 73,
73n, 74n, 202, 234
Amitayus, 74n, 221
Amoghasiddhi, 74n, 221
Ânanda, 14n, 170n, 173, 195,
220
Anandamayi Ma, 233

Angels, 63, 125, 179, 193, 217,
223
Angelus Silesius, 48n, 80n, 215
Animals, 21, 51, 54, 126, 140n
Anselm, 6n, 122n, 210
apatheia, apathy, 6n, 210
apocatastasis, 203
'*aql*, 170
Aquinas, Thomas, 44, 67, 214,
218, 224
'*ârif*, 172n
Aristotle, 225, 229
art: language of, 179; sacred, 16,
20, 143, 179
Artaxerxes, 92n, 223
asceticism, ascetics, 9, 37, 40n,
50, 70n, 127, 155, 213
Ashuku, 74n
ataraxia, 47
Athos, Holy Mountain of, 214
Âtmâ, 14n, 71, 156, 172n, 173,
174n, 188, 234
Augustine, 55n, 108, 133, 216,
224, 227
Aum, 65n
avarice, 27, 54
*avatâra, avatâra*s, 57, 142n, 204,
205, 211, 220, 233
avidyâ, 166
âyah, 71
Baal Shem, 133n, 227
bâlya, 125
Baptism, 6n, 143, 210, 218
barakah, 195
Barsanuphius, 6n, 210
barzakh, 61

bashar, 166
Basil the Great, 79n, 222, 227
Basilian spirituality, 135, 227
Basmalah, 71n
Bayazid (Abu Yazid) al-Bastami, 158n, 171n, 172n, 175n, 230
Beatrice, 9, 211
beauty, 14, 54, 127, 156-57, 157n, 201; divine, 154, 181, experience, sense of, 9, 183; of Buddhas, 20n, 144n; of character, soul, 8n, 93, 103; of woman, 157n; and love, 54, 193; and nature, 190; and perfection, 39; and Sufism, 46; and truth, 45, 103, 115; and virtue, 19, 19n, 62
Being: divine, 98, 117; as affirmation of Infinite, 167; as Name, Word, 61, 62, 66n; and beauty, 46; and Beyond-Being, 13-14, 60-61, 60-61n, 63; and God, 1, 13, 60n, 84, 168; and perfection, 62; and qualities, 83; and *sattva*, 49n; and Self, 170, 170n, 172, 173; and Trinity, 61n
belief, 109, 195; and faith, 5-7, 53
Benedict of Nursia, 164, 231
Bernadette of Lourdes, 126n, 226
Bernard of Clairvaux, 64n, 93, 136, 197, 217
Bernardino of Siena, 65n, 217
Beyond-Being, 13-14; and Being, 60-61, 60n, 63; and Non-Being, 83-84; and Self, 59

Bhagavad Gîtâ, 73, 220, 233
Bhaishajyaguru, 74n
bhakta, bhaktas, 43, 53, 136n, 170
bhakti, 43, 54n, 59, 72n, 160n
Bible, 7n, 64
Boethius, 108, 133, 224
Brahmâ, 221
Brahma, 3, 60n, 70, 71, 82, 158n, 205, 209, 220, 230, 234
Buddha, 20, 20n, 74, 143, 201, 221; bodies of, 203; invocation of, 61n; Names of, 60, 60n; Shakyamuni, 73, 221; Siddhartha Gautama as historical, 221. *See also* Amida (Amitabha)
Buddhas, 20n, 74n, 144n
Buddhi, 74n
Buddhism, 9, 9n, 20, 46, 154n; Japanese, 188; Northern, 16n; Pure Land, *xxii*, 38n
Cabala, Cabalists, 69n, 133n, 219, 227
Cabasilas, Nicholas, 65n, 218
Callistus of Xanthopoulos, 47, 214
Catherine of Siena, 137, 228
Chaitanya, 20n, 54n, 136n, 211
charity, 6n, 47n, 49, 50, 50n, 54-55, 86; prayer as act of, 2; sentimental, 126; social, 177; and holy anger, 111; and humility, veracity, *xxiii*, 19, 87, 95, 96, 109, 110; and knowledge (*gnosis*), 23, 40n, 44. *See also* love
childlikeness, holy, 32n, 125, 196, 213

Chit, 14n, 74n, 170n, 173

Chrismation. *See* Confirmation

Christianity, *xviii, xxii,* 9n, 46,
66, 66n, 67, 91, 136n, 159,
165, 186; and Cabala, 69n;
and deification, 82; and esoterism, 68-9, 218

Church, *xviii,* 142, 207, 212, 214

Clement of Alexandria, 215

Clovis, 147n, 229

combat, spiritual, 91, 155, 200

Communion, Holy. *See* Eucharist

complacency, 177

concentration, 13, 14, 62, 143,
157, 160, 184, 193, 201; intellectual, 192; mental, 10; pure,
59; techniques of, *xxiv;* on the
Real, 159, 187-88; and invocation, 188, 192

concupiscence, 1, 92

Confirmation, 143, 218

conscience, 114, 184, 224; voice
of, 164, 180

consciousness, 14-15, 40n, 62,
72, 95, 170, 172, 202; non-objectified, 117; spiritual, 87; of
God, 14; of Self, 3; and *Chit,*
173

consecration: formula of, 71,
220; and symbol, 142-43

contemplation, 6n, 25, 27, 47n,
54n, 62, 83n, 114, 151; intellective, 47, 48, 116; intelligence as, 44; pure, 69; as
act of knowledge, 40; of the
Divine, 115, 156; and action,
48, 48n, 151; and calm, 49n

cosmology, 139, 141

creation, 61, 61n, 71n, 77, 81,

85-86, 157; otherness of, 79;
and evil, 167

cross, symbolism of, 67, 174

Crusaders, 216

Curé d'Ars, 48n, 151n, 215

Cyril of Alexandria, 79n, 222

Dainichi, 74n

Dante Alighieri, 9n, 129n, 211,
226

al-Darqawi, Mawlay al-Arabi,
xviii (n)

darshana, 213

death, 2, 75, 87, 91, 120n, 154-
55, 180, 184, 200, 201; meditation on, 192; true and false,
181; and Last Judgment, 203;
and wrath of God, 167

deification, 66, 82, 135, 140, 222

deiformity, of man, 14, 110, 123

Desert Fathers, 210, 213

desire, 50n, 170n, 182; for *gnosis, xx;* for perfection, 110; for
union, 80n, 169

desires, 57, 137n, 146; soul,
53, 153; and images, 10; and
instincts, 1

detachment, 1, 210; and humility, 131; and renunciation, 8,
9, 160, 177

devil, 102, 105, 196, 234

dharma, 201

Dharmakara, 220

Dharmakâya, 74n

Dhât, 171

dhikr, 188, 197

Diadochos of Photike, 135n,
227

Diogenes of Sinope, 157n, 230

Dionysius the Areopagite, 143n,
229

dissipation, 48, 156, 181, 184, 198, 204

Dorotheus, 40n, 213

dream, 87; of ego, 183; of world, 206-207

dualism, 81

Eckhart, Meister, 9, 19n, 26, 37n, 62n, 79n, 82, 84n, 136, 159, 170n, 204, 210, 215, 217, 222

ecstasy, 20n, 223

ego, 53n, 145, 158, 171n, 183, 195, 199; cosmic aspect of, 142; empirical, 194; existential, 182; idea of, 30; inward and outward, 198; thinking, 44; true, 140; as distinct from Intellect, 169; as principle of illusion, 113; as principle of individuation, 164; as such, 59, 73n, 165; and world, 206

egocentrism, 125, 128, 129

Eliezer, Israel ben, 227

emptiness, 159, 160, 180; humility as, 135; idea of, 60; moral form of, 168; *vacare Deo* as, 45

esoterism, *xvii*, 68-69n, 69, 170, 186; bhaktic, 69; and exoterism, 142; and Christianity, 68-69, 218; and Islam, 68, 114, 165, 169, 218

eternity, 171n, 182, 207; reply to prayer in, 34; of God, 154; and death, 2, 75; and divine Name, 60

Eucharist, 65n, 67n, 143, 218, 222

Evagrius Ponticus, 6n, 40n, 47n, 49n, 210

evil: human, 22, 58n, 106; ignorance as root of, 165, 190; for psychoanalysts, 58n; and good, 106, 142, 155, 163; and nothingness, 67; and pride, 133; and will, 51, 187

exoterism, 68, 68n, 69, 80, 142; voluntaristic, 195

faith, 6-8, 6-8n, 40n, 44, 48, 62n, 68n; childlike, *xx* (n); as essence of prayer, 2; and Amidism, 73; and belief, 5-7, 53; and certitude, 5; and discernment, *gnosis*, knowledge, 52-53, 69, 69n, 122n; and Intellect, 122; and invocation, 199; and works, 92, 223

fanâ', 137n, 230, 232

Fâtihah, *xxi*, 29n, 197, 212

fear, 6n, 72, 195; devotional, 196; meditation based on, 154-55, 160; of God, 26, 72, 72n, 168

fitrah, 195

Francis of Sales, 151n, 229

Gautama, Siddhartha. *See* Buddha

generosity, 23, 90, 122-23; of soul, 46; and beauty, 54; and divine Goodness, 158; and humility, 177, 195; and trust, 16

al-Ghazzali, Abu Hamid Muhammad, 83n 137n, 223

gleichheit, 84n

gnosis, *xx*, 37, 44, 46-47, 49n, 71n, 97, 100, 135, 232; in Christian tradition, 66-69; of Alexandrians, 47n; and devotional perspective, 38; and

faith, 69n; and love, 40n, 43, 44, 47n, 114
gnostic, 43, 53, 175
God-Man, 29n
gopîs, 220
grace, 15, 58, 87, 102, 119, 135, 174, 185, 198; baptismal, 6n; sensible, 200; sanctifying, 143; and invocation, 187, 188; and method, 38, 38n, 39
Gregory of Nyssa, 37, 213
Gregory Palamas, 159, 215
hadîth, 8n, 46, 72n, 105n, 142n, 228, 234; divine, 171
al-Hallaj, Mansur, 52n, 68n, 216, 223
hanîf, 195
happiness, 2, 91-93, 167, 175n, 194-95; and the Name, 199
haqîqah, 68
al-Haqq, 171n, 172n
hayât, 170n
heart: eye of, 146n; hardened, 104, 181, 224; liquefaction of, 48n, 137n; prayer of, *xxi*, 63, 64, 210; and Intellect, 30, 113, 140; and Jesus Prayer, 41n; and love, 40, 48, 55, 211, 216; and microcosm, 14, 15, 26, 147; and Name, 62, 72, 188; and remembrance of God, 1; and Self, 41, 72
Heaven, 67, 91, 157, 175n, 182, 203; dialogue with, 92; elect of, 5; kingdom of, 157n, 191, 226; Son of, 152n; wrath of, 2; as degree of universe, 13
hell, 163, 175n
Hesychasm, Hesychasts, 6n, 41n, 47n, 64, 157n, 160n, 210, 214, 215
hesychia, 210, 215
himmah, 54n
Hinduism, Hindus, *xxii*, 16n, 163, 165, 177, 201, 220
Homer, 226
Horace, 226
houris, 64n, 217
hrî, 125
humility, *xxiii*, 72, 95n, 126-37, 151-52, 231; in Christianity and Islam, 166; as modesty, 125; as objectivity toward ego, 101; sin from, 127n, 226; and love (charity), truth (veracity), 19, 86-87, 95-96, 109-111
Huwa, 139n
Ibn al-Arif, 115, 225
Ibn al-Farid, Omar, 20n, 212
Ibn Arabi, Muhyi al-Din, 46, 82, 131n, 136n, 214
Ibrahim ibn Adham, 175n, 232
idolatry, 19, 92, 98, 115, 126, 166
Ignatius Loyola, 137, 228
Ignatius of Xanthopoulos, 47, 214
ihsân, 46, 70
illusion, 77, 87, 128, 158, 158n, 171n; cosmic, 9, 106, 140; ego as principle of, 113; of "I", individuality, 53, 159
'ilm, 170
imagination, 15, 122, 184, 198; subconscious, 59; and will, 201
imâm, 169
îmân, 8n, 70
immanence: mystery of, 93; universal, 174; and Self, 204; and transcendence, 204

immortality, 10, 58n, 93, 100,
181, 205; Edenic, 167
Incarnation, Christian doctrine
of, 67, 82, 222
Indians, American (Red), 14n,
60n, 198
individualism, 107, 114, 163,
183, 200
Infinite, divine Infinity, 47, 70,
77, 81n, 154n, 155, 164, 167,
202; and Absolute, 70, 159;
and creation, 167; and the
finite, 79, 81, 146n, 187; and
liberty, 85; and Name of Mary,
203; and Word, 77
initiation, 91, 142, 193; craft,
63n; and baptism, 6n
insân, 166
Intellect, 20-22, 33, 50n, 53, 60,
98, 125, 131, 135n, 145, 147,
158, 195, 198; Christ as, 40n,
66; created and uncreated,
26, 44, 170; divine, 47n, 53n,
59, 117, 170; supra-personal,
5; universal, 74n, 147; in soul,
82, 222; and faith, 122; and
heart, 113; and reason, 30-31,
43, 59, 97; and Spirit, 140-41
intellection, 10, 37, 39, 42, 154n,
213; miracle of, 7; pure, 38,
39; and divine "I", 117; and
peace, 47, 48; and reason, 26;
and virtue, 49n, 114, 116-17
intellectus, 82, 170n, 222
invocation, *xxii*, *xxii* (n), 61, 61-
62n, 81n, 186, 187, 194, 196,
199, 201-202; in Amidism, 73,
234; of divine Name, 62, 72,
144n, 188, 200; of Jesus-Mary,
235; and Eucharist, 65n; and

metaphysical discrimination,
60n; and virtue, 195
irâdah, 170n
Irenaeus, 66n, 169n, 218
Îshvara, 14n, 170n
Islam, 8, 69n, 70, 186; testimony,
testimonies of, 71n, 175, 219;
and esoterism, 68, 68n, 169,
218; and humility, 166; and
Name of God, 69
James, 47n, 163, 164
japa-yoga, *xxii*, 62n, 188
jejunium, 200
Jesu-Maria, 207, 235
Jesus Christ, *xix*, 47, 66n, 203;
Baptism of, 210; body of, 79-
80n, 159; Name of, 65n, 66-
68, 160n, 203, 217, 218; peace
of, 69; Real Presence of, *xxii*;
two natures of, 30n, 71n, 212;
as God, 144; as Intellect, 40n,
66; and childlikeness, 32n;
and esoterism, exoterism, 68,
68n; and *jîvan-mukta*, 204; and
Word, 127
Jesus Prayer, *xxii*, 41n, 207, 210,
214, 235
jiriki, 38n
jîvan-mukta, 142n, 203, 204-205
jnâna, 29n, 43, 59, 72n
jnânin, 29n, 43, 53
Joan of Arc, 5, 132n, 209
Jôdo-Shinshû, *xxii* (n), 38n, 62n,
234
John: the Baptist, 230; the Evan-
gelist, 229
John Climacus, 6n, 210
John of the Cross, 60n, 177n,
217
John the Hesychast, 6n, 210

Judaism, *xxii* (n), 9n, 71n
al-Junayd, Abu al-Qasim, 172n, 232
Kali, 37n, 212, 213
Kali-Yuga, 188, 204, 246
karma, 72n, 120, 189
Khayyam, Omar (Umar al-Khayyam), 106, 224
knowledge, 5, 15, 21-22, 26, 30, 49n, 146, 160, 164; divine, 117; false and true, 181; innate, 153; limits of, 175; metaphysical, 2, 25, 168, 185, 232; rights of, 130; Self as subject of, 40, 154; sensory, 41; as aim of meditation, 59; as discernment, 160; as imprescriptible, 131; as the true, 163; in perspective of *gnosis*, 44, 69, 135; in *Vedânta*, 46; of divine Name, 227; of God, 37-38, 40, 40n, 49, 51n, 52, 80, 113, 114, 132, 171n, 172n, 177; of Trinity, 40n; of *yogin*, 172n; and faith, 52-53, 122; and grace, 39; and humility, 97, 126, 129, 136; and Incarnation, 67; and love (charity), 40, 41, 40n, 43-47, 47n, 50, 52, 154n; and peace, 47n; and reason, 33; and volitive perspective, 42; and will, 51, 164; and *yin-yang*, 147n
Koran, 7n, 60n, 72, 212, 220
Krishna, 73, 204, 211, 220
Krita-Yuga, 204
Lakshmi, 73n, 220
Lanka, 73, 220
Layla, 9n, 211
Limbo, 226
Logos, 73, 212

Lossky, Vladimir, 6n, 40n, 210
love: creation by, 61n; depths of, 179; divine, 54n; earthly, 9; perspective of, 156-57; spiritual, 54; symbolism of, 144; as conformity to Truth, 6; as effective wisdom, 25; as mystery of union, 93; in Christianity, 46; of *Âtmâ*, 156n; of God, 1, 31n, 54, 72n, 108, 168, 175, 175n, 177, 216; of neighbor, *xxi*, 46, 54-55, 55n, 67, 72n, 108, 111n, 157, 178, 193, 216; and beauty, 54, 193, 201; and knowledge (*gnosis*), 25, 40-41, 40n, 43-47, 47n, 50, 50n, 52, 69, 101, 114, 154n; and Name of Christ, 67; and peace, 160n
Lucifer, 165
Ma Ananda Moyi, 189, 233
Macarius of Egypt, 40n, 80, 159, 213
macrocosm, 85, 91, 122, 140-41, 145, 158, 177
mahâpralaya, 203
Mahavairochana, 74n
Mahâyâna, 173n, 221
Maimonides, Moses, 163, 231
Majnun, 9n, 211
Makarios of Corinth, 225
manifestation: divine, 71n; limitation, illusion of, 77; symbol as, 142; universal, 13; in relation to Principle, 3, 10, 79, 85, 86, 134, 139, 141, 145, 146n, 171, 173; of Intellect, 31; of *Mâyâ*, 119; of Self, 85, 172; of Truth, 96; of Void, 60n, 202; and beauty, 103; and Word, 77, 140

mantra, xxii, 16n, 201, 202
Mara, 74n
marriage, 64n, 120n, 217
martyrdom, 10, 192
Mary, Blessed Virgin: icons of, 68n, 143; and *Mâyâ,* 91; Name of, 67-68, 203, 235; prayer to, 194; perfection of, 205
Mary Magdalene, 48n, 215
mason, 63n
materia prima, 63n
Maximus the Confessor, 37n, 47n, 49, 213
Mâyâ, 90, 91, 119, 169, 172, 173, 174n
meditation, 2, 153-160, 192, 201, 202; metaphysical, 30; themes of, *xxiii,* 15; as activity of intelligence, 13; as emptiness, plenitude, 159; as mode of prayer, 59; on death, 154-55, 192; on events of Christ's life, 228; on love, 156; on Scriptures, 135
mercy, divine, 2, 16, 38n, 61, 64, 67-68, 68n, 71, 71n, 92, 119, 157-58, 178, 181, 188, 196-97
metacosm, 85
metaphysician, 2, 122, 175
metaphysics, 23, 173n, 188; pure, 63n; and cosmology, 140; and faith, 53; and profane philosophy, 97
method: Hesychast, *xviii;* of intellective man, 42; of invocation, 143; of realization, *xviii;* and doctrine, 187; and grace, 38-39; and initiation, 91
microcosm, 14-15, 85, 113, 122, 140, 140n, 141-42, 144-45,

147, 158, 177
modesty, 100, 125, 133
monotheism, 81
moralism, moralist, 105n, 114, 115
morals, morality, 70n, 99, 125, 164
Moses, *xxii* (n), 60n, 217, 219, 223
mudrâ, 16n
mufrad, 72
Muhammad, 71, 234
muhsin, 46
mukta, 82
Muslims, 121; and esoterism, 68, 114, 165, 218; and exoterism, 68, 68n, 218; and *himmah,* 54n; and humility, 166; and the Intellect, 170; and sin, 165; and *tawakkul,* 201
mysticism, mystic, 47, 114, 165, 175, 200
Name: divine, 60, 143, 144n, 188-89, 199; given to Moses, *xxii* (n); master of, 227; supreme, 197, 206; as Being, 62; as isthmus, 61; in Islam, 69; of *Allâh,* 60n, 70-72, 72n; of Amida (Amitabha), *xxii* (n), 73, 220; of Beyond-Being, 61; of Buddha, 60; of Father, 62n; of Jesus Christ, 47, 65n, 67, 160n, 203, 217, 218; of Mary, 203; and *Basmalah,* 71n; and *oratio, jejunium,* 200; and remembrance (*dhikr*), 62, 188, 194
nembutsu, xxii
Nicaea, Council of, 215
nifâq, 71, 175n

Nikodimos of the Holy Mountain, 225
Nirvâna, 125, 127, 173n
niyama, 125
non-action, 152n
Non-Being, 83-84
nous, 213
Object, 83; divine, 40; of knowledge, 50; and Subject, 169, 173
objectivity: toward ego, 101; and human intelligence, 122
Origen, 54n, 55n, 215, 216
Ovid, 226
Palamite teaching, 48, 215
pantheism, 174n
Paradise, 5, 64n, 136n, 174-75, 175n, 203, 217; of Akshobhya, 74n; of Amitabha, 73, 220
Paramâtmâ, 14n
Parvati, 213
passions, 19, 104, 122, 146
Pater Noster, 29n, 207, 212, 235
path, 71, 172; mystical, 228; spiritual, 49, 144, 145n, 153, 197, 232, 233; Sufi, 223; of Union, 172; and divine Names, 74n; and humility, 136
Paul, Apostle, 25, 229
peace: of Christ, 47, 69, 160n, 214; spiritual, 2, 14, 47n, 48-49, 58, 72, 75, 156-57, 180-81, 192, 199
penance, sacrament of, 58, 114
perfection: active, passive, 62; ascending, 49n; aspiring to, 109, 110; divine, 99, 116, 202; God as, 133; human, 134; moral, 90, 178, 186, 202; Name as, 189; in faith, 8n; of

Being, 62; of Consciousness, 62; of ejaculatory prayer, 65; of humility, 134; of intelligence, 163; of macrocosm, 122; of necessity, 39
perseverance, 75, 143, 155, 160, 184, 200
Peter, Apostle, 58, 217
Philokalia, *xxii* (n), *xxiv* (n), 116n, 214, 225, 227
Plato, 223
Plutarch, 92n, 223, 230
pneumatikos, 175
pontifex, *xvi*, 110
possibility, 69n; universal, 23, 77, 106, 152, 174n
poverty, spiritual, 8, 10, 63
Prakriti, 14n
pralaya, 203
prapatti, 201
prayer: canonical, 57-58, 57n, 60, 197; continual, continuous, 6n, 54n, 135, 136; ejaculatory, invocatory, 60, 62, 63, 65, 183, 202, 207, 233; faith as essence of, 2; Hesychast method of, *xviii*; individual, personal, 57, 57n, 59, 186-87, 191, 200; Jesus, 41n, 207, 214, 235; levels of, *xx*, 228; life of, 92; Lord's, *xxi*, 207, 212, 235; meditative, 3; modes of, 16; ordinary, usual sense of, 29, 57; pure, 192; quintessential, 62; silent, 60n; as conversation, encounter with God, 1, 30; as petition, 58; of God-Man, 29n; of the heart, *xxi*, 63, 64, 210; to Blessed Virgin, 194; and action, 74-75; and

human existence, *xvi*, 182; and *jnâna*, 29n
predestination, 121
pride, 27, 27n, 43, 58n, 107-108, 126, 128-129, 131-33, 133n, 134-35, 136n, 151-52, 165-66
Principle: divine, 13, 31, 69n, 229; ontological, 170n, 173; supreme, 2, 3, 66; symbol as, 147; as cause of good, 156; and dignity, 152; and divine Name, 61; and manifestation, 3, 10, 13, 79, 85-86, 134, 139, 141, 145, 146n, 171, 173
Providence, 3, 71n
psyche, 140
psychoanalysis, 58n
psychology, 103, 140
Pure Land Buddhism, *xxii, xxii* (n), 38n, 220
purification, 9, 57, 87, 97, 113, 135, 153, 228
Purusha, 14n, 74n
al-Qushayri, Abu al-Qasim, 137n, 228
qutb, 232
Rabb, 169
Radha, 73, 220
Rama, 73, 73n, 204, 220, 221, 233
Ramakrishna, 20n, 37n, 60, 126, 189, 212, 213, 233
Ramana Maharshi, 204, 234
Ramanuja, 38n, 43, 54n, 213
Ramdas, Swami, 189, 233
Rasputin, 226
Ratnasambhava, 74n, 221
Ravana, 73, 220
Real Presence, *xxii*, 147n
Reality: absolute, 79; Allah as,

72; *Brahma* as, 3, 209; degrees of, 80; divine, *xxii*, 14, 33, 44, 52, 80, 81, 84, 139n, 142, 203; ego as inversion of, 199; God as, 181; infinite, 141; pre-ontological, 170n; Supreme, *xix* (n), 141; symbol as, 147; transcendent, 168; unity of, 174; and mind, 7, 106; and nothingness, 67, 78; and Self, 41, 43, 53, 170
realization: method of, *xviii*; spiritual, 32, 140, 154, 165, 177, 179, 189, 199; unitive, 171; in heart-Intellect, 113; of God, 116; of Self, 142n, 172; of union, 53; and concentration, 159; and *gnosis* (*jnâna*), 43, 46; and grace, 87; and Intellect, 141; and Paradise, 174; and psychology, 140
reason, 84, 121; temple of, 37n; and Intellect, 21, 26, 30, 31, 43, 50n, 59, 97, 122; and intelligence, 51; and sentiment, 30, 33, 50n, 122
religion, 20, 70n, 93, 194, 195
remembrance, of God, 1, 15, 27, 70, 72, 72n, 74-75, 92
Remy (Remigius), 147n, 229
repentance, 6n
resignation, 16, 58, 89, 119, 157, 157n
resurrection, 64n
retreat, spiritual, 194
revelation, 5, 61, 62, 86, 125, 142, 143; Islamic, 197; Mosaic, 71n; of method, 38; and divine Name, 188
Richard of Saint Victor, 55n, 216

ridhâ, 157n
risâlah, 68n
rites, 63, 64, 67n, 143, 166, 197
rosary, 151n
Rumi, Jalal al-Din, 20n, 212
sabr, 8
sacrament: of the Eucharist,
    65n, 79n, 159; of penance,
    58n
sâkshin, 170n
sâlik, 9
salvation, 61n, 64, 69n, 71n, 108,
    119, 168, 185; certitude of, 92;
    as remembrance of God, 70
samâdhi, 20n
samprasâda, 47n
samsâra, 173n
sanctity, 19, 106, 177, 179, 228;
    and esoterism, 68-69, 218
Sarasvati, 74n, 221
Sat, 14n, 49n, 170n, 173
Satan, 19
sattva, 49n
al-Saydlani, Abu Bakr, 172
Scheffler, Johannes. *See* Angelus
    Silesius
Scriptures, 7n, 135
sentiment, 23, 29-30, 33, 50n,
    54, 109, 122, 146, 180, 200
serenity, 1, 15, 26, 47, 47n, 49n,
    119, 195, 199
Shabistari, Mahmud, 72n, 220
al-Shadhili, Abu al-Hasan, *xviii*
    (n), 80n, 169, 222, 231
Shahâdah, 70, 71n, 188, 219, 234
shakti, 122, 220
Shakyamuni. *See* Buddha
Shankara (Shankaracharya), *xix*,
    29n, 38n, 43, 47n, 54n, 60n,
    82, 136n, 172n, 204, 209, 212,
    230

shânta, 47
shânti, 47
shaykh, *xviii* (n), 232
shema, *xxi*
al-Shibli, Abu Bakr, 172, 232
Shiva, 29n, 213
Shivananda, 189, 233
shuhûd, 170n
shûnya, 10
shûnyamûrti, 60n, 202
sidq, 8
Sifât, 171
silence, 60n, 73, 75, 199; divine,
    119; holy, 14, 47n, 215; vow of,
    212; as Name of Buddha, 60
Simeon the New Theologian,
    6n, 210
simplicity, 135, 136, 37, 151
sin, 11, 108, 163-67, 186, 193,
    207; mortal, 103; against the
    Holy Spirit, 195, 234; flight
    from, 72n; from humility,
    127n; of existence, 127, 142n;
    of pride, 133n; of the world,
    145; and fall, 163; and peni-
    tence, 114
sincerity, 3, 8, 68n, 96, 107-11,
    132, 199
Sita, 73, 73n, 220-21
sleep: and death, 203; and Ex-
    tinction, 62
sloth, 155, 204
sobriety, 196, 200
Son of God, 60n, 61n, 84n, 143,
    212, 214, 218, 219
Son of Heaven, 152n
soul: affective, 48; beauty of, 93,
    103, 156; contents, images,
    tendencies of, 1, 99, 135, 184;
    destiny of, 73; distinction

from body, 140; equilibrium of, 200; egoistic, 108; God in, 180; hatred of, 111n, 224; immortal, 2, 92, 96, 140, 141, 194; Intellect in, 82, 222; intelligent, reasonable, 47n, 49n; misfortunes, misery, suffering of, 119, 181, 189; profane, 49; purification, purity of, 57, 113, 135, 136, 181; Self in, 204; sensorial, 140, 141; spiritual, 108; transmutation of, 80; as desire, 53, 153; *in divinis*, 73n; and complexes, 109; and concentration, 10; and grace, 155; and knowledge of all, 117, 225; and Name, 72, 188; and prayer, 13, 16; and Spirit, 140, 141, 154

space: Absolute in, 66n; directions of, 74n; mental, 14, 15; and time, 121, 128, 180, 182

Spirit, 20, 23, 65, 144n, 154; divine, 61n, 140, 140n; Holy, 47n, 61n, 125, 147, 195, 234; universal, 141; world of, 86; as Self, 24; of God, 41n

sthûla-sharîra, 141

Stithatos, Nikitas, 47n, 214

subconscious, 31, 57, 59, 201

Subject, 67; absolute, 82, 82-83, 117, 141, 167, 173; Intellect as, 53n; Self as, 40, 83, 169

subjectivism, 107

suffering, 7-11, 89, 119, 154, 154n, 155, 157, 180-81, 192

Sufism, Sufis, *xviii*, 6n, 8, 19, 20n, 46, 61n, 110, 136n, 158n, 170n, 175, 195, 205, 232

Sukhâvatî, 73, 220

symbol, 62, 11, 142-45, 147-48, 154, 203; cross as, 67; definition of, 147; doctrinal, 7; initiatic, 142-43; Name as, 143; visual, 144n; voice as, 63; void in, 180; in macrocosm, 147; of *yin-yang*, 147n; and ego, 145, 158; and microcosm, 144

tanazzulah, 61n

tariki, 38n

Tathagata. *See* Buddha

tawakkul, 201

tawhîd, 172

temperament, 41-43, 45, 166

temptation, 9; of sadness, 202

Tenkalai, 38n

Teresa of Avila, 137, 217, 228

Teresa of the Child Jesus, 126n, 192, 226, 234

Tertullian, 122n, 225

tetragrammaton, xxii (n)

theogenesis, 145, 147

theology: antinomian, apophatic, 48, 80, 229; monotheistic, 170; and doctrines of identity, 80; and theosophy, 69n

theomorphism, of man, 66, 110, 152

Thérèse of Lisieux. *See* Teresa of the Child Jesus

Thomas, Apostle, 5, 209

Thomism, 137

time: Absolute in, 66; and remembrance of God, 72, 75; and space, 121, 128, 180, 182

al-Tirmidhi, Muhammad ibn Ali, 137n, 228

Torah, 60n, 133n

tradition: Christian, 66, 210; Far

Eastern, 152n; Islamic, *xviii*; quintessence of, 187; man of, 109; and sacred images, 143

transcendence: man as capable of, 122; of Creator, God, 1, 29; of Non-Being, 83; of knowledge, 47n; and immanence, 204

transmigration, 148

Trinity, 40n, 61n, 143n

Truth: Name *Allâh* as, 71; faith, love as adherence to, 6-7, 51; God as, 37n, 172n; Name of Christ as, 67; and humility, 137; and pure prayer, 192; and Way, 14, 108, 195

union, 62, 187; compressive, liberating, 204; God as, 45; Intellect as subject of, 171; non-dual (advaitic), 81, 169n; path, way of, 170, 172; realization of, 53; supreme, 175; of grace, 174; with Christ, 218; with God, the Real, 80n, 158, 169; with the Self, 203; and purification, perfection (expansion), 87, 97, 153, 228

unity: divine, 69-70, 80n, 171n, 174, 202; of man and God, 82; of the world, 87

universe, 5, 13-14, 122n, 174, 203

upâya, 202

Vadakalai, 38n

Vairochana, 74n, 221

Vedânta, 46, 80; *Advaita*, 209, 212

Vianney, Jean-Baptiste Marie. *See* Curé d'Ars

vichâra, 59

Virgil, 129n, 226

virtue: God in, 42, 54; human, natural, 100, 101, 116, 135; intrinsic, 116, 177; sentimental, 97; as abolition of egoism, 113; as idolatry, 126; and action, will, 115, 131; and beauty, 46, 62; and *dhikr*, invocation, 188, 195; and faith, 93; and intellection, 49n, 114, 116, 117; and Truth, Way, 95-96, 108, 113, 195

Vishnu, 220, 222

viveka, 59

void: divine, 1; manifestation of, 60n, 202; Reality as, 141; and Name, 188; and symbol, 180

Voltaire, 22, 212

war, holy, 31n

al-Wasiti, Abu Bakr Muhammad, 175n, 232

way, spiritual. *See* path, spiritual

will: free, 1, 51, 121-23, 164; spiritual, 48; as essence of man, 50n; as relative, 39; as sin, 164; of God, divine, 16, 22, 58, 64, 89-90, 119, 146, 180; and asceticism, 37, 50; and intellection, intelligence, 42, 121, 163; and knowledge, love, 51-52; and virtue, 131; and way, 14

wisdom: Son of God as, 61n; traditional, 139; and love, 25, 46; and religion, 195

woman, beauty of, 157n

works, 1; good, 177, 177n; and faith, 6n, 92, 223

wujûd, 170n

wu-wei, 152n

Yakushi, 74n

yama, 125
yantra, 16n, 144n
Yin-Yang, 147n, 203
yoga, 38

yogin, 172n, 205
Zen, 20n, 60n, 206
zuhd, 9

BIOGRAPHICAL NOTES

FRITHJOF SCHUON

Born in Basle, Switzerland in 1907, Frithjof Schuon was the twentieth century's pre-eminent spokesman for the perennialist school of comparative religious thought.

The leitmotif of Schuon's work was foreshadowed in an encounter during his youth with a marabout who had accompanied some members of his Senegalese village to Basle for the purpose of demonstrating their African culture. When Schuon talked with him, the venerable old man drew a circle with radii on the ground and explained: "God is the center; all paths lead to Him." Until his later years Schuon traveled widely, from India and the Middle East to America, experiencing traditional cultures and establishing lifelong friendships with Hindu, Buddhist, Christian, Muslim, and American Indian spiritual leaders.

A philosopher in the tradition of Plato, Shankara, and Eckhart, Schuon was a gifted artist and poet as well as the author of over twenty books on religion, metaphysics, sacred art, and the spiritual path. Describing his first book, *The Transcendent Unity of Religions*, T. S. Eliot wrote, "I have met with no more impressive work in the comparative study of Oriental and Occidental religion", and world-renowned religion scholar Huston Smith has said of Schuon that "the man is a living wonder; intellectually apropos religion, equally in depth and breadth, the paragon of our time". Schuon's books have been translated into over a dozen languages and are respected by academic and religious authorities alike.

More than a scholar and writer, Schuon was a spiritual guide for seekers from a wide variety of religions and backgrounds throughout the world. He died in 1998.

JAMES S. CUTSINGER (Ph.D., Harvard) is Professor of Theology and Religious Thought at the University of South Carolina and Secretary to the Foundation for Traditional Studies.

A widely recognized writer on the *sophia perennis* and the perennialist school, Professor Cutsinger is an Orthodox Christian and an authority on the theology and spirituality of the Christian East. His publications include *Advice to the Serious Seeker: Meditations on the Teaching of Frithjof Schuon, Reclaiming the Great Tradition: Evangelicals, Catholics, and Orthodox in Dialogue, Not of This World: A Treasury of Christian Mysticism, Paths to the Heart: Sufism and the Christian East,* and *The Fullness of God: Frithjof Schuon on Christianity.*

Prayer Fashions Man: Frithjof Schuon on the Spiritual Life is the second volume in a series of new anthologies compiled from Schuon's published and unpublished writings, and introduced and annotated by Professor Cutsinger.

PHILIP ZALESKI, a senior editor at *Parabola* magazine and editor of *The Best American Spiritual Writing* series, has taught religion and literature at Smith College, Wesleyan University, and Tufts University. His books include *The Language of Paradise* and *The Book of Heaven* (both with Carol Zaleski), as well as *Gifts of the Spirit* and *The Recollected Heart.* His articles on religion and culture have appeared in *The New York Times, First Things,* and many other national publications.